Basic Boat Building

RICHARD FRISBIE

Henry Regnery Company · Chicago

Library of Congress Cataloging in Publication Data

Frisbie, Richard P.
  Basic boat building.

  1. Boat-building. I. Title.
VM321.F73   623.82'3   74-23265
ISBN 0-8092-8390-5
ISBN 0-8092-8342-5 pbk.

To Evelyn, my mother-in-law,
who wouldn't let herself be dragged aboard
the boat I built by wild seahorses

Illustrations by Anne Celeste Frisbie

Copyright © 1975 by Richard Frisbie
All rights reserved
Published by Henry Regnery Company
180 North Michigan Avenue, Chicago, Illinois 60601
Manufactured in the United States of America
Library of Congress Catalog Card Number: 74-23265
International Standard Book Number: 0-8092-8390-5 (cloth)
                                    0-8092-8342-5 (paper)

Published simultaneously in Canada by
Fitzhenry & Whiteside Limited
150 Lesmill Road
Don Mills, Ontario M3B 2T5
Canada

Contents

1 A Chip off the Santa Maria

I HAVE built a ship with my own hands and sailed her. Some of my friends are impressed, supposing that I must be a craftsman who knows how to build a ship. Closer friends are more mystified than impressed. They know I took Latin in high school instead of shop, do not subscribe to *Popular Mechanics*, and rarely fix anything in my forty-five-year-old house until it falls on my foot. They think I'm crazy.

They don't understand that building a boat, like fathering a child, traveling in a foreign country, or planting a garden, is one of those experiences in life that a man ought to try at least once, undaunted by the odds that the results may be somewhat different from what he anticipated.

A person gets some pleasure in making anything of wood, but a built-in bar or a record cabinet just sits there; it doesn't have a life of its own. It doesn't dance around the end of a pier begging to be taken out. A boat wants to go on a voyage to far places, ghosting along the shores of tropical islands that somehow have drifted into Long Island Sound, Lake Michigan, or San Francisco Bay—where sales meetings, political campaigns, and freeway traffic seem exceedingly remote.

1-1. "Some kinds of ships are saltier than others. A sailboat is salt- than any powerboat. Square rig is saltier than fore-and-aft." (Photo *Nonsuch* replica courtesy of Hudson's Bay Company.)

When I'm out in a boat, I'm farther from land than I appear to those on shore. Just as sound travels faster through water than through air, distance over water is much greater than distance over land. If you're hiking in the woods and sit down for a snack, anyone else in sight seems intolerably close—almost as if his elbows are in your thermos of coffee. On the water, even on Sunday afternoons near cities—which scarcely offer the lonely sea and the sky that poets go down to—a boat is always surrounded by an immense psychological space.

So powerful is this quality of a boat that it can affect you right in your own basement before the boat itself is born. The voyage begins not when you cast off from the dock in the finished vessel but when you first spread out your plans on your workbench. You can almost imagine a seagull perching on your vise.

The ancients understood that there was romance in building a boat as well as in sailing it over the horizon. When Hieron II of Syracuse (a wise man said to have ruled for fifty-four years without killing, exiling, or injuring a single citizen) decided to build a pleasure boat, he turned over the project to his friend Archimedes. The ruler and the scientist spent many pleasant hours watching the carpenters at work. The yacht was 407 feet long, with sixty cabins, a gymnasium, a marble bath, and gardens—rather too large to build in the average garage, but an inspiration nevertheless. If Archimedes himself could turn his mind to the building of a pleasure boat, such work cannot be dismissed as entirely frivolous.

The Vikings so loved their ships that they insisted on being buried in them. The curator of the Oslo museum that owns the Oseberg and Gokstad Viking ships has compared the obsession of the old Norse with the feeling of the nineteenth-century British aristocracy for horses. A man too poor to own a ship was laid away among stones placed to outline the shape of a ship. His heirs were lucky; they didn't have to stand the expense of digging a hole seventy or eighty feet long and perhaps twenty feet deep. And fortunately for the economy, even kings did not demand a hole deep enough to include mast and sail.

Viking builders worked without plans, shaping the overlap-

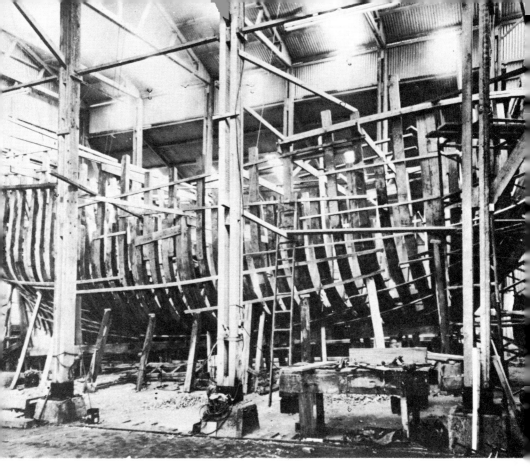

Fig. 1-2. Traditional ship-building methods depended on skilled shipwrights. Modern materials, such as epoxy glue and marine plywood, enable beginners to construct satisfactory hulls. (Photo of *Nonsuch* replica under construction courtesy of Hudson's Bay Company.)

ping planks by eye until the graceful shell was finished, then fitting ribs for reinforcement. Below the waterline, ribs and planking were lashed together with spruce roots, making the ship flexible in heavy seas. The ship wasn't considered complete until an artisan had decorated it with intricate carving.

There still are psychological as well as practical rewards for building a boat, especially for someone whose usual work is to deal in abstractions. Monday through Friday you are an accountant or a copywriter, Saturdays a Viking, with your half-finished dragon ship already growling on the stocks.

Life developed in the sea. When the first amphibians crawled ashore, they brought part of the sea with them in the salt balance of their body fluids. To this day, every air-breathing creature, including man, carries in its body a tiny drop of that primeval sea, however diluted by gin from generation to generation and species to species since Paleozoic times. Perhaps that's why water still fascinates us.

In the navy, there is—or used to be—a word to describe the appearance of a sailor who looks and acts experienced. In contrast to the recruits, he's "salty." At sea, some methods of doing things are saltier than others, which is another way of saying less lubberly. Likewise, some kinds of ships are saltier than others. A sailboat is saltier than any powerboat. Square rig is saltier than fore-and-aft (see Figure 1-1). A small schooner, ketch, or yawl is saltier than a large sloop or cutter. A gaff-rigged mainsail is saltier than a Bermuda rig. And, of course, building a boat is infinitely saltier than buying one.

Not that the practical advantages are to be ignored. It is cheaper to build than to buy a boat unless one spoils an extraordinary amount of expensive material. Even in factories, where much of a boat is molded in fiberglass-reinforced plastic, a lot of costly handwork still runs the price up. Some authorities claim that do-it-yourself shipwrights can save 30 to 50 percent of the retail price of a comparable boat.

Weighing various practical considerations against desired degrees of saltiness, I decided a few years ago to build a small cruising sloop, sixteen feet, five inches long overall with a small cabin and two bunks. This book tells how I did it, with the suggestion that if I can build a boat, anyone can. For some people, a powerboat or a houseboat may be salty enough. Details of construction for these boats would be different, as shown in their plans. But the basic techniques and problems are the same, so this book should be useful to anyone who wants to build any kind of boat—or to savor the idea by reading about it without going to all the trouble.

It is considerable trouble. I put in 702 hours, spread over two years and four months, from January, 1970, through April, 1972. The costs were as follows:

Plans	$ 25.00
Lumber and plywood	608.72
Marine hardware and fastenings	283.75
Glue, paint, and fiberglassing materials	245.99
Tools and materials bought specifically for boat building	242.79
Rigging and turnbuckles	86.93
Aluminum mast, boom, and fittings[1]	159.33
Sails: main, large jib, and small jib	150.00
Cordage	19.00
Trailer	284.48
	$2,105.99

1. Wooden spars are saltier than aluminum ones, but making them scarcely pays. For my ship, mast grade Sitka spruce would have cost $45; sail track, $18; nails and glue, $3; total, $66. A comparable aluminum mast cost $63; boom, $27; total, $90. The extruded aluminum spars require no sail track because the rope-bound edges of the mainsail slide into a built-in groove. Other fittings would be the same for either type of mast, so the aluminum spars cost only $24 more than wood. But the aluminum comes ready to use and requires no future maintenance, while spruce has to be fabricated and glued up, then varnished and revarnished year after year. Also, aluminum is about 6 percent lighter in weight, a substantial factor considering the multiplying effect of a tall mast's leverage.

Since no factory-built boat is exactly comparable to mine, I can't be sure how much I saved. Considering the prices of stock boats approximately the same size with similar features, I'm sure I saved a few hundred dollars. I might even have earned as much as a dollar an hour.

This boat could have been built with less expenditure of time and money, for I spent half the 702 hours staring at the plans and scratching my head. If I built another boat the same size, I think I could do it in about 400 hours.

I could have purchased materials more cheaply if I had bought them all at once and shopped harder for bargains. I bought materials in small batches as I was ready for them so I wouldn't have a lot of money tied up in the project right from the beginning.

"I could have purchased materials more cheaply if I had bought them all at once and shopped harder for bargains."

As for scrounging for bargains, I didn't have time for that, since I was too busy staring at the plans and scratching my head.

A man in Texas built a boat just inches larger than mine for more than $300 less. He is a professional remodeling contractor who didn't have to buy any tools and could get professional discounts on some items. In addition, he used galvanized instead of bronze fastenings and merely painted the plywood hull instead of fiberglassing it. Being a professional, he also worked much faster and completed his ship in 300 hours.

A Pennsylvanian built a seventeen-footer for $900 less than my costs, also with galvanized fastenings and fiberglass only on the plywood seams. His secret was a single-minded dedication to scrounging materials and finding the lowest prices on earth. He persuaded local factories to give him various kinds of free scrap, which he converted into fittings. His sails were made in Hong Kong.

But it's the psychology of spending that most favors building a boat yourself. If you merely go to the boat store and write a large check for the boat you want, you have to shake off the image of yourself as an overgrown boy blowing his allowance at the toy store. In building a boat, you easily persuade yourself that by laboring with your own two hands you are earning it. You may even be able to persuade your wife.

Many of the great solo voyagers have also been boat builders. Joshua Slocum, the first man to sail around the world single-handed, rebuilt a rotting hulk beginning with a new oak keel from a tree he felled himself. The job lasted thirteen months and cost $553.62 at 1894 prices. His *Spray* was thirty-six feet, nine inches long, a big boat for one man, but Slocum planned to live aboard for a long time.

In recent years, Robert Manry extensively remodeled the cockpit and cabin of his thirteen-and-one-half-foot *Tinkerbelle* before sailing her from Falmouth, Massachusetts, to Falmouth, England. Only the extreme smallness of *Tinkerbelle* made this exploit news-worthy, for craft only slightly larger, built by amateurs and carrying enough crew to stand watch around the clock, routinely cross the oceans without attracting much attention.

Fig. 1-3. Captain's cabin on an old square-rigger: one of the saltiest places on earth.

Some homemade boats have disappeared at sea, including the famous *Spray* on a second voyage to South America, but that happens to big steel ships, too. Experts consider a staunch, well-handled small boat at least as safe as a big ship in a storm at sea.

I think my decision to build a boat was made one fall afternoon when I was sailing my aluminum canoe around the Horn—that is, there was rather more wind on Pistakee Lake than a canoe is designed for. By careful attention to wind, waves, balance, and other variables of sailing, I avoided capsizing. As we beat into the wind against the chop, there was nothing I could do about the water that splashed into the boat but heave to and bail whenever the water inside got almost as deep as the water outside.

With my lunch (fortunately wrapped in plastic) floating around my knees among the kapok cushions, I began to design a detachable foredeck to shed the spray flung up by the bow. It had to be detachable so I could still carry the canoe without help and use it for river trips. Then I realized it would be smarter to build a complete boat instead of trying to attach anything more to the canoe. In sheltered waters under reasonable conditions, a sailing canoe handles well and provides plenty of sport; however, all the dozen or so sailing fittings have to be assembled and disassembled every time you go out. So I would build a boat, or, rather, a small ship.

In normal usage, a "ship" is a large, seagoing vessel. A "boat" is a watercraft that can be hoisted aboard a ship, except on the Great Lakes, where huge ore carriers larger than the cargo ships using the St. Lawrence Seaway are nevertheless called "boats." My definition is different. I consider any vessel on which a person can eat and sleep for a short cruise to be a ship. Under sail, it makes any port in the world theoretically accessible. The ship I built is substantially larger than *Tinkerbelle*, which crossed the Atlantic.

The owner's attitude qualifies the definition. A 100-foot diesel yacht is only a boat if used mainly for entertaining. But, unlike some purists, I accept a powerboat as a ship if its owner thinks salty. He may be compromising with his children's fondness for water skiing or the desire to go to and from favorite fishing grounds with more dispatch than sail affords.

"I consider any vessel on which a person can eat and sleep for a short cruise to be a ship."

The trouble with most small power cruisers is that they guzzle fuel. They can't risk exploring unfamiliar waters where there may not be a convenient marina without careful planning and auxiliary tanks. And a speck of dirt in the carburetor can make them a rescue case for the Coast Guard.

My qualifications for ship building were slim, although not nonexistent. Once, years ago, I was appointed assistant feature editor of a newspaper, a job that consisted mostly of editing and makeup with certain writing duties, including a weekly column on men's fashions (at the time I was an admirer of the late Heywood Broun's "unmade bed" look) and a weekly column on do-it-yourself projects (I had never hammered a nail straight in my life).

One adapts. I stopped wearing my red hunting cap to the office and began to consult experts and books on home handicrafts. Having grown up in an apartment where all household repairs were handled with a lightweight crating hammer, a well-rounded screwdriver, a beer can opener, a kick, and a cuss, I was astonished to learn about refinements like screwdrivers that come in sizes to fit the screws and chisels that stay sharp because you don't pry open paint cans with them.

Later, as owner of an aging house, I found myself reading my own clippings for a refresher on how to replace sash cords or fix roof leaks or lay floor tile. In time I acquired the tools for most home repair jobs and considerable practice using them.

But I didn't plunge into ship building. My first step toward laying the keel was to panel the walls around the back stairs with prefinished plywood. This achieved two important results: it put my wife in a more favorable frame of mind toward the ship project, and it gave me needed practice with my saber saw. And until you have used a saber saw for a while and got the feel of it, trying to make accurate cuts is like threading a needle with an electric eggbeater.

I was not a fool who didn't know what he was getting into; I was a fool who did. Once before I had been involved with an amateur boat yard. When I was a senior in high school I joined a friend in purchasing an aged seventeen-foot sloop. We each put up twenty-five dollars.

She was free of rot, but needed caulking, painting, and repairs to the laminated wood mast, which towered thirty feet above the deck. She probably had been built by an amateur. Except for the mast, as will be explained, the builder did a good job. A keel of sheet steel, weighted with a removable blob of lead, counterbalanced the big spread of sail. There was enough flotation in the wood hull to keep her from sinking when she filled up at her mooring from rainwater and a chronic slow leak. The deck was covered with green canvas in good condition, and the roomy cockpit was protected with a mahogany coaming. *Aurora* was her name most of the time; we kept changing it.

As noted previously, I wouldn't have had the faintest notion where to begin with the repairs, but my partner, Jack, had worked for a couple of summers as a deckhand on a fifty-foot yawl that sailed in the Mackinac Race and he knew what to do. My role was to pay half the expenses and help with the less skilled kinds of work, like lifting, fetching, sanding, and painting.

We transported the *Aurora* from the former owner's backyard to Jack's by improvising a dolly and promising eventual cruises to seven or eight of our more muscular friends. It seems to me I spent most of that spring in the space under the foredeck with a paintbrush. But I didn't mind; I was sustained by a vision of myself taking my turn at the helm while *Aurora* wrought a seachange on the Chicago lakefront.

By the time *Aurora* was ready for the water it was later in June than we had intended. The plan was to turn out the muscle crew again, load her on the strengthened dolly, and drag it about a mile to the water's edge. From there it would be a two-mile sail with all hands to our anchorage in Jackson Park Harbor.

All the anchorages had been taken for the season, but the ways of the Chicago Park District have ever been Byzantine. In the end, we were allowed to make fast to the stern of the *Santa Maria*, a replica of Columbus's ship that had been rotting at the edge of the harbor since the world's fair in 1893. It was not the most desirable location, since pieces of the *Santa Maria* sometimes fell off in storms, but it cost us only the legal anchorage fee and the time expended on inquiring after the health of people who knew people.

On launching day we never reached the harbor. Arriving at the beach, we found a fine breeze accompanied by a formidable chop. With considerable exertion we managed to drag the dolly across the sand, turn *Aurora* on her side, bolt on the lead ballast, and shove her through the waves out past the surf line. With her fixed keel, she drew about three and a half feet. Four of the launch crew stood in water up to their shoulders to steady the hull while two or three of us tried to keep our balance on the deck long enough to step the mast.

Aurora resisted, throwing spray to make everything slippery and pitching until the tall, unwieldy mast went overboard time after time, taking the deck crew with it. Finally, the crew tired of diving frantically to the bottom to avoid being brained every time the mast crashed down, and they went home to dinner, leaving Jack and me to beach *Aurora* on her side and give up for the day.

In the morning we returned, lashed the spars to the deck, and paddled the two miles to the harbor where, in the calm shelter of the *Santa Maria*, we raised the mast without difficulty. (Since we didn't have a dinghy, we would stand on the end of a nearby pier and catch some protruding part of the boat with a lariat loop, then pull it over to us. *The Aurora*'s mooring line was weighted so that ordinarily she would swing clear of both the *Santa Maria* and the pier. Some members of the Jackson Park Yacht Club obviously were pained to observe such lubberly maneuvers in progress in the shadow of the *Santa Maria*, but Columbus never complained.)

Every boat has its quirks and crotchets. The original *Santa Maria*, unlike *Niña* and *Pinta*, was a willful tub who ran herself aground. My first boat, a plywood kayak with buoyancy compartments, liked to spit out the little corks that plugged the vents in the deck. *Aurora's* problem was her mast. We didn't realize this at first. Our sea-trial cruise met with only a light breeze. *Aurora* handled well, and we were delighted. On the second cruise we were fooled by an evening breeze, which took us miles out on the lake and died away. Night came on with a drizzle, still windless, and we had to paddle back, arriving home late and wet. But that was scarcely *Aurora's* fault.

Then we put to sea on a day when a stiff breeze promised fast sailing and flying spray. Almost immediately we heard an ominous crack from high on the mast, where an earlier break had been repaired. We quickly furled the big mainsail and came creeping home gingerly on the jib alone. Not knowing what else to do, Jack and I took the mast to a carpenter shop, walking two or three miles with the thirty-foot spar on our shoulders. The carpenter knew nothing of nautical construction, but he fixed it the best he could, replacing cracked pieces, gluing them in, and bracing the mend with a steel collar. This took a couple of weeks, and by the time *Aurora's* mast was back in place, it was August.

For our first trial of the repaired mast we had a hot, sunny Sunday afternoon, perfect for most kinds of outings. For sailors it was a day of challenge. The wind blew strong, gusty, and unpredictable from shore, a variety of Chicago's late summer weather notorious for upsetting sailboats into bone-chilling water and keeping the Coast Guard busy.

We romped, exhilarated, for four or five miles across water blown flat by the wind. Then came an especially strong gust. *Aurora* was a stable boat with a broad beam, the hard chines of a dory, and plenty of external ballast. Instead of heeling over on her beam ends, she snapped her mast. It broke off entirely about twenty feet up—just above the carpenter's steel collar—and tumbled into the water in a tangle of sails and stays. We hauled the mess aboard, made it fast, and started paddling with our single emergency paddle. But against that wind we could make no progress with such a heavy boat. We were still drifting slowly toward the distant Michigan side of the lake. Downwind, the voyage would have been about seventy-five miles across water that was quite rough away from shore.

But our predicament was obvious to every other boat in sight and several came to our rescue. A large inboard cruiser eventually towed us all the way back to our anchorage. Her captain, in the finest tradition of the sea, succored the castaways with chicken sandwiches on the way.

That was *Aurora*'s last cruise, ending a frustratingly short season. Before we could scrape up funds for another attempt at mast repair, we were back in school. Increasingly urgent telephone messages began coming from the harbormaster, insisting that we get our boat out of his harbor. Thanksgiving was coming on, and the season was over.

This was a problem we hadn't thought through. In the spring a boat owner can find scores of friends eager to help, but in the fall they don't recognize him on the street. Without a crew to help, Jack and I couldn't haul the boat on the dolly all the way from the harbor, and we couldn't sail her anywhere without the mast.

Finally, Jack's father, who was in the coal business, provided a coal truck and its crew on a cold, rainy Saturday. The truck dragged *Aurora* ashore on a towline. We unbolted the ballast. Then all of us together, three men and two boys, barely managed to lift her onto the truck. That was the last time I saw her, riding away ignominiously on the back of a coal truck with the coal dust already sifting over her paint.

With the war on, there were no more leisurely summers of sailing. *Aurora* sat neglected on a coal dock while Jack and I went off to college and the navy. When, years later, the *Aurora*'s crew reassembled in Chicago, *Aurora* had vanished.

"It's almost harder to decide what kind of ship to build than to do the building."

2 Bicycle off the Port Bow

Ducks are poor swimmers because their hull shape is hydrodynamically inefficient. Research at Duke University showed that a mallard wastes all but 5 percent of his energy in swimming at top speed, while a well-designed ship converts power to speed with 20 to 30 percent efficiency. The researchers concluded that ducks sacrifice some hydrodynamic efficiency to improve their performance in the air.

This is a good illustration of a basic principle of boat design. For almost every advantage of a particular boat, the builder has to sacrifice something else (and not just money). If a boat is going to cut through the water like a clipper ship, you can't expect it also to bob its nose underwater to chase minnows and waddle ashore at night.

It's almost harder to decide what kind of ship to build than to do the building. I think it's smart to begin by building a small boat such as a dinghy or a pram. You can find out whether you really have the patience for boat building before you fill the garage with several hundred dollars' worth of materials. You can get the feel of tools and learn not to split planks by nailing too close to the ends or knock out plywood cores by planing edges in the wrong direction.

And you can discipline yourself to check every measurement twice. Until I became thoroughly used to being careful with measurements, I often found myself forgetting the dimension I had just ruled off and confusing it with my shoe size or a football game score or some other distraction.

Although small rowing boats lack the dignity of the cruiser you may build later, they are salty enough in their own right. Just the other day I felt an itch to build a quahogger—a New England fishing boat—merely because of its name. Small boats can trace the winding water trails of a marsh or laze along the current of a stream, where the mystery of the unknown waits around every bend. In a larger craft, the skipper is concerned to stay away from land for fear he'll run into it.

The only reason I didn't start small myself was that I already had an aluminum canoe. There is one problem for the shipwright who already has a small boat: on fine spring mornings he has to decide whether to continue working toward the future launching of a new vessel or drop everything and go boating right now.

Perhaps the small boat you build first will become the tender for the yacht to follow if your delusions of grandeur are sufficiently strong.

Eventually, you have to resolve the question of what you really like to do best on the water—and realistically can expect to be able to do. There's no point in building a ship designed especially for a round-the-world cruise when the boss will never give you more than a week of vacation at a time. It's fairly common for builders to think expansively — and expensively — about spacious cruising accommodations or heavy-duty deep sea construction that they'll never use. Still, if you're going to be strictly practical, you won't even enjoy owning a boat, never mind building one.

What usually restores a sense of reality is thinking about where you will do the building and keep the boat after it's built. For a boat of modest size, half of a two-car garage is adequate. A larger boat may require a special boat shed, which you can construct inexpensively of polyethylene over an A-frame of lumber. (The trick with polyethylene is to nail through a lath over the plastic and into the supporting frame. This shades the stress points from the deteriorating effects of sunlight and prevents the polyethylene from tearing loose around nailheads or staples.) Zoning laws in many communities do not permit such temporary edifices in residential areas, so you may have a problem if you are planning a boat too big to build in the garage. A man in Elk Rapids, Michigan, at this writing was building a thirty-footer in his living room. At the proper time, he plans to knock out a wall. He figures that will cost less than building or renting a large permanent building for a year or two.

There is a persistent myth that people frequently build boats in their basements, not realizing until too late that there is no way to get the finished boat out, but I have never been able to document a case. When pressed, people will always confess that their story of the cellar sailor is secondhand, and they cannot furnish an address where I could go to see for myself the frigate behind the furnace.

When I asked Stuart Nystrom, head of the International Amateur Boat Building Society, he could not think of a single example of a boat built in a basement (except on purpose by someone who had already planned a way to get it out), although the registration figures from the various states show that amateurs are building 30,000 boats a year. Seeing so many opportunities for bungling, one must conclude that here and there around the country are houses with unusual equipment: a boat in the basement to use when the drains back up.

Sources of Plans

Companies in the business of supplying plans for amateur boat builders advertise in boating magazines, and the magazines themselves publish collections of plans. Naval architects sell plans, and the International Amateur Boat Building Society collects and publishes them. Some suppliers also sell kits, which range from just the frames to complete sets of parts requiring only assembly.

Reading plan descriptions is fun. At various times I have been entranced by the thought of building a Chinese junk eighteen feet long and a two-masted catboat of comparable dimensions. One doesn't see many boats around with this much character, because racing designs have exerted so much influence over cruisers.

Many skippers say that what they enjoy about sailing is getting out under the big sky, away from the competitive pressures of modern life. So they join a racing club and spend their weekends hanging over the side of a high-performance sailboat trying to beat the other refugees from the Rat Race across the finish line by half a length. There's a racing class on the Chesapeake whose rules specify that as soon as the boats round the buoy for the downwind leg the whole crew except the helmsman jumps overboard and swims ashore to save weight.

The requirements of racing joined to those of manufacturing tend to make stock boats all look alike. But if the last half knot of speed theoretically possible isn't vital to your sense of self-worth, building your own boat permits you to indulge your taste for a bowsprit or a lugsail or whatever other detail strikes you as properly salty. Somewhere there's sure to be a plan for it.

You have to be careful to choose plans drawn by a designer who doesn't expect the builder who uses them to be a skilled old-time-craftsman-the-kind-you-can't-find-anymore. Some plans lay everything out simply and clearly. Others call for virtuoso accomplishments like cutting an accurate rabbet the entire length of the keel (on both sides!) or fitting and caulking innumerable narrow planks. Watch for such encouraging phrases as "designed for the amateur builder," "requires only basic tools," "ideal first boat for a couple of boys," and the like.

All such claims, naturally, are overstated, but a plan that doesn't even claim to be easy might give you a nervous breakdown. The easiest plans are those that call for marine plywood planking and provide a full-size pattern for cutting out the frame components.

Following are some observations on the main differences in types of boats to take into consideration in choosing the design to build.

Hulls

Flat bottom.   A flat-bottomed boat, in its simplest form, is a

Fig. 2-1. Flat-bottomed hull.

watertight box, which is a good description of the johnboats common on the Upper Mississippi and other rivers. (See Figure 2-1.) The square bow makes a johnboat easy to get into and out of against a steep bank. The broad, flat bottom is stable and provides plenty of room in the boat. This is the easiest and least expensive hull form to build. The disadvantage of a flat bottom becomes apparent if you try to sail one in open waters where the wind kicks up waves. The boat rocks alarmingly and pounds against the water, particularly under power, as each wave lifts the bow.

Consequently, over the years shipwrights have experimented with flat bottoms so that they shade gradually into other hull shapes. Punts, dories, sharpies, and other familiar types modify the basic box form in some way. The bow is pointed, the sides set at an angle, the keel bent upward (rockered) fore and aft.

Many fairly large sailing ships for coastal work were essentially flat-bottomed, and Grand Banks fishing dories are famous for their seaworthiness. Nevertheless, the general rule is that flat bottoms are for rivers and sheltered waters where you don't have to fight large waves.

V bottom. If you make the bottom of a dory narrower and narrower, it finally disappears. (See Figure 2-2.) A boat with a V bottom slices into the waves instead of slapping against them. Under power, it is faster than a comparable round-bottomed hull.

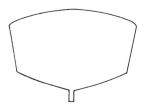

Fig. 2-2. V-bottomed hull.

Fore and aft, it rides comfortably; but side to side, the V shape permits the boat to roll back and forth with a snap at the end of each movement cycle. You can't beach a V-bottomed boat. It falls over on its side.

The shipwright's answer was to modify the Vs. Adding planes to a V bottom makes it behave more like a round-bottomed hull. (See Figure 2-3.) Some powerboats are V-shaped forward to slice the water, then flatten out aft so the boat has something to sit on when it planes.

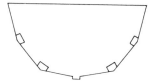

Fig. 2-3. A multichine hull can approximate the shape of a round-bottomed hull.

Round bottom.   A rounded hull is generally considered superior to flat-bottomed or V-bottomed hulls in rough water because its response is less violent. (See Figure 2-4.) A sailboat slides along more efficiently with a round bottom. But a round bottom is hardest to build; you can't use plywood planking, and you do have to steam bend the frames to shape. As will be discussed later, steam bending is perhaps less difficult than amateurs usually think, but it is extra work.

The cross section is not all that determines the performance of

Fig. 2-4. Round-bottomed hull.

a hull. Its shape fore and aft and the width of beam at various points also make a big difference. A planing hull is broad at the stern. Most powerboats and a few lightweight sailboats (in enough wind) are designed to rise up out of the water and skim along the surface going much faster than they could otherwise. At low speeds, however, planing hulls drag along inefficiently.

A displacement hull resists planing. Above a certain speed, more power merely pushes its stern deeper into the water. I have many times noticed this phenomenon using a 3.5 horsepower outboard on a canoe. A smaller motor, say 1.5 horsepower, would be much more efficient.

Without a second passenger or a load of camping gear, the canoe needs a bucket of sand or stones in the bow to keep her from rearing up on her tailbone, which is about eight inches wide, and rolling over. I can tell when I open the throttle too far because the stern settles into the water until the bracket that holds the motor starts scooping up water and flinging it into the boat.

There is a formula for calculating the maximum speed of a displacement hull: The speed in knots equals 1.34 times the square root of the length of boat at waterline.

The waterline length of my canoe is roughly 16 feet, with a square root of 4. Applying the formula, you find that the maximum hull speed is 5.36 knots or a bit over 6 miles per hour (a knot equals 1.15 miles per hour). One day I noted the time and sailed the canoe a distance of 2 miles according to the chart in 20 minutes. I was surprised. There was a good, steady breeze, but it hadn't seemed especially strong; yet it was driving the canoe at the hull's top speed. I was amused to consider how my outboard would roar and thrash trying to drive the boat that fast—if it could. To use full power on the canoe requires ballasting the bow, but too much ballast slows the boat; getting the precise balance is troublesome.

Such is the operation of this waterline principle that when I use the same outboard on the sloop, which has about the same waterline length, it goes almost as fast as the canoe, although the sloop is so much wider and heavier.

Fast powerboats are by far the most popular. A planing boat with a big engine can pull a couple of water skiers and is exhilarating to drive if the water is calm. As mentioned before, it also uses a lot of fuel. A big, fast power cruiser making seventeen knots may be using a gallon of gasoline a mile. A slower cruiser designed to cruise at ten knots might use only half as much gas, enjoy twice the cruising range with the same size tank, and ride more comfortably in rough water.

As Thor Heyerdahl demonstrated when he sailed across the Atlantic on a big bale of hay, from the time of the ancient Egyptians to the present there has been a wide variety of opinion among shipwrights as to what a sailing craft should look like. It isn't enough for a shipwright to choose between round and flat bottoms. He also has to consider the other complexities of a sailing craft hull.

One objective of yacht design is to reduce the area of hull that drags against the friction of the water (*wetted surface*, the experts call it). Since a sailboat heels with the wind, wetted surface varies according to the angle of heel. Too much wetted surface makes a boat slow. Obviously, a sailboat with a broad beam will have more wetted surface than a slim, rakish craft. But a broad beam isn't necessarily a disadvantage. By making the boat more stable, it increases the driving power of the sails and the efficiency of the keel.

A boat gains stability also from the amount and location of ballast it carries. Deep sea boats usually have heavy ballast concentrated at the bottoms of their keels, where the weight can exert maximum leverage. Boats of this type have been rolled entirely over in typhoons. With hatches securely fastened, they righted themselves and survived.

An amateur can't really conclude much about a boat's performance from looking at the hull plans. Almost any generalization has to be qualified. For example, a double-ended hull form is generally considered especially seaworthy. Many lifeboats are built this way. Without a flat transom across the stern, they are less vulnerable to a dangerous smack from a following wave. But a double-ended design is hard to work out without a curve at the quarter-beam buttock that increases the size of the quarter wave created by the passage of the hull through the water. In rough water, a large quarter wave may superimpose itself on a following wave and make it break. So the sharp stern contributes to the exact situation it was intended to avoid—a big breaker coming over the stern and smashing things up.

Multihulls

Catamarans and trimarans are different from other sailboats. They're much faster, and the lightweight construction is relatively inexpensive. The disadvantages are that a trimaran, for example, is about as wide as it is long, so it is difficult to house, transport, and moor; it is also vulnerable to damage. A multihull is stable, but if you ever tip one over, which is not impossible, you are upside down to stay.

In choosing a hull—once you've eliminated alternatives that aren't sufficiently salty for you—it helps to observe boats at harbors and marinas. That's a guide to what the sea lets skippers get away with in your area. You can almost judge the climate by the prevalence of houseboats. Among powerboats, the spaciousness of houseboats makes them ideal for cruising. With big enough engines they can even run fast, but their broad, flat bottoms and the high wind resistance of their superstructures make them unsuitable for a place where the wind often blows hard and kicks up big waves.

Rigs

The Marconi or Bermuda rig is almost universal for modern small sailing ships. Such a sloop, its mast braced with spreaders and stays, is more efficient than other rigs sailing to windward. The tall mainsail usually has a boom short enough to swing inside a permanently fixed backstay. (See Figure 2-5.)

Fig. 2-5. Marconi or Bermuda rig.

Fig. 2-6. Gaff rig.

Gaff-rigged sloops have a saltier look. (See Figure 2-6.) They also sail better downwind (which is why you see so many spinnakers with Bermuda rigs), and they heel less than a comparable Bermuda sloop. But you have to fiddle with an extra halyard for the gaff, and you will probably have to contend with running backstays.

Both kinds of sloops can be sailed with a variety of headsails —large or small jibs and spinnakers.

A catboat is a sloop with the mast set so far forward that no headsail is needed to balance the main. (See Figure 2-7.) You have

Fig. 2-7. Catboat.

to handle only one sail, which you can reef according to the wind velocity. Twenty-five feet is considered about the maximum length for a catboat because the single sail for a larger boat would be too hard to handle.

The lateen sail seen on so many sailboards has salty antecedents, having been copied from ships that rode the monsoons to India in ancient times. (See Figure 2-8.) A lateen rig provides a lot of sail area for a relatively short mast. Its main disadvantage is that it sails better on one tack than on the other.

There's no theoretical reason why a small ship, under thirty

Fig. 2-8. Lateen rig.

Fig. 2-9. Yawl.

feet, can't have more than one mast. The practical reason is that the extra mast and its rigging clutter up a small deck to an unreasonable degree. The advantage of additional masts is that they permit hanging out a wider variety of sails to suit weather conditions. If the boat is quite small, there's scarcely room to stow those sails and accommodate the additional members of the crew needed to wrestle with them.

A yawl is basically a sloop with a small mizzen at the stern. (See Figure 2-9.) Skippers argue over whether the tiny mizzen on most yawls accomplishes anything, except in a race with a light breeze, when it does seem to help work to windward.

Fig. 2-10. Ketch.

Ketches, with mizzens almost as large as the main, are well thought of for cruising but not for racing, since a sloop will beat a ketch on the upwind leg. (See Figure 2-10.)

A schooner is a ketch backward. That is, instead of a large mainsail forward and a smaller mizzen aft, a schooner has its mainsail aft and a smaller foresail, plus the usual headsails. (See Figure 2-11.) My personal opinion is that a gaff-rigged schooner is the saltiest looking rig of all, and I may build one yet.

Fig. 2-11. Schooner.

Keels and Centerboards

There are four solutions to the problem of preventing a sailboat from blowing sideways through the water: a keel (Figure 2-12), a centerboard (Figure 2-13), twin keels (Figure 2-14), and a ballasted centerboard. Oceangoing yachts usually rely on a heavily ballasted fixed keel, for such a boat is almost impossible to capsize. If swamped, however, it probably will sink from the weight of the ballast. The depth of the keel makes the boat difficult to launch from a trailer. You can't run it up on the beach for lunch, and in shallow waters you have to pay close attention to the chart or you'll go aground. I'm looking at the plans for one small ship, only eighteen feet long, with a fixed keel that gives it a draft of three and a half feet. The same boat with a centerboard will float in one foot of water, although with the centerboard all the way down she draws five feet.

If knocked down by a sudden gust, a centerboarder usually is

Fig. 2-12. Deep keel.

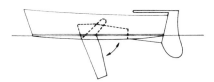

Fig. 2-13. Retractable centerboard.

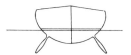

Fig. 2-14. Twin keels.

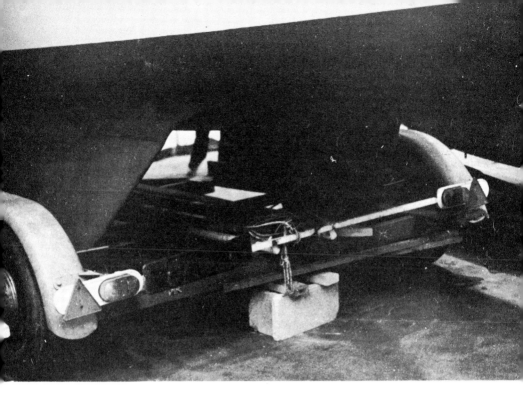

Fig. 2-15. Extra wide trailer accommodates a twin-keel hull.

not self-righting; it's likely to leak, at least a little, around the bottom of the centerboard case; and the case takes up space smack in the middle of the cabin. Nevertheless, a centerboarder provides flexible performance. Sailing downwind, you retract the centerboard entirely and sail faster. In gusty weather, you can retract it partly and cushion the gusts by sliding sideways a bit. Experts can use a centerboard to feel their way around a shoal or twisting channel. And a centerboard hull is easiest to trail. (Larboards, a Dutch invention, are, in effect, twin centerboards that hang over the sides.)

A compromise popular in England and Scandinavia, where there's a wide tidal range, is the twin keel. The two keels allow the boat to sit upright on the mud when the tide runs out of the harbor. The boat can be made self-righting and isn't too difficult to handle on a special low-slung trailer. But the extra keel adds wetted surface, slowing the boat, and requires heavier construction in the hull.

In amateur boat building circles, there is reported to be growing interest in twin-keel cruising sloops about eighteen feet long—large enough for basic accommodations and small enough to be hauled on a trailer. Amateurs used to prefer building auxiliary cruisers about twenty-six feet long, but the problems of maintaining larger boats and finding mooring space make a self-righting boat that can be trailed look better and better.

Another compromise found on a few designs is the ballasted centerboard. It has a heavy weight on the end like a fixed keel, but can be retracted like a centerboard. Because of the weight, it requires a winch to crank it up.

I charted all these considerations and brooded over them for several weeks. I was limited by the fact that I would have to work in one side of a double garage 26½ by 17½ feet in area and take the finished ship out through a door 94½ inches wide by 84 inches high. There was a further limit on length because I had to leave room in the garage for half a dozen bicycles, the lawn mower, and —oh yes—the car.

I am enough of a purist to be attracted by the idea of traditional construction, which begins with "lofting"—transferring the lines of the ship from the plans to full size on the floor of the work space. (This will be explained in more detail later on.) But my garage isn't heated. I planned to construct the frames in the basement during the winter, then begin assembling the hull in the garage when the weather warmed. Plans are available that include full-size patterns for the frames and eliminate the need for lofting.

To get the features I wanted into a small ship required efficient, compact design. That eliminated salty folderol like bowsprits and extra masts and argued for a conventional sloop.

I rejected the idea of assembling a fiberglass kit offered by one major supplier. The twenty-foot size was too big for the garage, and the sixteen-foot size offered only twenty-eight inches of headroom in the cabin. I can't sit up in twenty-eight inches. Besides, I wanted to *build* the boat, not assemble it. A popular seventeen-foot model offered by a leading plan source included several attractive fea-

Fig. 2-16. Depending on the hull design, keels take a variety of shapes.

tures. It could be built of marine plywood over wood frames and coated with fiberglass. But the cockpit was only five feet, six inches long.

Many small sailing ships offer too much cabin in proportion to cockpit. This encourages visions of adventurous overnight voyages, but ignores the fact that cruisers are actually used most of the time as day sailers. In any case, I thought the cockpit deck should be longer so that it could be used for extra sleeping space under a boom tent.

Finally, I settled on a stock plan that offered several satisfactory compromises. With a length of 16 feet, 5 inches, it would leave room in the garage for all the bikes. Its beam of 7 feet, 4 inches would fit through the door with $3\frac{1}{4}$ inches to spare on each side.

The hull would approximate the appearance and performance of a round bottom by using a series of narrow flat planes to make the V look more like a U. "Multichined" is the technical phrase.

I wrote to the plan source and learned that they advised raising the cabin headroom by a maximum of four inches if necessary to a total of forty inches. That doesn't add to the windage too much, although it did make the cabin look a little boxy. But at least my sons and I can sit in it without knocking our heads with every wave. The cabin contains two bunks and a head plus a little extra space that can be used to unfold a table for cooking or spreading out part of a chart. Even so, the cockpit is six feet long.

From the beginning, there was only one possible name for the new ship. All of our family has enjoyed reading the Narnia stories by C. S. Lewis. One of them, *The Voyage of the Dawn Treader*, chronicles an adventurous cruise by merry companions aboard an able ship. So we would build another *Dawn Treader* and supply the merry shipmates, too.

In 1694 the British agreed upon a formula for computing the size of a ship: tonnage equals length times beam times depth of hold divided by 100. Under this formula, taking the hold measurement from the deck to the bilge and ignoring the fact that she actually weighs only a little over 800 pounds, the *Dawn*

Treader can be described as a three-ton ship. That sounds salty enough to make up for her lack of a quarter deck for the captain to pace.

"I confess to a prejudice against concretes, plasters, grouts, mortars, and all other goops."

3 Materials: Ivory, Apes, and Seacocks

Working with traditional boat building materials provides esthetic pleasure. I noticed this as soon as I opened the first package of bronze screws, bright and golden like freshly minted doubloons. I loved the look of the dark Philippine mahogany, a dense heartwood so deep-hued that even the sawdust is a rich red-brown.

But I can't say I relished the *taste* of Philippine mahogany sawdust. It has a weak bouquet and a slightly bitter aftertaste. Personally, I prefer Ponderosa pine or even Douglas fir for flavor, although fir is rather bland. This is not an inconsequential consideration; during a boat building project, you are likely to sample more than a soupçon of sawdust.

Tasting the product as you go is not the only similarity between boat building and cooking. The shipwright is no freer to substitute materials than a cook is to meddle with a recipe. Of course, when things turn out badly a cook may still be able to eat the results. The *Wall Street Journal* reported that a man in Vancouver whose ferrocement hull came out underdone had to have a bulldozer come and bury it in his backyard.

You can't make a final decision on the plan you prefer

33

without thinking about the materials it calls for and the construction methods involved. No ship building material is so superior to others that it has won universal favor among shipwrights. Each, including fiberglass-reinforced plastic, offers advantages and disadvantages.

Ferrocement

The big advantage of ferrocement for amateur boat builders is that it drastically reduces hull cost in the larger sizes—thirty to forty feet and up. The hull curves are defined with ordinary half-inch water pipe, bent to shape with a plumber's pipe-bender. Next, reinforcing rods are welded to the framing pipes like the longitudinal ribs in wooden construction.

Over this framework, the shipwright fastens wire mesh with twisted wire loops. The procedure is something like putting up wire mesh fencing. When all the metal has been fastened down and shaped, the mesh is filled and covered inside and out with a fine-mix concrete, a job that sounds something like plastering a gymnasium ceiling all in one day. (See Figure 3-1).

John Samson and Geoff Wellens, two enthusiastic promoters of this material, concede in their book, *How to Build a Ferrocement Boat*, that "the final plastering of the boat or the

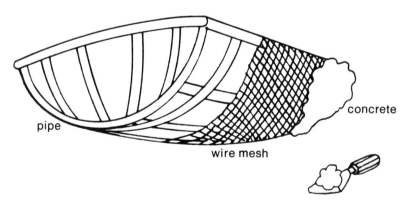

Fig. 3-1. The ferrocement method: Over a framework of piping go wire mesh reinforcing and a skin of fine-mix concrete that must be applied all at one time.

cementing does require special attention. The finish of the boat depends entirely on the success of this one-shot operation and it is always advisable in this area to have a professional man on hand."

So, on the big day, you need six to ten friends—one or two of whom just happen to be professional plasterers or cement finishers —willing to work all day and perhaps into the night. They have to slather goop into every crevice of the mesh so that it will set in one unblemished piece, with no gaps, cracks, or thin spots anywhere.

I confess to a prejudice against concretes, plasters, grouts, mortars, and all other goops. So many of the projects involving them require their use at a crucial step before you've had a chance to become experienced at mixing just the right consistency. With wood, you cut a piece to a certain size and that's that. With goop, if it doesn't all run down your arm and drip off your elbow because you added too much water, you can't tell whether you've accomplished anything until it sets.

A typical ferrocement yacht has a hull thickness of about three-quarters of an inch. For a hull less than about sixty feet long that makes ferrocement heavier than other materials.

The advantages of ferrocement seem to become persuasive somewhere over thirty feet. At forty feet, a ferrocement hull is said to cost only a fourth or a fifth as much as aluminum, less than half as much as steel, slightly more than half as much as wood. No frames are needed, and ferrocement is so much thinner than comparable wood planking that the interior of the hull is noticeably roomier. Ferrocement is unaffected by shipworms, salt water, or spilled gin in the bilge, and it grows stronger with age.

One owner of a forty-two-foot ferrocement powerboat tells of knocking a big chip off a reef at eleven knots with no more damage to the hull than a long scrape mark.

If you haven't built a ship before, a thirty- or forty-foot hull is too ambitious a project. Besides, I doubt that you have six friends who are willing to work all day with wet concrete. The only time any skipper has six friends is on a beautiful summer afternoon when the ship is all fitted out and waiting at the pier for the party to come aboard and cast off.

Steel

Although steel is the standard material for large ships, it is generally considered impractical for small vessels, and few designs are available. Steel is heavy, and for a hull shorter than about forty feet, the plates have to be very thin—so thin they could rust through without constant attention.

Yet small boats have been built of steel successfully by amateur boat builders who have welding equipment and other tools for working steel. It may well become more popular as designers provide plans, because steel is strong, easy to make absolutely watertight, and easy to repair if you have the equipment. Craftsmen who can repair wood or fiberglass hulls are scarce, but there are plenty of body and fender men, welders, and others who understand steel work.

Aluminum

Forty percent of all boats under sixteen feet long are made of aluminum. It's lightweight, strong, corrosion-resistant, and durable. I've paddled, sailed, and motored the same aluminum canoe since 1964. It has scraped over rocks, driven up on beaches through surf and run aground with a heavy load of camping equipment countless times. Nevertheless, it has never been damaged or required any maintenance whatever.

The trouble with aluminum is that it's difficult to work with outside a well-equipped factory. The plates have to be riveted and then sealed with a bedding compound, or welded with equipment to which few amateur shipwrights would have access. Besides these technical difficulties, the material itself is costly. I almost never hear of an amateur building his own boat of aluminum. The best applications for aluminum seem to be small mass-produced boats and custom yachts over forty feet or so, welded in boat yards that specialize in aluminum construction.

Fiberglass

Plastic reinforced with fiberglass has become the standard material for pleasure boat hulls. In factories, where hull after hull can be formed with the same mold, it can be cheaper than wood or metal construction. Much of the cabin, down to toothbrush holders, can be molded the same way. Unless you're a fanatic, fiberglass is too much trouble for an amateur building just one boat. The usual process requires making a male mold, then making a female mold from the male mold and laying up layers of wet, resin-impregnated fiberglass cloth inside the female mold. It sounds as if you could make three wooden ships while you were making the molds and laying up the hull for one of fiberglass.

There is a new method that simplifies the process somewhat. (See Figure 3-2.) You begin by building frames with the cheapest

Fig. 3-2. The urethane method: Sheets of thin urethane are stitched together over a hull shaped of common lumber strips. Then the urethane is coated with fiberglass and resin. At the end, the wooden framing is lifted out and used to make another hull or disposed of.

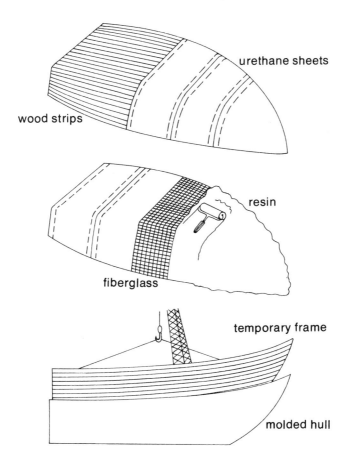

lumber you can find, since they won't be part of the finished hull. You set them up in position and cover them with thin wood strips —also of disposable lumber—running fore and aft about an inch apart. Four-by-eight sheets of urethane are stitched to the strips with a special outsize needle and thread. This gives you a mold.

Over the urethane go layers of fiberglass and resin. When the final coat of resin has set, the mold is lifted out of the fiberglass skin and whatever reinforcing is called for by the plans is put in. Needed wood parts are fastened to the fiberglass hull with more fiberglass and resin.

As always, the hull must have been designed with this method of construction in mind. A U-shaped cross section permits the mold to be removed. If the sides of the hull flare out and curve back in anywhere, you'll have a problem. Also, first-time builders aren't used to the material. (Remember, I warned you about goops.) You could easily wind up with weak places in the hull where the fiberglass wasn't sufficiently saturated with resin.

For amateur boat builders, the best use of fiberglass is probably as a coating over a plywood hull. It greatly strengthens the ship and is not unduly difficult to apply. Mistakes are not fatal and can be repaired. The process will be described in more detail later on.

Fiberglass is an excellent boat building material. Salt water and shipworms can't hurt it; the strength/weight ratio is equivalent to that of steel; and it won't rot. Little maintenance is required, although this point is sometimes overstated. Fiberglass does occasionally delaminate or develop cracks. And eventually the surface gets so scruffy that most owners paint it.

Wood

Although wood requires more maintenance than the other materials mentioned, it is still the choice of the vast majority of amateur shipwrights. Almost everyone has had some woodworking experience and probably already owns many of the tools he will need. Other tools are available at better hardware stores and can be used for other purposes around the house after the boat is finished.

Just as wood paneling adds warmth to a room, wood is a friendly material to work. There's something almost affectionate about the way wood curls up behind the edge of a plane and grasps at your fingers. I don't get any friendly vibrations from a pot of evil-smelling resin. Also, wood is salty. Its use links your ship to her ancestors, like the Oseberg Viking ship, which has endured since the ninth century in oak, and the great ships of the age of exploration. Is it really possible to think of yourself as a grizzled seadog when your ship looks like a plastic bathtub?

Different species of wood, of course, offer quite different characteristics. Some are unsuited to nautical applications because they rot or crack easily. Choosing among woods that make good boats, you must consider their availability. New Zealand shipwrights favor kauri, rimu, and totara for rot-resistant framing, but don't bother to ask your lumber dealer for a quote on totara timbers. Teak is superb, but you can't afford it.

In general, the best wood for boat building is the dense heartwood cut from the interior of a log of the proper species, air-dried rather than kiln-dried. In the old days, it took three or four years to build a ship and the lumber seasoned itself just lying around the shipyard.

For the framing of the *Dawn Treader*, I was able to obtain from a small dealer specializing in marine supplies a quantity of good Philippine mahogany. (See Figure 3-3.) I could tell it was

Fig. 3-3. The framing of every hull is different, as specified by the designer. Shown here is the framing of the *Dawn Treader,* following the blueprints drawn by R. T. Hartley of New Zealand.

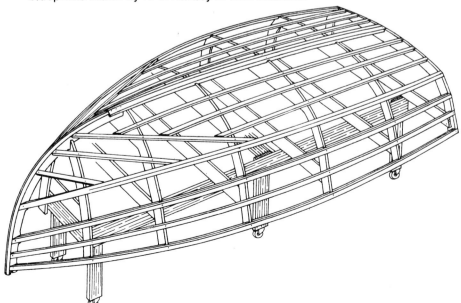

good lumber because of its straight grain, density, and dark color. I couldn't be sure it was air-dried, but it didn't give me any trouble.

Wood for boat building can't be purchased at the ordinary lumber yard. You have to find a source who knows what boat lumber is and can get it for you. Of the 140 species illustrated in a field guide to North American trees, many have been used successfully for boat building at one time or another. Cherry, locust, and rock elm, for example, are all excellent framing materials—strong and rot-resistant—but they are seldom used today. Redwood, which should be good because it's rot-resistant, turns out to be brittle and resistant to steam bending.

Judging from the price lists of firms specializing in boat lumber, the species most widely used and most readily available now are African mahogany, Alaskan yellow cedar, Honduran mahogany, oak, Philippine mahogany, Sitka spruce, teak, Virginia white cedar, western red cedar, and yellow pine. Availability changes from time to time. I recall a sudden influx of yellow pine into the Chicago construction market about fifteen years ago when certain southern forests reached maturity and mills stepped up production. I was writing advertising for a lumber dealer account, and we had a lot of yellow pine to sell.

The cedars.   Cedars are used mainly for planking. Cedar is rot-resistant and swells readily when wet, which is what you want planking to do. Cedar is not strong enough to use for framing.

Sitka spruce.   This wood has a high strength/weight ratio and comes in long, clear pieces. It is the almost universal choice for wooden spars.

Oak.   Oak includes several species, of which white oak is best—the traditional framing lumber of the age of sail. It's the one wood that sometimes is used green because unseasoned white oak is easier to steam bend than is seasoned stock.

The mahoganies.   African and Honduran mahoganies are like oak—suitable for any part of the boat because they're dense, strong, and rot-resistant. Honduran mahogany is stronger than African, but the African wood is usually handsomer.

Philippine mahogany. "Philippine mahogany" is a trade name covering several species, none of which is a true mahogany. Preferred for boat building is the dark red variety, and vast quantities of this wood are used for boat frames because it's such a good value. It's strong and rot-resistant, holds fastenings well, and isn't especially difficult to work. It's cheaper than oak or true mahogany.

Teak. This is the wood that increases a boat's value. Besides being extremely hard, dense, and strong, it holds a natural oil in its pores that makes it impervious to rot. It won't absorb water or swell. A teak deck is the finest there is, and it is customarily left unpainted and unvarnished. (Painting teak would be as barbaric as painting marble.)

The trouble with teak is that it grinds down your bank account even faster than it dulls your tools. The last time I looked, teak cost three or four times as much as Philippine mahogany.

Yellow pine. Yellow pine—the long-leaf species—is much harder and stronger than other pines. Some builders consider it almost as good as oak, and it costs less. Inspect individual pieces for pockets of pitch, and reject those that have them.

Boat building lumber sometimes is sold in flitches, which are planks cut the full width of the log with the bark left on the edges. No boat lumber is cut to standard sizes, such as two-by-fours, because so many different dimensions are specified in boat plans.

The question arises at this point whether to have your supplier mill your lumber for you to the sizes you need or to do it yourself. The answer depends on whether you own a good table saw with plenty of room around it for ripping long pieces.

Except for ripping raw stock, a table saw isn't especially useful in boat building. There are too few straight lines. I didn't want a table saw around the place, so I ordered my lumber cut to the sizes specified in my plans. This saved me time as well as the cost of expensive equipment for which I had no other use.

If you decide to do your own ripping, don't skimp on the lumber order. You're sure to make some mistakes figuring the most efficient cuts. Ordering a bit too much is no problem; you'll find a use for anything left over. If you run short, the whole project will have to stop while you wait for another order to be filled.

Plywood

No one denies that AA marine plywood is the best product for marine use, apart from cost. Both faces are clear, and care is taken to make the core solid, with no gaps. A gap in the core could weaken a hull at a crucial point or collect water and start rot.

Ordinary plywood is not made with waterproof glue; hence it delaminates when wet. As for exterior grade plywood, there is a controversy as to how far you can go using it afloat. The kind that is most widely marketed has only one good face; the back is full of knots and defects. Some builders, however, use an AB grade exterior plywood, which has a back almost as good as the face, when they plan to coat and strengthen the hull with fiberglass.

An experienced craftsman who has built several boats and enjoys virtuoso control over his materials can get away with some shortcuts. The beginning shipwright working on his first hull is better advised to stick to thoroughly dependable materials. I used only marine plywood in the *Dawn Treader*, although the dealer occasionally asked me if I wanted my order gift-wrapped to take or delivered by armored car.

Standard plywood is made of Douglas fir, but marine plywood is made from other species as well. Philippine mahogany plywood is about the same price as fir and provides a better surface for finishing if you intend to paint or varnish it. Philippine mahogany is heavier than fir, however, and increases the weight of the hull.

Shipwrights with a taste for salty traditions will be interested to know that the mills laminate thin teak planks to a plywood base. You can have a teak deck that goes on fast, won't leak, and costs only about four times as much as fir marine plywood.

Marine plywood also is available with a fiberglass coating applied at the mill, but I doubt whether much is sold. You still have to do something about the seams and edges, and that's the hard part.

Fastenings

Your plans should specify the proper size of boat nails and screws to use for each part. Ordinary fasteners from the corner hardware store won't do in a boat because they'll rust away, especially in salt water. Whether to use galvanized or bronze fasteners is a matter of controversy, boat building being one of those delightful fields in which experts disagree, casting more than a few aspersions on the intelligence of members of opposing schools.

Here are the considerations: galvanized fasteners resist rust, but they do rust eventually lying at a mooring in salt water season after season. In a boat used on weekends in fresh water and stored on a trailer in the garage during the week, it seems unlikely that galvanized fasteners will ever have to be replaced. Bronze endures, salt water or fresh.

Life being what it is, the spring after you finish building a boat with galvanized fasteners you'll be transferred to a place on the Gulf Coast where there's a long sailing season and convenient moorings—in salt water. As time passes, your sleep will be troubled by dreams in which your usual pastime of trying to outrun rhinos, trolls, or IRS agents will be interrupted by visions of galvanized screws corroding, molecule by molecule.

That's why there is wide support for the view that basic hull fastenings should be of bronze, which will last as long as the ship. Although bronze fastenings cost about two and a half times as much as galvanized ones and add many dollars to the price of a small ship, the portion of the total cost invested in fastenings is small.

Planking is usually fastened with special annular boat nails. (See Figure 3-4). The rings around the shank greatly increase the

 Fig. 3-4. Boat nail.

holding power. Bronze boat nails come in two grades—"commercial bronze" and "silicon bronze"—and the latter is harder and more expensive.

Remember how far back in history the Bronze Age lies? Conservative generals who liked to refight the previous war with bronze weapons received rude shocks when new enemies came along armed with iron. The iron usually put quite a dent in their excellencies' bronze helmets. Even with silicon bronze, you have to drill pilot holes for every nail, for bronze nails are easy to bend while being hammered into hardwood if you're not careful.

Never use brass in hull construction. It's too soft; you can easily twist off the head of a screw while trying to drive it; and it corrodes underwater.

Monel, an alloy of copper and nickel, is available in boat nails of superior strength and holding power. Like bronze, it lasts forever, and it is as strong and unbending as steel, but it costs more than silicon bronze.

All the hull fastenings in the *Dawn Treader* are of silicon bronze, although I don't expect that to make the Midwestern sailing season more like that of the Gulf Coast.

In most boats, large timbers are bolted together, other framing members are fastened with flat-head wood screws, and planking, decking, and bulkheads are nailed on. The largest bolt in the *Dawn Treader* is seven inches long and $5/8$-inch thick. Several others are nearly as large. When I opened the package from the mail order supplier, I was somewhat awed by their size, perhaps even a little intimidated. They looked like parts left over from a suspension bridge.

That seven-inch bolt made a good symbol of the magnitude of my ship building project. And, with matching nut but no washer, it cost about five dollars. Another apt symbol.

Above the waterline, stainless steel is widely used. It is protected from rust by an invisibly thin coating of oxide that forms in the air. Underwater there's no coating, and it corrodes like other steels. Stainless costs as much as a third more than bronze in the smallest sizes. Fortunately, the recommended applications for stainless are mainly fastening deck and spar hardware, for which not many screws are required.

Electrolysis

Shipwrights who like to meditate on the Bible should turn at this point to Matthew 6:19-20, where you learn about what happens to treasures that aren't laid up in heaven. They rust—especially if you have used more than one kind of metal in your hull. Dissimilar metals adjacent to each other in water become the anode and cathode of an electrolytic system. The metal that is lower on the galvanic totem pole disintegrates. That's why you can't switch to galvanized planking nails halfway through because you ran out of bronze or vice versa.

However, when metals are close to each other in the galvanic series the galvanic action is weak and you can safely mix them. Stainless steel fittings are customarily fastened to aluminum masts with stainless steel self-tapping screws, for example, but copper and brass should be kept well away from any aluminum.

Table 1

Common Metals Ranked from Electro-Negative to Electro-Positive

1.	Mercury, mercury paint	11.	Stainless steel
2.	Monel	12.	Cast iron
3.	Nickel	13.	Wrought iron
4.	Silicon bronze	14.	Mild steel
5.	Copper, copper paint	15.	Aluminum
6.	Yellow brass	16.	Cadmium
7.	Phosphor bronze	17.	Galvanized iron and steel
8.	Manganese bronze	18.	Zinc
9.	Tin	19.	Magnesium
10.	Lead		

One of the main electrolytic risks on a ship is fastening ballast to the bottom of a keel. With iron ballast castings, only galvanized bolts should be used. If the ballast casting is lead, use bronze or Monel bolts. The wrong combination may eventually cause the ballast to drop off, which could spill the skipper's coffee mug, to say the least, in a breeze you ordinarily wouldn't pay much attention to.

Obviously, it is not always possible to make everything below the waterline of the same metal. *Dawn Treader* has a steel centerboard pivoting on a bronze bolt. No doubt the steel will corrode in time, but a heavy plate $5/16$ inch thick should last a long time.

Sometimes an engine propeller and other fittings of dissimilar metals come through the hull. If they're separated by considerable distance, you probably won't have any trouble. If they're within a foot of each other, the solution is to fasten a zinc sacrificial plate about two inches square to the hull. The plate takes over as cathode and begins to disintegrate instead of your valuable fittings. It is replaced as necessary.

Before leaving the subject of fastenings, I should mention that it is possible to build a plywood hull almost without nails or screws. The method, best known for its use in Mirror dinghies, consists of cutting plywood panels to a pattern and stitching them together with copper wire. The seams have battens on the inside and are covered with fiberglass tape on the outside. The hull has to be designed for this type of construction from the beginning, and I know of only one cruising design currently available. Unfortunately, despite its apparent construction virtues, I don't like its looks. (Readers fascinated with the idea of sewing a hull together can obtain the plan through the International Amateur Boat Building Society. For address, see Appendix.)

Adhesives

There are three kinds of glue used by boat builders—plastic resin, resorcinol, and epoxy.

Plastic resin comes in powder form and is mixed with water in small batches. The pot life is about four hours. It reacts badly with oak and is less durable than the others, but it has been used successfully in many boats. It is by far the cheapest.

Resorcinol is a liquid activated by a catalyst powder that turns it purple. It is completely waterproof. Like plastic resin, it should be used at temperatures no lower than seventy degrees with joints that fit snugly.

Epoxy is the strongest and most expensive. It consists of two syrupy liquids that are mixed together, the darker one being the catalyst. (See Figure 3-5.) Epoxy can be formulated for use at temperatures as low as about forty degrees. It is tolerant of joints that don't fit as snugly as they might, and it can be thickened with filler and used as a putty to fill gaps and compensate for errors. I can't understand why an amateur shipwright would consider gluing with anything but epoxy. (See further discussion in Chapter 5.)

Fig. 3-5. Epoxy is now marketed with the resin and the catalyst in squeeze bottles, convenient to use. You also get a plastic measuring cup, a set of wooden tongue depressors for stirring and spreading, and a quantity of thickener for making epoxy putty to fill gaps.

Other Materials

In any boat, you'll have a use for caulking and bedding compound. Hardware and paint stores carry several grades, and the labels identify the kinds intended for marine applications. This is the material you squirt along the seam between the cabin sides and the deck with a caulking gun. You use it under the centerboard casing and wherever a fitting or a bolt passes through the deck or hull. It's supposed to stay resilient and pliable so that it can shrink or expand and twist with the boat while retaining its ability to keep out water.

You'll probably make your own cabin windows, which requires coping with Plexiglas or Lucite (acrylic plastic). Some of the marine mail order suppliers carry the proper thicknesses for boat work. The material stocked at hardware stores and lumber yards for storm windows is too thin.

Acrylic plastic can be drilled and sawed. For drilling, back the plastic with scrap wood to avoid chipping as the drill bit breaks through the back. Saws should have fine-toothed blades. After sawing, file the edges smooth. Plexiglass (with a double *s* it's not a brand name) has a tendency to crack if left with a notch in the edge.

Although marine materials are invariably costly and it's folly to overbuild, it never pays to skimp. When I was building the *Dawn Treader,* I considered using fiberglass tape on the seams and merely painting the rest of the plywood hull. Instead, I decided to fiberglass the whole hull, although not the decks or cabin. The second or third time I sailed her I had occasion to be glad.

On a beautiful afternoon in spring I was returning to the harbor at Waukegan, Illinois, after a pleasant sail on Lake Michigan. The wind was from the north, not especially strong, but steady. Sailing alone, I had taken down the jib off the harbor's mouth. Now I was halfway in, paralleling a long concrete jetty.

I have to confess that in my mind I was still sailing a canoe, which can usually be preserved from a collision disaster with a quick thrust of a paddle or by sticking out a leg and kicking away from the menace. That explains the stupid maneuvers that followed.

I decided it was time to drop the main and start my outboard to motor to the trailer slips. There are always too many boats at close quarters to sail all the way. I should have started the motor before giving up the sail, but I didn't have a topping lift yet. The rigging plan hadn't shown one, and I didn't know how badly I would need it. Consequently, as soon as I loosed the main halyard the boom dropped into the cockpit along with the sail, trailing the main sheet and the traveler over the transom. These lines, dragging in the water, would have fouled the propeller immediately if the engine had been running.

It took only a brief moment to unbend the sail, roll it up, and stuff it into the sailbag. Then I could use the main halyard to hold up the end of the boom. I yanked the engine cord, once to prime, once to start. Nothing happened. In the excitement of launching a new boat I had been negligent about changing the spark plug.

While I fiddled with the engine, the wind inexorably pushed the *Dawn Treader* toward the jetty. I should have stopped tinkering long enough to rig some boat cushions as temporary fenders. Instead, since the engine was beginning to make encouraging noises, I kept trying to start it until I could hear the *Dawn Treader*'s port side beginning to scrape against the rough concrete lip of the jetty, up and down with each ripple.

I wished fervently that I had a crewman aboard to fend off. Single-handing provides little margin for stupidity. If I had felt impelled to throw somebody overboard as a human sacrifice to the sea gods, there would have been no one to offer but the skipper himself. Fortunately, the engine sputtered to life finally and hauled us free just in time.

Later, with hull safely up on the trailer, I inspected the damage. The paint was scraped off in several places. Underneath, the fiberglass coating seemed unharmed. I had no difficulty at home sanding the scraped places and touching them up with matching paint. I'm afraid that plywood protected only by paint, as I once intended, would have been deeply gouged.

In the annals of the sea many a mariner has drifted helplessly down on a reef with unfavorable wind or current. After the *Dawn Treader*'s brush with the jetty, I could empathize. I had a sinking feeling.

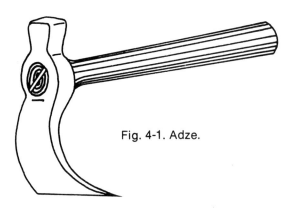

Fig. 4-1. Adze.

4 Tools: The Shark's Teeth and Seashell Game

ONE reason the British blockade in the Revolutionary War wasn't more effective was that colonial ship builders could set up operations along almost any stream deep enough to float the finished vessels. There was timber everywhere. Owners of the shipyard would dig a saw pit just past the first bend, out of sight from the sea, and provide two-man saws and heavy mallets. The ship carpenters brought their own hand tools—axes, adzes (see Figure 4-1), augers, and plumb lines plus chisels, handsaws, planes, and squares. New blockade runners were spawned like salmon.

The simplicity of this equipment suggests that boat building tools today needn't be elaborate. If you live in a house and have to cope with such things as broken shutters and endless demands for more shelving, you probably already own most of the tools needed. There are only a few special boat building tools that you almost certainly will have to go out and buy.

The ancient Polynesians had only stone, shell, and shark's teeth with which to build their famous seventy-foot seagoing canoes, which were faster and more seaworthy than European ships up to rather recent times. Seafarers in those days weren't too interested in blazing speed. Since there were no charts, the faster a ship went the faster it could get into trouble in treacherous waters.

While I'm digressing, I'll mention the corollary: too small a ship can get into trouble because of her slow speed. As noted previously, the maximum speed of a displacement hull is determined by the length of the waterline. One ocean racing expert gives the example of a fourteen-footer beating into the wind at a forty-five degree angle. Although sailing at top speed, she is actually making good 2 knots toward her destination. Under identical conditions, a seventeen-footer could make good 2.8 knots. Depending on currents and other conditions, the larger vessel might claw her way home before a storm broke while the smaller one failed to make progress or even lost ground.

We observed this principle on one of *Dawn Treader's* first cruises—three days on Lake Winnebago, which empties into Green Bay and Lake Michigan. When we woke up on the morning of the second day, the wind was already blowing strong from the south. Our four-dollar cabin radio gave the morning forecast: wind southwest fifteen to twenty-five miles per hour. (Later, the evening news broadcast informed us that wind velocity actually reached thirty.)

Our first thought was that with such a strong wind blowing we could reach the north end of the lake easily by afternoon. That seemed like a good idea lying at anchor in a sheltered cove with breakfast over and a hot mug of tea in hand.

We started out with the small jib up and a big reef rolled into the main. Sailing downwind was glorious, with the shoreline sliding past at five miles an hour, according to the chart, and big waves lifting under the transom and thrusting us ahead. After a while, we shook the reef out of the main and went even faster.

A little past Oshkosh, I began to pay more attention to the waves, which were already running over three feet and probably soon would be four. I thought about our situation if the strong southerly winds lasted another day. Beating into the wind and those waves to return to our car and trailer at the south end of the lake would be unrewarding. Our outboard auxiliary wouldn't be much help; the propeller would be out of the water half the time.

So I picked a snug cove on the chart and put about into the wind. Now we were beating into the Straits of Magellan with Andean williwaws howling around our ears. Heeled far over, the *Dawn Treader* smashed into the waves, the spray drenching the forward cabin windows.

To make good a quarter of a mile of southing and round the point into the cove took two tacks and half an hour. From the cove back to our trailer the distance was eighteen miles. At the rate we had just sailed it would take thirty-six hours. If we had continued to the north end of the lake past Neenah as originally planned and the wind didn't change, returning to our trailer would have been a voyage of fifty or sixty hours—more time than we had available for our cruise.

A ship with a twenty-five-foot waterline would have been 25 percent faster. It could have covered the entire distance we had originally charted in the time available, although the return voyage would have been tedious; beating into the wind always is.

Since the hurricane was blowing against us, we dropped anchor in the cove, furled the sails, and made lunch. While the sea worked itself up into a rage, we bobbed comfortably in the lee of the forested shore. We lounged in the cockpit in the shade of the cabin, dozed, and read books from the ship's library. For once, they had nothing whatever to do with ship building or sailing.

To return to the subject, books can be valuable tools for boat building as well as pleasant diversions at anchor. Following are several useful references that go beyond the scope of this volume.

Boatbuilding by Howard I. Chapelle (W. W. Norton, 1941) has for a generation been the basic wood boat building manual. It doesn't, however, cover the new techniques made possible by such modern materials as epoxy and fiberglass.

Complete Amateur Boat Building by Michael Verney (MacMillan, second edition, 1967) covers many useful details, although the title is something of an overstatement. The principles are illustrated by the specifics of building three small boats. Originally written for a British audience, it can be opaque here and there for

American readers. Amateurs have enough trouble with such nautical terms as *chine*, *futtock*, or *skeg* without also having to stumble over Britishisms like *knotting* for shellac, *GRP* for fiberglass, and *sellotape* for masking tape.

Skene's Elements of Yacht Design, revised by Francis S. Kinney (Dodd, Mead, eighth edition, 1973), emphasizes why boats sail and perform in certain ways more than how to build them. It contains charts and tables providing such technical information as how to determine the aluminum equivalent of a wooden spar and how much force is required to capsize a particular hull.

All of these authors are naval architects or engineers. During the building of *Dawn Treader*, I frequently turned to one or another of them (or all of them) for advice on some difficult point. The trouble with experts is that they tend to assume that the reader has capabilities that he does not in fact possess. They lightly describe methods relying on intricate joinery I wouldn't attempt even after successfully completing the *Dawn Treader* and acquiring lots of practice with my tools. Verney, for example, likes stems rabbeted to receive the ends of planking. And he recommends dovetailing deck beams into their supports. Easier methods also work if the design provides for them and if you have proper materials.

Cutting

For cutting, power tools will never completely replace hand tools. Quite often, it's far easier to use a hand tool for a moment than to take the trouble of setting up a power tool—changing blades, running an extension cord from the nearest outlet, clamping on a cutting guide, and the like.

So you'll need a crosscut saw and a ripsaw, the standard hand models used by carpenters everywhere. For some work, the regular crosscut saw with about eight points per inch will be too coarse. The answer is a second crosscut saw with ten or eleven points per inch. For these finer cuts, I found the box saw that came with an inexpensive miter box set just right.

Handsaws must be kept sharp or they tend to drift off the cutting line. If you're going to build a ship, start out right by bundling up all your handsaws and taking them to the hardware store for sharpening.

For a boat built with plywood, a saber saw is the most useful power tool. You'll spend hours cutting out curves and intricate gusset shapes from large plywood panels; doing it by hand would be tedious. Get new blades periodically, for a dull saber saw blade, like a handsaw blade, becomes increasingly hard to control.

Other kinds of power saws aren't of much use with a plywood boat unless you decide to rip your own lumber. There are few straight lines. Although it is possible to approximate a curve using a rotary saw to make a series of short, straight cuts, the process is scarcely labor-saving, and it wastes material.

It's nice to own a full set of chisels, including a big one two inches or more wide, sometimes called a "slick" and much used by some shipwrights for shaping planking. My chisel collection consists of only two sizes—½ inch and ¾ inch. I had a ¼-inch chisel once, but when I went to look for it just now I couldn't find it. I can't remember when I saw it last and can't say I've missed it. This suggests that ½- and ¾-inch chisels were adequate for a ship the size of *Dawn Treader*.

Once you start using chisels you need a sharpening stone. The correct angle of a chisel bevel is from twenty to twenty-five degrees. There is a tool that clamps chisel and plane blades to the proper angle for sharpening, which some find useful. I bought one, then decided that sharpening the bevel seems to go faster by hand.

The sharpening stone should be lubricated with light machine oil before use, to maintain its bite. Sooner or later it will become glazed, and you must clean it with ammonia, then touch up the surface with fine sandpaper wrapped around a wood block.

Chisels should be used to take off only a little wood at a time. There's a temptation to chisel off too much in a chunk, sometimes splitting the wood in the process. You know, of course, that a chisel turned one way digs in too far and makes a deep gouge; turned the other way it doesn't dig in enough, comes up unexpectedly, and stabs your left knee.

The best quality tools do the work better and save time. This is particularly true of any tool with a cutting edge. A good one stays sharp longer.

Drilling

Every fastener used in a boat needs a pilot hole drilled for it. Even the boat nails need pilot holes; otherwise they tend to bend over when you try to hammer them. All this drilling calls for a ¼-inch electric drill, an essential timesaver.

Sometimes the home handyman working with a soft wood like pine is tempted to cheat and drill only one pilot hole for a screw through two pieces of wood. This works only if the wood pieces are clamped together while the screw is turned and if the tightness of the joint is not crucial. You can't get away with this in boat building, where the tightness of the joint *is* crucial. You have to drill one hole the proper diameter for the threads through the piece to be fastened and into the base piece. Then you drill a second, larger hole in which the shank of the screw can move freely. A third pass with a countersink bit recesses the wood to accommodate the screw head.

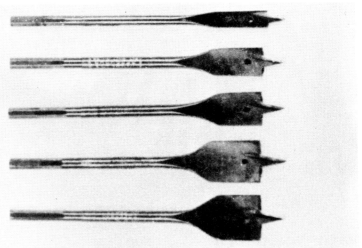

Fig. 4-2. Drill team: useful bits for fast, deep holes in wood with a power drill. But always back the work with a piece of scrap to avoid splintering when the bit emerges on the far side.

Changing bits constantly becomes irksome. One solution is to have an extra drill handy, power or otherwise. Another is to use special bits that bore the thread hole, shank hole, and countersink in one operation. I used three of these in building the *Dawn Treader*, sized to match number 8, 10, and 12 wood screws. One drawback of these bits is that, although the thread drill's length can be adjusted with a tiny set screw, the shank cutter is not as long as the shank of a bronze screw by $\frac{1}{4}$ inch or so. In some circumstances, when you have to fasten thicker pieces of wood, it is still necessary to drill a separate hole for the shank.

An awl is a useful accessory for drilling. The rotary action of the electric drill tends to make it crawl when you start to drill into something hard. Use the awl to make a starter hole for the tip of the drill bit exactly where you want it.

This can lead to an amusing chain of events:

1. Mark the spot with a pencil.
2. Make a starter hole with an awl.
3. Drill the pilot hole, using a $\frac{7}{64}$ bit for a number 10 screw.
4. Unclamp the top piece of wood and drill a shank hole with a $\frac{3}{16}$ bit.
5. Change bits again and countersink for the screw head.
6. Forget to lubricate the screw with soap and break off the head trying to turn it.
7. Start over in another place.

The old-fashioned brace and bit has not been outmoded by power. Sometimes the shorter power drill bits of the same diameter aren't long enough to do the job.

Fastening

A brace with a screwdriver bit is the ideal way to drive screws. (See Figure 4-3.) Once started, you want to keep them moving in hardwood so they don't freeze. I prefer the brace to the power-driven alternatives: a variable-speed electric drill or a gear-down accessory for single-speed electric drill, which can also be used with a screwdriver bit. With the leverage of the brace handle, I can exert ample torque. This eliminates extra fumbling with power drill

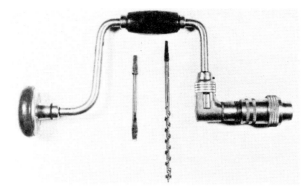

Fig. 4-3. There are screwdriver bits for use with a brace as well as the usual auger bits.

chucks. The power drill can be kept ready to drill the next hole.

Seating a series of number 10 or 12 screws in hardwood with a screwdriver is strenuous; you'll get blisters. Use your brace instead.

The most common mistake with screwdrivers and screwdriver bits is using a size too small for the slot and damaging it. Bronze ship screws are softer and more vulnerable to damage than the steel screws used for most other jobs, so it's especially important to keep on hand a full set of the necessary sizes. If any of the blades get nicked or twisted, retire them.

While waiting their turn (apt phrase), screws should be kept in a dish with a chunk of soap and a little water. The water keeps evaporating, but the same chunk of soap will last for the construction of an entire vessel. (It helps to be able to economize here and there.)

Use a nailset to finish driving boat nails. You don't want to bang dents into the planking with the hammerhead. Also, nail heads should be driven a little below the surface of the wood so they can be puttied with wood dough.

Very little fastening can be accomplished on a boat without C clamps. (See Figure 4-4.) Usually, the wood is sprung into a curve and has to be held while holes are drilled, screws driven, and glue allowed to set.

No shipwright ever has too many C clamps. Besides being useful, they're expensive. I kept resisting purchasing additional clamps until I would find myself in desperate circumstances and have to send a child biking to the hardware store for another, like Balto, the sled dog, bringing serum to the settlers.

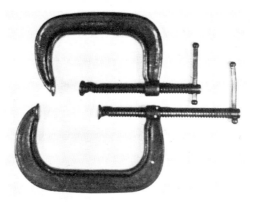

Fig. 4-4. Indispensable C clamps. You'll need a minimum of one for each frame in your hull.

I finally learned that the minimum number of C clamps needed was the same as the number of points at which a longitudinal timber could be attached to the frame. The *Dawn Treader* needed seven, one for the stem, one for the transom, and five for the intervening frames.

C clamps with four-inch jaws sufficed for most jobs, but more than once I was grateful that I had picked up a pair of six inchers on one of the emergency runs when the hardware store was out of four inchers.

There's a versatile product you should know about sold at most hardware stores under the brand name "Redibolt." It consists of long steel rods threaded the entire length to fit standard nut sizes. A pair of these can be used in innumerable ways to clamp and control things.

I used them to install the heavy centerboard case. (See Figure 4-5.) It had to be maneuvered up and under the centerboard slot cut in the upside-down keel and held while holes for permanent bolts were drilled from above.

So I drilled holes just large enough for the Redibolt in scrap lumber, which I placed under the nuts like huge washers. Then all I had to do to lift and position the case was to turn the two nuts on the two rods projecting through the centerboard slot.

Fig. 4-5. Homemade tool: a length of Redibolt, a couple of nuts, and grippers of scrap wood can handle many jobs, including maneuvering the centerboard case into position while the hull is upside down.

Shaping

Every task has its representative tool. One associates the ax with the log cabin, the hammer and saw with a frame house, and the trowel with masonry, although other tools are needed in each case. The saltiest tool in ship building is the plane. I spent many hours shaving thin red curls of mahogany from the timbers of the *Dawn Treader* to prepare a surface for affixing planking.

Before building the *Dawn Treader,* my experience with planes had been limited to fixing doors that tended to stick. I soon learned that in serious planing there are a couple of temptations to resist. One is to plane an edge lower on one side. The other is to plane the ends lower than the middle.

Most of the planing on a boat involves beveling a longitudinal timber. To avoid overdoing it, keep checking your progress with a bevel gauge set to the desired angle.

The basic plane for ship work is the longest jack plane you can find. Mine, with a fourteen-inch base, was satisfactory. Some builders use still longer ones and swear that old-fashioned planes with base shoes of wood, creating less friction than steel, are the smoothest and best of all.

A long plane is for shaping bevels and smoothing, working along the grain. To work across the grain at the end of a timber you need a block plane. Planing cross grain is much harder; the plane needs to be kept extra sharp and adjusted to barely cut.

For certain steps I found a small rabbet plane indispensable. The rabbet plane's advantage is that its blade runs the full width of the tool. I could lay its cheek against the beveled surface of a longitudinal timber and bevel the edge of a piece of plywood planking to match. Other planes don't cut right up to the edge because their blades protrude through a base shoe, which surrounds the blade on all sides.

As you plane—always toward the left if possible—keep your head above the handle and transfer your weight to your left foot. Lift the blade on the return stroke to avoid dulling it. You'll develop a rhythmical swing and shuffle that could be set to music. Always plane from the ends toward the middle. When beginning to plane at the end consciously bear down on the knob of the plane to help keep the sole in line with the surface.

You'll find that your plane blade requires frequent sharpening. Don't think, "Oh, I'll just finish this and sharpen the blade tomorrow." It really saves time and trouble to stop at once and get out the sharpening stone when you notice that the plane is losing its edge.

A plane cuts better if it is held at an angle so the blade can slice. This is especially true with a plywood edge, which otherwise is difficult to plane. Avoid planing all the way across the end of a piece of wood with the block plane. The blade may catch on the last few wood fibers of the far edge and split it off. The solution, if you plane in only one direction, is to clamp on a backing block of scrap wood.

I think some builders might find a power plane useful. I didn't buy one because they cost over sixty dollars and because I was afraid that, in the critical process of preparing the ribs for planking, a power tool might get away from me.

Every time I worked on the *Dawn Treader*, I began by slipping a wood rasp into my hip pocket. It was that useful (although rather disagreeable to sit on absent-mindedly). You use a rasp (Figure 4-6) to smooth cut edges, especially on plywood, to make minor bevels, and to improve the fit of pieces that were cut a hair too long.

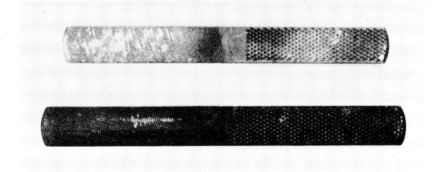

Fig. 4-6. Wood rasps.

Halfway between a plane and a rasp is a Surform (Figure 4-7). It can be used in places where planing is awkward, and it takes down wood faster than a rasp.

The adze (Figure 4-1) and the drawknife (Figure 4-8) were popular with old-time shipwrights for shaping the heavy timbers of stem and keel. Never having seen either in stock in the hardware stores I frequent, I had to make do with other tools, including my teeth.

Power sanders come in three types: belt, orbital, and disk. None is perfect for ship building. Belt sanders are heavy and hard to use on a curved surface. Orbital sanders are lighter, but don't cut as fast. Their motion makes whirl marks in the wood unsuitable for finishing with varnish. One variation of the orbital sander converts to a straight line reciprocating sander, which gives wood grain a fine finish and can be used next to vertical projections. Disk sanders also make whirl marks, but can cut fast and work over curved or irregular surfaces.

Not wishing to buy a heavy-duty sander, I used a disk sanding attachment on my electric drill plus hand sanding on the hard-to-reach places and the few parts I intended to varnish. It did the job.

Of course, an electric drill is not made for sustained sanding. It overheats after a while. Fortunately, I have both a $\frac{1}{4}$-inch drill and a more powerful $\frac{3}{8}$-inch one. As soon as one began to feel warm, I switched the sanding attachment to the other.

Restraint must be used with all power sanders. When running with medium or coarse grit, they can easily dig in and bite off more wood than you intended.

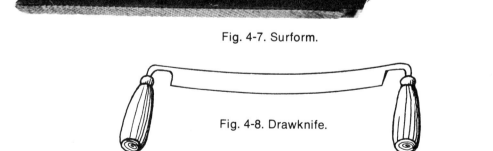

Fig. 4-7. Surform.

Fig. 4-8. Drawknife.

Metalworking

The aluminum alloy used for spars is only a little harder than the "do it yourself" aluminum tube and bar stock sold in hardware stores. It's easy enough to drill with an electric drill and to cut with a hacksaw. Stainless steel is the metal that tests your mettle, like breaking out of jail and other forms of real metalworking.

My journal notes that drilling two stainless steel crosstrees (spreaders), tapping the holes, and completing the assembly took half a day. And I broke two drill bits.

Fortunately, I had my $\frac{3}{8}$-inch drill, which runs more slowly than $\frac{1}{4}$-inch drills. Slower speeds are more effective for working hard materials. Cutting oil helps by cooling the cutting tip and preventing the metal chips from flying around so much. You should always wear plastic safety goggles when using any kind of power tool on metal.

My $\frac{3}{8}$ drill has a variable speed trigger, which simplifies starting a hole in metal. Even so, despite what the ads say, I found it necessary to start each hole with a center punch. Thin metal is easier to saw or drill if clamped to a backing of scrap lumber, and metal edges have to be filed smooth before you cut yourself on them.

Measuring

Steel tape measures come in various lengths up to sixteen feet. The six-foot size is worthless for ship building. Eight feet is the minimum, ten feet is better. Never use a cloth tape measure, which you might be tempted to do in measuring along a curve; it has too much stretch in it.

A metal yardstick is worth having, not only for measuring but also to use as a straightedge in marking and to brace the saber saw against while making straight cuts.

You'll need a pair of dividers—the kind with two sharp-pointed legs and a screw adjustment. (See Figure 4-9.) As will be explained later on, there are several steps that scarcely can be managed without dividers.

Another essential measuring tool is an adjustable bevel gauge,

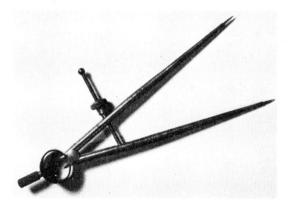

Fig. 4-9. Dividers.

which you use to figure out the proper bevels, then to mark the piece to be beveled. (See Figure 4-10.) As mentioned earlier, you also use it to keep checking on your planing. You have to have a

Fig. 4-10. Sliding bevel gauge is shown in scale with try squares. You can't build a boat without this tool.

square for marking right angles. A level is essential for certain stages, and you also need a plumb bob once or twice; maybe you can borrow one instead of buying it.

Miscellaneous Tool Needs

Some unexpected items complete the shipwright's tool kit: wooden tongue depressors for stirring paint and mixing and spreading epoxy, spring clothespins for holding slippery glue-

Fig. 4-11. To plug holes with dowels coated with glue, grip them with a spring clothespin and hammer in.

covered dowels (Figure 4-11), and a bicycle tire pump for blowing sawdust away when you're ready to spread glue.

For some gluing-up operations, you'll need every clamp you can find. Don't overlook such auxiliary clamps as the net holders from the Ping Pong table, the base of the food grinder, and the reading lamp from the headboard of the bed.

Decide on a permanent boat building costume. Anything you wear around the shipyard will become spotted and stiffened with epoxy, which never washes out.

Since you usually have to take the tools to the work instead of conveniently bringing the work to your bench, you'll need portable lighting to show you what you're doing and a couple of old tomato baskets or other tool toters. Once you turn the hull right side up and begin working inside the boat you'll particularly appreciate toters that help you keep an assortment of the most-used tools with you as you move about.

It's frustrating to be lying under the deck beams in the bow out in the garage when you realize that the chisel you need is lying on the workbench down in the basement. Because it's so much trouble to climb out and fetch it, you delay a moment. Maybe you imagine yourself already at anchor in the lee of an isle—"palm girt," I believe, is considered the best kind. You're lying on what will become a bunk, and you nap.

That's why it takes some builders longer than others to finish a ship.

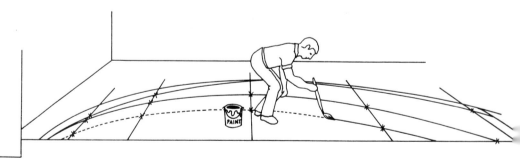

Fig. 5-1. "Lofting" (reproducing the plans full-size on a large bare floor) is the salty way to begin building a boat, but the amateur building a hull less than twenty feet long will usually prefer to use plans that include a full-size paper pattern for the frames. This makes lofting unnecessary.

5 Framing:
Epoxy Vobiscum

To understand the importance of a boat's frames, take a cucumber and amputate the ends. Then set aside slices from the rest of the cucumber at equal intervals of, say, an inch and a half. Feed what's left to the fishes or eat it yourself to help ward off scurvy. With the two ends and the slices you saved, spaced an inch and a half apart with toothpicks, you could reconstruct the exact shape of the entire cucumber.

Similarly, frames define the shape of a boat. Whatever you decide to build, the plans will show you the right slice for each cross section and how far apart to space them.

This method makes boat building easier than it used to be. The Swedes built the *Vasa* the old-fashioned way, by instinct instead of with plans, and as soon as they launched her, she turned over and sank, drowning some of the crew and spoiling the smorgasbord.

Lofting vs. Full-Size Plans

There are two ways to begin. One, called lofting, requires painting a full-size copy of the plans on the garage floor. Although I followed the other method, I'll describe lofting because it's the professional way, and saltier. (See Figure 5-1.) Professional plans show the hull as viewed from underneath, from the side, and from the ends, with appropriate cross sections. They also provide a table of offsets, giving the measurement to various key points from the centerline out and the base line up.

Instead of painting on the floor, some builders use four-by-eight sheets of white beaverboard or one-eighth-inch plywood taped together so they can be folded up out of the way.

To reproduce plans full size you need a straightedge eight or ten feet long, a large plywood square, and two or more long thin strips of wood, flexible and straight-grained. The strips are for drawing curves. You get points along the curve from the table of offsets. Then the strips are used to connect the points in a natural curve. But you don't nail through the wood strips; you hold them with finishing nails tacked in on either side (an argument for using a plywood base instead of working directly on a concrete floor).

It is customary to put down end views, side views, and bottom views overlapping but painted in different colors to reduce confusion. Although lofting is a bit tedious at the start, it saves you time later on when you just lay parts on top of the painted lines and mark where to cut.

With boats shorter than about twenty feet, the builder often has the option of buying plans that include a full-size paper pattern for the frames. (See Figure 5-2.) By pasting two large plan sheets

Fig. 5-2. Full-size plans provide patterns for half of each frame and curved deck beam. Shown with one of the half-frames is a plywood gusset cut to fit over the joint.

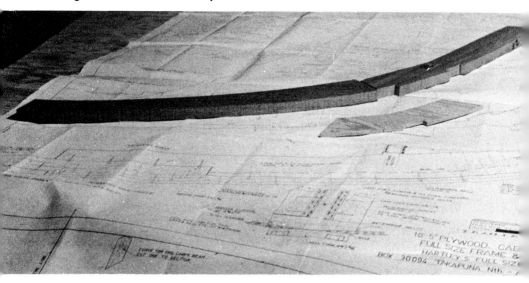

together carefully, you get large enough patterns to define the shape of half of each cross section. The other half, of course, is the same.

If you don't have a large, uncluttered floor space that won't be needed for other purposes for a long time, you'll probably decide to pass up the salty challenge of lofting in favor of a paper pattern unless the plans you want don't come that way.

Sawed Frames and Gussets

In ancient times, boat builders liked to make their frames out of wood that grew naturally to the proper curve. Today, the neighbors wouldn't understand if you cut down the oak in their front yard because you liked the shape of its knees. The modern alternatives are to steam the wood and bend it to the desired curve or to saw frame parts to shape out of wide planks and glue them together.

Steam bending requires constructing a mold of cheap lumber on which to shape each frame. A boat yard can use the same molds over and over, but building molds and steam bending the timbers is a lot of extra work for just one boat.

To saw out a whole frame in one piece you'd need a sequoia-sized plank. So it's not done that way. The frames are cut in pieces, then joined with overlapping strengtheners of plywood called gussets. To complete the arc from the gunwale on one side to the gunwale on the other may require four pieces of timber for the larger frames. They are joined by gussets at the keel and at the sharpest turn in the hull cross section.

There's a saying, "Don't bust a gusset," which seems an appropriate admonition to a boat builder. A broken gusset certainly would weaken the hull. Apparently derived from an old word meaning "nutshell," *gusset* originally referred to joint-pieces in a suit of armor, then to similar parts of other kinds of apparel. So perhaps it's not surprising that the arts of dressmaking and boat building share common techniques.

For example, dressmakers use a toothed wheel to transfer patterns to fabric. A similar tool, somewhat larger, is available for boat builders to mark through the patterns to the wood. (Personally, I prefer to tap along the pattern lines with a hammer and a small nail, making tiny holes an inch or two apart. My wheel tended to wander off the lines.)

Working with a paper pattern, you don't need a lot of space to make the frames, so you can start with the frames in your workshop and move your shipyard operation to the garage or outdoors later on.

One night in January, I went down to the basement and began building the *Dawn Treader*. Out in the garage, where the final assembly would take place, a ship could be caught in the ice floes until spring. Here in the basement, near the furnace, the air was tropical. I would be comfortable while I assembled the frames.

I approached the job cautiously. Altering the lines of a ship by botching the framing could turn a graceful sea sprite into a Caliban coal barge. I knew I would have to overcome my accustomed attitude toward woodworking, which was that a multitude of mistakes could be covered by a dab of putty and paint. I realized that the real knack in boat building isn't possessing any great amount of skill with tools but disciplining yourself to give up lubberly habits and take the pains to do things right at each stage.

Lewis Mumford, writing in *The Pentagon of Power,* expresses his belief that this is good for people anyway, and not just boat builders. "If, as many anthropologists still hold, the making and using of tools was one of the chief sources of primitive man's intellectual development, is it not time that we asked ourselves what will happen to man if he departs as completely as he now threatens to do from his primal polytechnic occupations?"

I think the answer to Mumford's question is already clear. Men who are quite able at the office become a menace when they pick up a tool. By the time they've spoiled enough material, it's their lumber dealer who winds up with a yacht.

I have sailed in those waters. Besides taking you step by step through the construction of a typical small ship, I'm pointing out some of the places where I ran aground so you can go and not do likewise. Although details of construction vary with the plans for every boat, the opportunities for stupid mistakes are similar for all designs.

Most of that first night I spent getting organized and looking at the plans. Howard I. Chapelle wrote in his classic work on boat building that every shipwright should have a "moaning chair . . . a comfortable seat from which the boat can be easily seen and in which the builder can sit, smoke, chew, drink or swear as the moment demands. Here he should rest often and think about his next job. The plans should be at hand and here he can lay out his work. By doing so he will often be able to see mistakes before they are serious . . ."

Besides my moaning chair, one of my most useful tools from the beginning proved to be a mechanic's trouble light with a 100-watt bulb and a long cord. I didn't always know what I was doing, but with a bright, portable light at hand I could at least see the problem.

I didn't quit my job or abandon my family to work on the ship. I usually spent a couple of hours aboard about three nights a week, with a longer stint on Saturday afternoon. The entire project averaged out to roughly six hours a week, more in summer, less in winter.

In the enthusiasm of beginning, I found something to do almost every night. As described earlier, I transferred the pattern to the wood with tiny, closely spaced nail holes. Then I removed the pattern and connected the holes with a legible black pencil line to follow with my saber saw. As I cut each piece, I labeled it to avoid confusing myself later and trying to attach the equivalent of a foot to a wrist.

After three weeks I had the pieces cut and ready to assemble. (See Figure 5-3.)

Making the Stem

What gave me the most trouble was the stem, the big, curved timber that defines the bow and flows back into the keel. It was composed of eight overlapping sections that had to be laminated together in four plies to form a stout timber. (See Figure 5-4.) This was done with waterproof glue, bronze screws, and all the C clamps I could lay hands on. With large pieces of heavy wood, screws do

Fig. 5-3. It looks like a pile of scrap lumber stored under the workbench, but it's actually all the frame parts and gussets for the whole ship.

not pull up tight enough by themselves to hold the joint. It is necessary to use clamps, give the screws a final turn, and leave the clamps on until the glue sets.

Once the stem was fabricated, the next step was to bevel it all around so planking could be attached. I soon discovered there was no good way to do this. The angle of the bevel changed as it followed the curve of the bow. I couldn't use my ripsaw because it wouldn't bend around the curves. My power saw couldn't follow two curves at once. I tried a coping saw but it kept threatening to bite too deep. Making such deep cuts in heavy timber taxed its thin, flexible blade even under maximum tension.

Michael Verney, whose book was cited earlier, writes that "an adze is really the best tool for shaping the cutwater and the lower part of the stem," adding the warning, "it pays to watch an expert in a boatyard for a while before trying it." The adze is notorious for biting the hand that wields it, or at least the leg under the hand, when allowed to escape from the museums where adzes are usually kept.

So I resorted to a sort of dicing technique (Figure 5-5), in

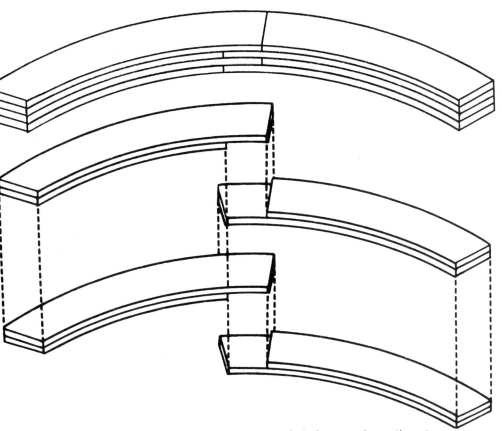

Fig. 5-4. One way to make a large curved timber, such as the stem, without looking for a tree that grew the right shape: saw components to shape out of a plank. Then laminate them with screws and waterproof glue.

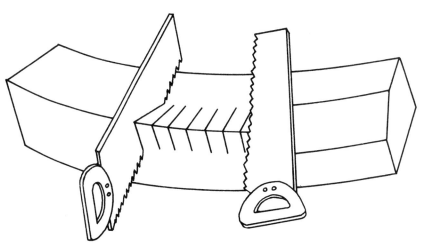

Fig. 5-5. A method for cutting the bevel around the outside of the curved stem: Slice in as far as the bevel line with a crosscut saw. Then take off each wedge-shaped piece in turn with a ripsaw. This allows the ripsaw to follow the curve.

which a crosscut saw was used to slice in from the edge to the guidelines every inch or two. Then when I used a ripsaw along the curve, the little triangular bits of wood dropped off, allowing the ripsaw to follow the curves—more or less. This wasn't the perfect answer, either, since it left a great deal of finishing to do with plane and rasp. In the end, I felt that I had gnawed out the stem like a beaver. My journal shows that beveling the stem took me four hours.

Assembling the Frames

Then it was time to begin assembling the frames. (For a labeled version, see Figure 5-6.) In addition to the stem, the hull skeleton included five frames and the transom, the flat section across the stern.

Each frame consisted of two or four curved ribs cut out of Philippine mahogany with marine plywood gussets overlapping and securing the joints. The plans detailed the size and shape of each rib and gusset. The procedure was to lay two of the rib pieces on top of the plans so they would meet at the correct angle. Then I drilled nail holes through the appropriate gusset into the mahogany. That positioned everything as well as making sure the hardwood wouldn't split or the relatively soft bronze nails bend when I nailed them in.

Each gusset had to be glued to the frames as well as nailed. After a few early experiments with resorcinol, I concluded that epoxy, although expensive, is the only possible glue for boat building, since it can be formulated for use at colder than room temperatures and can be thickened a bit with filler and used like putty to fill gaps. It dries clear (resorcinol is purple).

The first epoxy I used came in screw-top cans. Having read somewhere that epoxy doesn't stick to polyethylene, I turned a small polyethylene bowl into a permanent glue pot with fill levels crayoned on the outside. I discovered that a wooden tongue depressor with the rounded end snapped off flat made the ideal tool for stirring and spreading epoxy. A little later, I found that it was worth the trouble to decant the epoxy and the catalyst from the

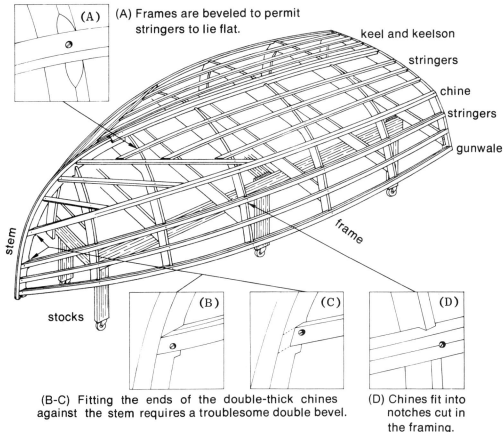

(A) Frames are beveled to permit stringers to lie flat.

keel and keelson

stringers

chine

stringers

gunwale

frame

stem

stocks

(B)

(C)

(D)

(B-C) Fitting the ends of the double-thick chines against the stem requires a troublesome double bevel.

(D) Chines fit into notches cut in the framing.

Fig. 5-6. Framing.

screw-top cans into a couple of plastic squeeze bottles ordinarily sold for dispensing catsup or honey. Both epoxy and the catalyst are highly viscous.

My next batch of epoxy came in cans with pry-off lids like paint cans, and I made note of my ingenious discoveries for inclusion in this book. But by the time I reordered again, other imaginations had been at work. The epoxy and the catalyst came in a little kit: two plastic squeeze bottles, a container of thickener, several tongue depressors, and a small polyethylene cup graduated in ounces and milliliters! (There's an illustration of the kit back in Chapter 3.)

In making difficult joints, most amateur boat builders fall short of machine-shop precision. The answer is to butter both surfaces well with epoxy. (Wear rubber gloves unless you want permanently sticky fingers.) The excess epoxy will be squeezed out and can be wiped off when the joint is clamped, having filled small gaps and made the joint secure. Resorcinol doesn't tolerate tolerances.

When I started assembling the first frame, I made a pencil mark on the mahogany to show exactly how far to spread the glue to line up with the back of the gusset and not slop over. But even with the pencil mark for a guide I had a hard time lining up the pilot holes for the nails once both surfaces were coated with glue. Wet epoxy is sticky and slippery at the same time. I learned that it was necessary to start two nails through the gusset before applying the epoxy. Then I could use the two nail points, slightly protruding through the gusset, to feel around for the holes in the mahogany. Once they were lined up it was easy to drive the rest of the nails. (See Figure 5-7.)

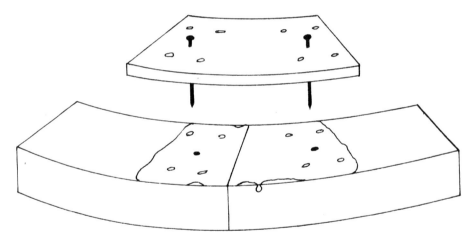

Fig. 5-7. Before trying to line up the predrilled nail holes when joining sawn frames with a gusset, start two of the nails through the gusset. This overcomes the tendency of the slippery surfaces to slide out of alignment when you begin to hammer.

To glue and nail together all the frames and gussets took 12½ hours, spread over a week. I couldn't have done them any faster without buying all the C clamps in North America. Working slowly, I could let each session's production set, thoroughly clamped up, then use the same clamps for the next batch.

When assembled, each complete frame was shaped like a shallow U. The next step was to attach a crosspiece connecting the two arms of each frame at the precise place specified by the plans. These crosspieces, not actually part of the ship, were of ordinary construction grade lumber fastened only with screws, *not* glued, because they would have to come off later. Their function was to hold the frame upside down on the stocks while the planking was applied to the hull. (See Figure 5-8.)

Fig. 5-8. All the frames assembled, with plywood gussets nailed and glued in place. The crosspieces with knots in them are temporary spreaders to hold the frames in place on top of the stocks.

Building the Stocks

One prefers to think of a ship taking shape on the stocks right side up. Upside down seems ignominious, even ominous in the case of a sailing vessel. Boats longer than about twenty feet are built right side up because they're too heavy to turn over later, but upside down is much the easier way to work.

The stocks for a small ship are a rectangular framework built of common lumber as specified in the ship plans. (See Figure 5-9.) If the stocks are accurately built, placing the inverted frames in the proper places on the stocks guarantees that the frames will be set up in proper relation to one another.

Fig. 5-9. The stocks, built according to the blueprints for the ship itself. It proved convenient to add extra bracing and dolly wheels so the whole project could be moved around the garage.

Because of the importance of this step, I took my time—five hours to assemble the stocks, five hours to brace up the frames temporarily in position with a couple of long, thin pieces of common lumber. The frames had to be centered on the stocks and perfectly plumb, except for the transom frame, which was set at a specified angle. Once the frames are fastened in place, the shipwright is just about finished using the plumb line or level. There are very few straight lines anywhere in a boat outside the cabin.

I brooded about the small amount of working space—adequate but cramped—I would have between the hull and the garage wall. So I took time out to give the stocks extra bracing, jack up the whole works, and mount it on heavy-duty dolly wheels. This allowed me to move the project around in the garage to suit my convenience, and it suited my convenience very well.

Longitudinal Ribs

After the frames were mounted in place on the stocks, it was time to begin attaching the longitudinal timbers. These had come in a big bundle of thin pieces of Philippine mahogany, delivered personally by my supplier in—and on—his battered station wagon. I laid them all out in the driveway, studied the plan specifications, and figured out which piece was for what part. Then I labeled each piece with a black felt-tip marker to avoid mix-ups later. Otherwise, it would be easy some night to cut a short part out of the last piece that was long enough to reach from bow to stern and have to order more lumber.

Each longitudinal was fastened to each frame with a bronze screw and a dollop of epoxy. Since each curving longitudinal crossed each frame at an angle, it was necessary to make bevels on the frames at each point of attachment to provide flat surfaces for the longitudinals to be glued to.

To find the proper bevel for each point, I clamped the longitudinal in place and copied the angle with my sliding bevel gauge, removed the longitudinal to get it out of the way, and cut the bevel into the frame—repeatedly checking the angle with my gauge. For the *Dawn Treader*, this had to be done at seventy-nine points. In most places the angle of the bevel was so slight that using a chisel would have been overkill. The most appropriate tool turned out to be my trusty wood rasp.

Beveling the frames is one step that would have been easier if the plans had been lofted. The bevels then could have been copied from the painted lines without all the clamping and unclamping of the actual wood.

I might have known I would have the most trouble at the stem, which had already been such a struggle to make. There were four kinds of longitudinals to deal with: the keelson, a wide, thick plank running from the base of the stem aft to the bottom of the transom; the chines, which provide bracing at the angles where the planes of the hull intersect; the stringers, which add strength between chines; and the gunwales.

The keelson was no problem. The pattern for the stem left a notch for it, and all I had to do was bevel the frames a little and fasten it down. But the chines, stringers, and gunwales all had to be beveled in two directions at once to fit against the side of the stem. The fit had to be good to avoid interfering with the plywood planking that would come later.

In time, I would lie on the foredeck of the *Dawn Treader* with my head hanging over her bow and admire the gracefulness with which it slit the water. It's like watching fish, soothing and timeless —as long as my eldest son is at the helm. When some of the younger helmsmen are on watch, I prefer to be back in the cockpit.

There was nothing soothing about constructing the bow, however. I began by somehow getting confused and marking the bevels wrong. Then, having corrected that error, I found that cutting a bevel in two directions at once is difficult. For small operations like beveling a thin piece of wood, hand tools are usually less trouble than a power tool, but my dexterity with a box saw wasn't sufficient to keep it from straying off one of the guidelines somewhere.

The best solution turned out to be tilting the saber saw to match one angle while I followed the pencil mark for the other angle across the wood as if making a straight cut. (See Figure 5-10.) This required careful measuring, using the sliding bevel tool to

Fig. 5-10. The best way to cut a double bevel is to tilt the base of your saber saw.

transfer the angle of the bevel to the saber saw blade and clamping down the wood in a convenient location while cutting.

Fortunately, the longitudinals came a foot or two longer than necessary, and I hadn't cut any of them to length before making the bevels. This gave me extra wood to make mistakes with. My journal records that it took me four hours to pick up the knack.

Boat building, pursued to the end, teaches you to be unflustered and philosophical. A friend of mine who is a highly inventive engineer and skilled craftsman once bought a plywood boat kit from a company that was going out of business, more because it cost only fifty dollars than because he lusted to build a boat. Involved with his numerous other interests, he had little time left for boat building, but every spring he would move the framework out of its storage space, work on it a little on long summer evenings, then put it away in the fall.

After several years of slow progress, he banged a shin on it in the dark for the hundredth time while entertaining friends in the backyard. After solemn discussion, he and his guests voted to send the stillborn boat to Valhalla with rites befitting the dignity of a wooden vessel. Flammables were procured, a spark lit, and the boat dispatched to the stars in a glorious display of flame and sparks. Unfortunately, the dance around the pyre was interrupted by the unexpected arrival of fire engines, and my friend was saved from considerable embarrassment only by the fortunate circumstance that the village police and fire commissioner was among his guests.

On the other hand, it is recorded that as early as the summer of 1836 Henry David Thoreau built a boat for a trip on the Sudbury River. I'm sure his perseverance in this project helped develop the quality of serenity he captured years later in the pages of *Walden*.

Because the longitudinals of the *Dawn Treader* were curved and springy, and because of the bevels on the frames, the clamps couldn't be made to hold the longitudinals in exactly the right places. There was a danger that as I worked back from the bow, frame by frame, the screw holes wouldn't line up. So at each frame I drilled pilot holes and fastened the joint with a steel screw of the proper size (no glue yet) before drilling at the next frame. When the entire stringer or chine had been installed in this way, I backed out the screws, covered the joints with epoxy, and put the longitudinal back on to stay with bronze screws. (See Figure 5-11.)

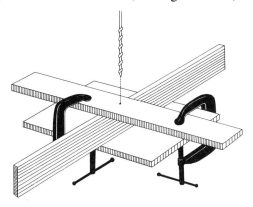

Fig. 5-11. When clamping longitudinals to the frames, you'll find that the natural place to fasten a C clamp is on the very spot where you want to put a screw. The solution is to use two C clamps and a piece of scrap lumber to create a clamping contraption that doesn't interfere with drilling.

I used steel screws temporarily because the softer bronze screws sometimes sustained damage to the slot or broke off while being backed out. Considerable force is required to turn large screws in hardwood. As I mentioned before, I always kept at hand a small plastic box containing a chunk of soap and a little water. I counted out the necessary screws into the box and let them slosh in the soapy water to become lubricated before I used them.

Another trick I learned at this stage was to use a tire pump to blow sawdust out of joints before applying epoxy. I also became somewhat ingenious, through necessity, in devising clamping contraptions. Often a big C clamp holding a chine to the frame occupied the exact spot where I wanted to drill. The solution was to put a thick piece of scrap behind the frame and tighten the chine against it with two C clamps, one on each side of the drilling spot. (The British refer to clamps as "cramps," a bit of unconscious poetry that evokes some of the situations you get into in using them.)

Installing the longitudinals took nearly seventy hours and occupied my spare time from March to July. Completion of the basic
frame was a moment to exult (Figure 5-12); the *Dawn Treader* already looked like a ship. I was gladdened to see that, even upside
down, she had a lovely sheer line. While all the framework was still
exposed, I sloshed every piece with wood preservative to prevent
dry rot. Then I stood back and tried to visualize about where the
bow wave would curl up the sides as she trod the seas, escorted by
dolphins and seabirds.

Fig. 5-12. View of completed framing shows triumphal solutions to main
problems arising in the early stages of construction. In the foreground is
the heavy curved stem, gnawed into shape by a tame beaver. Attached
to it are gunwales, chines, and stringers beveled in two directions at
once. Slight imperfections add the traditional charm of the hand-crafted
object.

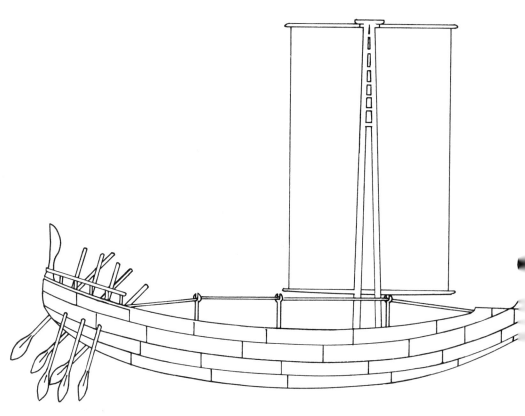

Fig. 6-1. You can tell that the Egyptians were bricklayers before they were shipwrights.

6 Planking:
Floating Like a Pyramid

THE ancient Egyptians, who got their start with masonry, built ships with short, wide planks. (See Figure 6-1.) In their subconscious, they probably were still laying up courses of stone or baked mud blocks. This produced hulls with more joints than a picket fence. Nevertheless, these ships served them well and can still be seen in museums, encouraging the amateur shipwright in his attempt to build a hull that will keep the water out permanently. There are quite a few ways to do this.

Canvas. Canvas can be stretched over the wood framing, an approach that is also as old as the pyramids but still good for building small boats such as kayaks and sailing dinghies. It's significant that canvas curraghs are still in use by fishermen along the Atlantic coast of Ireland.

A typical curragh (Figure 6-2) is about eighteen or twenty feet long, with a rather narrow beam, a round bottom, and no keel. Fore and aft, it's curved (rockered) like a banana, to make the bow and stern ride high. All the curraghs I've seen now have a well for a small outboard motor, placed farther forward than you would expect.

This is a lesson in design. The most convenient place to put an

85

Fig. 6-2. An argument for light planking: Curraghs on the west coast of Ireland with tarred canvas over the framing withstand violent seas on a rugged coast.

outboard on a sailing vessel is over the transom, out of the way. But that's not such a good idea when you're depending on the motor to bring you home in rough water—the natural habitat of curraghs—for the propeller would be chewing on air much of the time. Placing the well for the outboard forward of the helmsman puts the outboard propeller about where the propeller of an inboard engine would be, deep under the hull and never out of the water. (See Figure 6-3.)

The wood framing is not flimsy, but with tarred canvas instead of planking a curragh is light enough for its crew to carry up a steep ramp to safety from the huge Atlantic swells that pound against Ireland's rocks and cliffs. The theory is that no planking could be made strong enough to survive coming ashore on that coast out of control, so a boat might as well be light enough to snatch away from the breakers and run with. If you make a minor mistake, canvas is also easy to repair.

Fig. 6-3. The outboard well on a curragh is located rather far forward, so that the propeller stays in the water when the waves are steep.

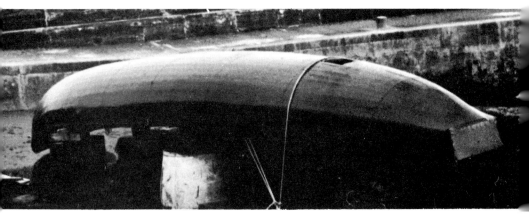

Lapstrake planking.   Lapstrake planking, also called clinker planking (Figure 6-4), overlaps. The edge of the underlying plank is planed to make a perfectly flat surface for the overlying plank to fit against. Closely spaced fasteners can make the hull tight without caulking, especially after the wood has a chance to swell. A lapstrake hull looks salty enough to fly the Jolly Roger, but if you ever have to replace a plank you'll wish you could walk it instead.

In addition, the fitting becomes rather complicated toward the bow. The edges of the planks cannot remain parallel from stem to stern because nearly all hull shapes rise at the bow and flatten out toward the stern. It is usually necessary to fit extra planks called nibs at crucial points. All this is rather demanding for a shipwright who only recently installed a shelf in the upstairs bathroom that somehow turned out not to be level.

Carvel planking. Carvel planking (Figure 6-5) consists of planks butted against one another, with caulking in the seams. Most wooden boats are carvel planked, and this method has the same problem as lapstrake planking when it comes to fitting at the bow.

Strip planking.   This kind of planking (Figure 6-6) has become practical for amateurs with the development of resorcinol and epoxy glues. It consists of narrow strips of suitable wood, perhaps $\frac{7}{8}$ inch by $1\frac{1}{8}$ inch, depending on the size of the boat. The strips are nailed to one another as well as to the frame, and all the surfaces are glued to one another. Each strip is planed so that the next one will fit against it snugly. The glue makes a strip-planked hull all one piece, so it never needs caulking and it doesn't dry out and become leaky when stored out of the water. Even on a round-bottomed hull with continuously curved frames you can get a tight fit by using milled strips that come convex on one side and concave on the other.

Strip planking seems to be increasingly popular with amateur shipwrights who decide not to use plywood. Of course, the plans

Fig. 6-4. Lapstrake planking.

Fig. 6-5. Carvel planking.

Fig. 6-6. Strip planking.

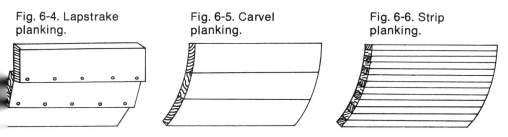

usually limit the planking options. When you're making a choice of one planking method over another, you're also deciding on a design that permits that particular material. (In a sense, this whole book, with its discussion of alternate methods and materials, is about how to choose a plan.)

Plywood planking.   This is still the easiest way for an amateur to keep the water out of his shoes while cruising. A plywood hull is rigid and strong, considering its light weight, and easier to maintain than lapstrake or carvel planking. It is thin in comparison with conventional planking for an equivalent hull and more vulnerable to damage from a rock or a submerged log, but any damage is easier to repair.

So use plywood and keep a good lookout. We had an experience in the *Dawn Treader* that demonstrated the wisdom of that proviso. One evening when we were already at anchor the sun dropped quietly over the horizon, leaving only the pale glow of a sky washed clear by a late afternoon shower. A steady breeze sprang up, blowing in the right direction, and the moon was rising full. We packed a thermos of hot tea and upped anchor.

The moon provided ample light for steering and handling the gear. We could see the islands and headlands we had to avoid looming above the light-flecked ripples like woodcuts. In the cockpit there was enough light to read the compass, and I even discovered a pair of loose screws on the tiller extension and tightened them without a flashlight.

We watched for a lighted buoy shown on the chart. All we had to do to make the next harbor was put ourselves on a direct line between the buoy and the harbor light, which we could already see on the horizon. But the buoy never materialized.

The silent serenity of sailing by moonlight makes it a sacrilege to speak. For a long time the only sound was the soft gurgle of the ripples curling back from the bow. Then it became apparent that, without the buoy, we were off course. A headland cut off our path; we were too close to shore. We had to discuss my small store of sailing lore. When a point ends in a cliff, the water next to it is likely to be deep. When a point grades off in a narrow, low-lying spit, you are justified in suspecting shallows off the end of the point.

We changed course to clear the low point by a respectful distance, but it wasn't far enough. Suddenly, the centerboard began clanking across rock and bucking on its pivot bolt. We hurriedly hauled on the centerboard tackle until the clatter stopped. With shallower draft, we steered farther out to sea and sailed on, once more in silence.

A ship with a fixed keel would have gone aground because of the absence of the buoy. A centerboarder takes care of herself to some extent. Good thing. I have to confess that in the moonlight, although I could see every detail of sky and land, I couldn't tell much about the black water. We easily could have run into floating logs or killer whales or Loch Ness monsters. Since we didn't, I can say that moonlight sailing is well worth a moment or two of concern about the plywood skin.

Regardless of the planking material to be used, the first step is to fair up the framing. Fairing means planing every piece of framing so that the planking can lie flat against it at every point of contact. (See Figure 6-7.) Except with a round-bottomed hull, the cross section changes angles at several points. Wherever that occurs, the longitudinal framing member has to be marked down the center and planed at two different angles.

There's no mystery to this in practice. Take a scrap piece of plywood and lay it across the framing members to which a single piece of planking is supposed to be attached. You can immediately see where the framing has to be planed down.

After you've worked at it a while, the framing will be almost fair, with high spots here and there. Identify them with your piece of scrap and mark the high spots with crisscross lines in pencil or chalk. Then you'll know exactly where to plane and can avoid taking too much off in the wrong places.

Fairing up a whole hull requires hours of planing, and the blade of your plane has to be sharpened repeatedly. Watch out for the heads of the screws that fasten the longitudinal members to the

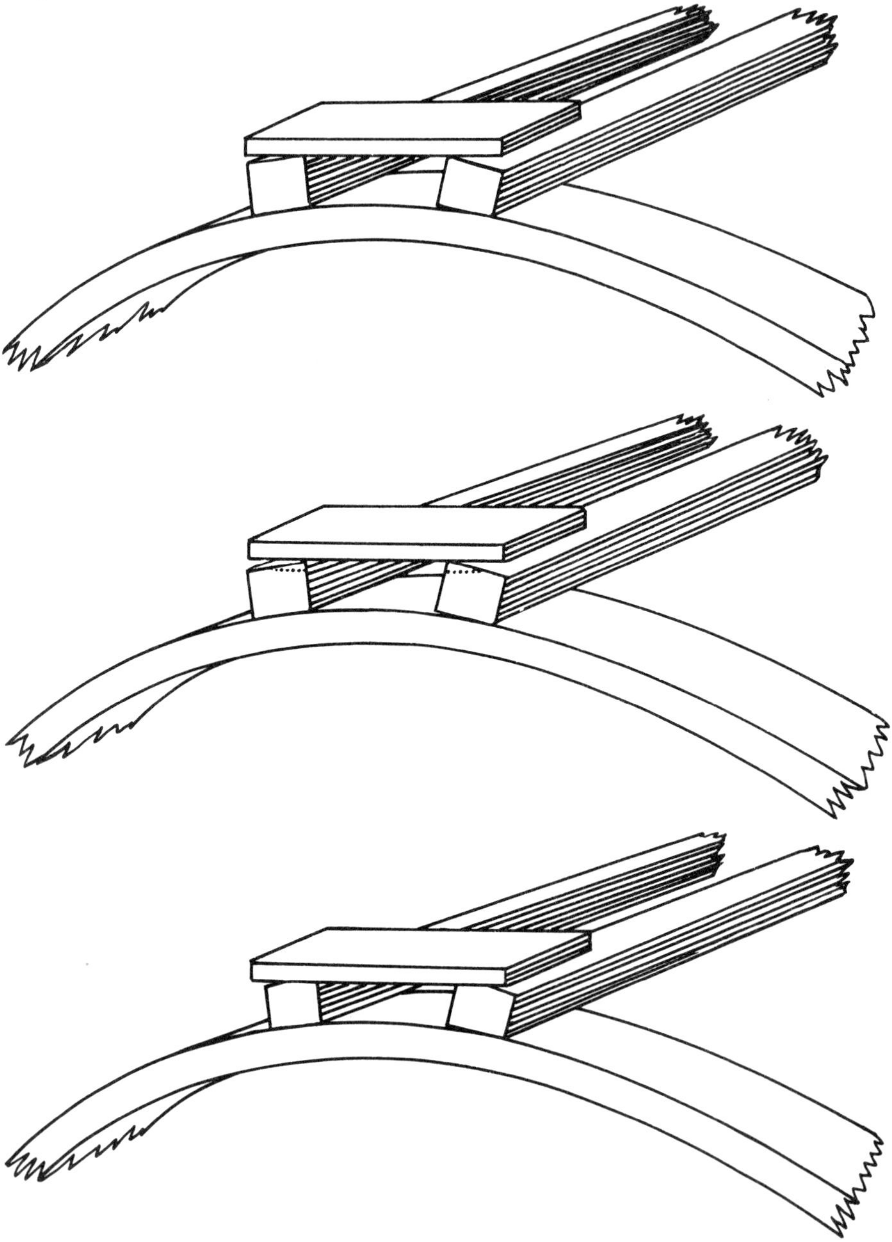

Fig. 6-7. Plywood planking has to lie flat against chines, so you plane the chines—carefully. Keep testing the angle by laying a piece of scrap across two chines.

transverse ribs. Most of them should have been countersunk enough to be out of the way, but in places there'll be screw heads obstructing the plane as you take the wood down. Instead of nicking the blade of your plane (as I did), file down the screw head and use a rasp on the wood for a couple of inches on either side.

If you find out that plywood can be obtained in longer lengths than the usual four-by-eight panels, you may be tempted to try to buy pieces long enough to reach the entire length of your hull. Forget it. You'll find that eight-foot pieces are as much as you can handle, and making the joints with shorter pieces isn't difficult.

The first piece of planking to apply is the transom, because the other planking covers its edge. Fortunately, this is the easiest one to fit. You just clamp a plywood panel to the hull and mark the shape to cut with a pencil.

When using a saber saw, always cut a little to the outside of the mark. The saw is sure to get away from you occasionally and the kerf will wobble a little. If you keep the cut outside the mark at all times, you can plane down the excess when the piece is in position and get a good fit.

In constructing the *Dawn Treader* I failed to label the transom plank and forgot which was port and starboard. Having two options, I naturally installed it the wrong way. Fortunately, I had achieved a high degree of bilateral symmetry with the frame and had cut the transom a bit oversize, so it fit anyway.

Fig. 6-8. This photo illustrates a principle: Whenever anybody wants to help, let him. The author is holding up a large piece of plywood while an assistant marks the outline for cutting out the transom.

When a piece of plywood planking has been cut to size, you should clamp it in place, crawl inside the hull, and outline the framing on the planking with a pencil. Then you unclamp the planking and drill pilot holes for nails from the inside out, centering them between the pencil lines. Clamp the plank in place again and drill the pilot holes into the framing through the holes already drilled.

Off comes the plank again. Now you use the pencil lines as a guide for spreading glue. You also spread glue on the corresponding section of framing. Remember the trick of starting a couple of nails through the plywood so that the slipperiness of the glue doesn't prevent you from keeping the pilot holes in the plank and in the framing lined up while you're nailing.

This is one of the tests of character that arise in ship building. You'll be tempted to eliminate some of the clamping and unclamping. The thought will occur to you that it would be easier to drill all the pilot holes at one time, from the outside of the plank into the framing. But that is the voice of the Devil; do not listen. If you try to take a shortcut, you'll surely find yourself drilling a few pilot holes at places where there is no framing underneath. The framing curves and, once out of your sight beneath the planking, writhes out of the way of pilot holes placed in a straight row.

The plans of the *Dawn Treader* specified $5/16$-inch plywood for the planking, but I couldn't get this size from my dealer. So I ordered $3/8$-inch, reasoning that because I was using Douglas fir instead of the heavier mahogany plywood the extra $1/16$ inch wouldn't do any harm. Since then I have read one authority who says that when a plywood hull is to be coated with fiberglass, as the *Dawn Treader* was, the planking thickness can be reduced by $1/8$ inch. If he's right, I could have built a lighter and faster hull with $1/4$-inch plywood.

Still, I'm not sorry to have the additional thickness. More than once, lying in my bunk when off watch and listening to the centerboard suddenly scrape over an unexpectedly shallow bottom, I have thought how thin a wall was keeping the water out of my ears.

Even with pilot holes properly drilled, a nail will sometimes strike a recalcitrant drift of grain and start to bend. Bronze boat nails are relatively soft and subject to bending. Their annular rings make them difficult to withdraw. If a nail seems determined to bend, give up. Pull it out before it goes any deeper. Or break it off, which is almost too easy, and drill another pilot hole nearby. Drive the nail home with a nail set. A putty knife scraped across a row of nail heads should not tick any of them.

Bow Planking

After the transom, the next piece of planking to apply is one of the lower bow pieces, which are the most difficult of all. Some builders make a pattern of brown paper or cheap ⅛-inch hardboard rather than starting with the plywood itself.

One of the problems is that the bow is the most highly curved part of the hull. You can clamp one edge of the plywood to the framing, but the other—not having been cut to shape yet—projects far beyond its proper place. Considerable force is required to bend the sheet enough to mark where to cut it.

I was able to use a pair of automated, self-adjusting, remote-controlled clamps—two teen-age boys who stood on the work as directed. First, I soaked the plywood with a hose. Water makes plywood more pliable. A refinement, if necessary, is to keep the panel covered for half an hour with rags soaked in boiling water.

For all planking cuts except the transom, make the pieces at least half an inch larger all round than appears necessary. Because of the curves, a piece of plywood clamped here and there is somehow sprung to a different shape than it holds when securely fastened every two inches.

I have always believed that the story of Pinocchio is based on fact. In the beginning, the piece of wood later fashioned into a puppet by the old woodcarver twists in his hand and raps him across the shin. That's how wood acts when it gets a chance—sneaky and subversive.

The first bow piece is struggle enough; the second one is worse. With the first one, you can clamp it down all around while you nail it. When you start to put the second one on, you find that the first piece covers all the clamping bases along the most crucial edge, the keel and stem. That's when you really need your automated, self-adjusting, remote-controlled clamps. Or, if you don't have big boys handy, you can fasten a wire to the planking and tighten it down with a turnbuckle or a Spanish windlass (Figure 6-9: a stick inserted between two wires or ropes and twisted). To

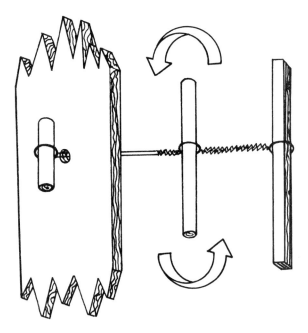

Fig. 6-9. Principle of the Spanish windlass: twisting the cords pulls planking into place.

fasten the wire, you lead it through a small hole in the planking and around a piece of scrap on the other side. The hole can be plugged later with a dowel.

It's difficult to drive the nails tight against the resistance of the bent plywood, which can't be clamped everywhere. It's essential that the edge along the keel and stem—which can't be clamped on the second piece—be nailed first with the clamps on the opposite edge loosened as much as possible. Then the clamps can be tightened while the remaining nails are driven.

I wish I had followed the suggestion of making a pattern for these two bow planks instead of going ahead with the plywood itself. I'm sure it would have been easier in the long run.

Edge Joints

With the transom and lower bow planks in place, planking proceeds from bow to stern and from the keel to the gunwale. (See Figure 6-10.) Keep an eye on the plywood grain. Occasional flaws

Fig. 6-10. Planking proceeds from bow to stern and from keel to gunwale.

in the surface are filled by the mill with an oval plug. You should avoid allowing one of these plugs to fall at a joint or at the sharpest part of a curve. The outer grain of the planking should always run fore and aft.

There are two kinds of joints to be made. The longitudinal joints come together over the center of longitudinal framing members. The planking panels won't butt against each other without being beveled.

Fig. 6-11. Where plywood planking joins along a chine you don't have to bevel both edges. Lay a rabbet plane against the chine (which has already been planed to the proper angle) and use it as a guide to bevel the edge of the first piece of plywood. The adjoining plywood will then fit snugly without beveling.

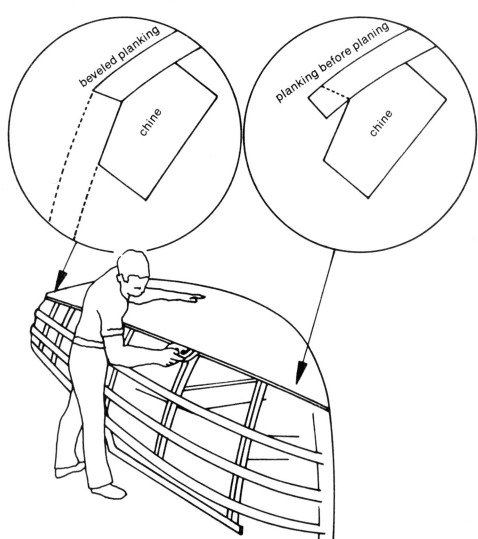

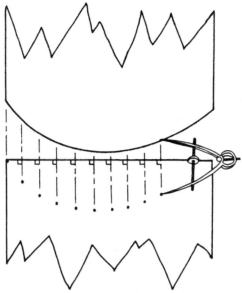

Fig. 6-12. When you copy a curve with the dividers, you keep the dividers at ninety degrees to the edge of the uncut material. If you swing the dividers with the curve, the new piece won't fit.

To solve this problem, you use a rabbeting planc. As explained in Chapter 4, a rabbet plane has a blade that cuts all the way across the full width of the tool. You can lay the rabbet plane against the framing (which has already been planed to the proper angle) and use the framing as a guide to bevel the edge of the plywood that has been nailed and glued in place. (See Figure 6-11.) The adjoining piece of plywood will then fit snugly without beveling.

In Chapter 4, I also told you to buy a pair of dividers. Now is the time to discuss their use. Visualize the situation. You have clamped a piece of plywood to the frame adjoining planking already installed. The straight edge of the new piece doesn't fit at all against the curved (and beveled) edge already in place. So you set the dividers to slightly more than the width of the widest gap. Then you use the dividers to copy the curve onto the new plank. The sharp point should prick the wood at intervals of about one inch. (See Figure 6-12.)

Draw the curve with a heavy pencil line from point to point. Before doing anything else, cut the curve with your saber saw.

Now the new plank should fit more or less snugly against the old one. Actually, because of the difficulty of achieving perfect control over a saber saw cut, there probably will be small gaps here and there. Gaps up to ⅛ inch can be filled by thickening your epoxy glue to a putty with the thickener usually provided in a glue kit or with sawdust.

Don't overdo using epoxy as a putty. It dries extremely hard. It dulls tools, gobbles up sandpaper, and erodes your patience.

The piece of planking we have been talking about also has another edge, which hasn't been mentioned yet. Once you have the curve described above worked out, you can clamp the plank in its final location and outline the framing from the inside. When you take the plank off again to cut it you have an opportunity to make a disastrous mistake.

The farthest line marked on the plywood is not the cutting line. Rather, it is a line distant from the actual cutting line by one half the width of the longitudinal framing member to which it is to be fastened. The planking meets in the center of the ribs.

To avoid cutting along the wrong lines and wasting material, I tried to get in the habit of labeling everything "port," "starboard," "inside," "outside," "up," "down," "glue," "no glue," "chine edge," "cutting line," or whatever the circumstances required.

When a curved line is not the actual cutting line, you use the dividers—in this instance set to half the width of the framing member—to run along the pencil line and establish the cutting line.

This all becomes perfectly clear when you have the actual materials in hand—as long as you remember to keep track of what you're doing.

Butt Joints

The second kind of plywood planking joint occurs along a course of planking wherever you come to the end of an eight-foot length. You just butt another piece of planking and back up the joint with another piece of plywood the same thickness as the planking and extending for four to six inches on both sides of the joint, depending on which authority you follow. I was conservative and used twelve-inch butt blocks. (See Figure 6-13.) Each block extends the full width between longitudinal framing members and is beveled if necessary to fit snugly between them.

Fig. 6-13. Joints in plywood planking are backed by butt blocks fitted between the framing members and securely glued. (Lubberly touch: the C clamp ought to be separated from the planking by a piece of scrap to avoid marring the planking.)

The trick with butt blocks is to draw them tight to the planking while the glue sets. Most of them can't be clamped. One solution I read about and tried was to drill holes for machine screws with nuts and washers, then remove the screws after the epoxy had set and plug the holes with dowels. Unfortunately, this method is ridiculous for anyone with arms less than twelve feet long. After the planking has been glued in the way, it isn't easy to hold the nut on the inside and back out the screw with a screwdriver on the outside at the same time.

My boat plans advised holding the butt blocks with copper nails, clenched. I didn't like that idea, partly because of the appearance of the clenched nails on the inside and partly because I was dubious about pulling up the butt blocks tightly enough with clenched nails. (Clenched teeth and clenched fists I'm used to, especially after a bad day in the shipyard, but I've never had much experience with clenched nails.)

In the end, I decided that the best way to hold the butt blocks was with round-headed wood screws and washers. When the glue set, I backed out the screws and drilled holes for pieces of dowels. I coated the dowels with epoxy before driving them in. (See Figure 6-14.)

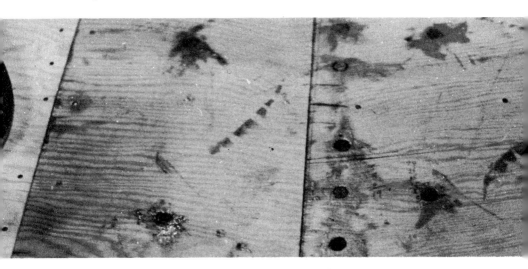

Fig. 6-14. Use round-headed wood screws to draw the planking tight to the butt blocks while the glue sets. Then back out the screws and plug the holes with glued-in doweling as shown.

At first, it proved difficult to get the dowels in the holes because they were so sticky with glue. Then I discovered that the perfect way to hold a gooey dowel is with a spring clip clothespin. Once gripped in the jaws of the clothes pin and lined up with a hole, the dowel could be banged in quite easily.

My journal shows that I began fairing the framing on July 11, when I had already put in 141½ hours since the beginning of the year. It took 106½ hours to complete all the fairing and fasten the planking. I put the last piece of planking in place on October 17.

Keel

Next, following the plans, I planed a flat place on the bottom of the hull the exact width to receive a long, heavy mahogany plank that became the keel. I also planed the bow where the edges of the planking were fastened to the stem. A piece of mahogany capping was supposed to fit there.

At this step, I think I made another mistake. The hull proper was finished, and the next step should have been to fiberglass it *before* applying the stem capping, the keel, and the skeg (the tailfin that fits under the stern in most sailboats). Getting fiberglass to stick on the rounded surface of the hull itself is much easier than covering projections with several planes at ninety degrees to each other. These projecting parts could have been applied over the fiberglass.

Centerboard Case

I had another problem on my mind. I had to decide whether to install the centerboard case while the hull was still upside down or wait until it was turned right side up. The case had been assembled in the basement during the winter. I took care to paint the inside while I could still get at it, knowing that once it was assembled I would have a hard time getting paint inside a slot only ¾ inch wide. Subsequently, I learned that some builders assemble centerboard cases with screws and bedding compound so they can be taken apart for maintenance. Not knowing this at the time, I followed the plans and built mine for eternity with epoxy.

I concluded that the centerboard case should be installed upside down, which I learned later is not the orthodox procedure. I wanted to avoid having to lie on the garage floor under the keel countersinking the bolt heads and washers with sawdust drifting into my eyes and mouth.

It's impossible to work the bottom of the centerboard case into a perfect curve that will fit snugly against the inside of the hull at every point, although you should try to come as close as you can.

The plans give you the theoretical curve. Then you do some trial and error fitting and final planing. To prevent the final result from leaking, the centerboard case is bedded in mastic rather than glue. You use the kind of rubberized caulking compound that stays pliable.

A series of heavy bronze bolts fastens the centerboard case and the skeg to the hull. Nuts are on the inside where they can be tightened from time to time if necessary.

Tradition says that all centerboard hulls leak eventually, and I found the *Dawn Treader* no exception. The first season my home town tore up the street in front of my house for the summer, so *Dawn Treader* had to be kept in a slip at a marina. I don't know whether it was my fine craftsmanship or the wood swelling in the water or both, but she didn't leak a drop all summer. Unless there was rain, the bilge would be as dry as the Sahara from one weekend to the next.

The second season, *Dawn Treader* was anchored in my garage between voyages. This gave the wood a chance to dry out. More voyages gave the centerboard more opportunity to exert its tremendous leverage from side to side on the case. So it finally began to leak.

I wasn't dismayed. I had read that it would leak, and I expected it to leak. When the leak finally came, I was ready to pounce on it with my new hand pump and feel salty. ("Man the pumps." "Aye, aye, captain.") The trouble was that it wouldn't leak enough. In a whole afternoon of sailing there wouldn't be enough water in the bilge to get at with the pump. I could only mop it out with a sponge, more like a housemaid than a proper seaman.

To make room for the centerboard case, I had to remove a couple of the temporary spreaders supporting the hull in its position, upside down on the stocks. The other spreaders were left in place as long as they weren't in the way, even after the hull was righted, to strengthen the hull until deck beams could be installed.

I drilled and sawed the slot in the keel and matched it with the centerboard case slot. I pulled the heavy centerboard case into place with two lengths of Redibolt turned into a special giant clamp with nuts, washers, and crosspieces of scrap timber, as described previously.

Keel Bolts

Then I drilled the bolt holes, using one of those flat drill bits that look like chisels. The bits were long enough to pass through the hull and bite into the centerboard case logs, but not long enough to complete the boring. So, after the locations of all the holes were marked, I removed the centerboard case and finished the boring at my workbench.

Boring deep holes with a hand drill requires concentration. The bit will be less likely to wander off course if you back it out after several turns and blow the accumulated chips out of the hole with a tire pump. However, it will probably still wander a little, so allow for that. If perfect accuracy is necessary, use a drill press or build a jig that will hold the drill shaft perpendicular to the work.

When a big drill bit emerges from the other side of the wood, it can tear out big chunks of wood from around the hole. One way to avoid this is to back up the work with a piece of scrap. Or, if this is not feasible, you can watch for the tip of the bit to come through. Then stop and drill back the other way, using the hole made by the tip as a pilot hole.

The hardest drilling I did was in the skeg. I had to drill three ⅜-inch bolt holes through a piece of timber 1½ inches wide. If I strayed off the center, the skeg would be lopsided when bolted to the keel. So I worked slowly and carefully by hand with brace and bit instead of galloping ahead with my power drill and perhaps botching it. Besides, my auger bit was two inches longer than my flat bit of the same diameter.

You should be aware, in case you run into deep boring problems, that in addition to the bit extensions sold in hardware stores there is such a thing as a ship auger—a special kind of bit that comes up to twenty inches long.

The last piece of wood to apply to the hull was a tapered plank of mahogany curving around the stem and covering the edges of the planking. The theory of the designer was that while a ¾-inch piece could not be bent to that curve, the same thickness and strength could be achieved with two much more flexible ⅜-inch pieces, one glued over the other.

When I tried it the first time, the ⅜-inch piece just cracked. The second time I prepared by soaking the board overnight in the bathtub, then pouring boiling water over when I was ready to use it. It cracked anyway.

Steam Bending

Then I realized I was going to have to build a steam bending apparatus after all, which turned out to be rather simple. (See Figure 6-15.) For a heat source, I had a charcoal grill with short legs.

Fig. 6-15. Steam bending: A charcoal fire in the grill boils water in an old gasoline can. Steam passes into a box made of scrap plywood through the spout and a hole in the bottom of the box.

For a boiler, I used an old two-gallon gasoline can with a long metal spout. I nailed together a steam box made of scrap lumber and plywood, with a hole in the bottom just big enough to admit the spout of the can.

The rule of thumb is one hour of steaming for each square inch of cross section in the piece to be bent. My piece was 2½ inches wide and ¾ inch thick—a cross section of 1⅞ square inches for which two hours of steaming should do nicely.

My boiler should have been larger. It boiled dry and I had to add fresh water before the two hours passed. But it worked beautifully. I took out the hot, moist wood (with gloves) and fastened it at one end with a screw, for which pilot holes had been drilled in advance. Then I bent it easily around the curve and clamped it at the tip of the bow.

By morning, it had assumed its new curved shape and was as easy to glue and nail as any straight piece in the ship. The hull was now ready to paint, if I wished, or, as I decided, to cover with fiberglass.

There have been some improvements in materials since the days of the Pharaohs, and shipwrights should keep up with them. In fact, I used something newer than fiberglass, as I shall explain, to "fiberglass" the *Dawn Treader*.

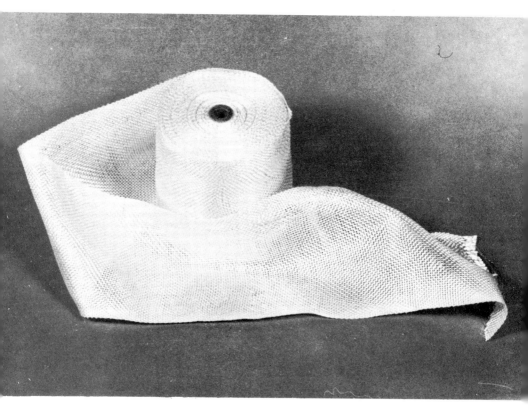

Fig. 7-1. Fiberglass tape is a porous material that's readily saturated with resin.

7 Fiberglassing: The Right Deed for the Right Resin

L ET's consider for a moment how far we have come. The hull, still upside down on the stocks, is completely planked. Here and there along the plywood seams where the fit could have been better the gaps are filled with epoxy putty and sanded down. Now is the time to decide whether to paint the hull or to fiberglass it.

As mentioned earlier, fiberglass is an excellent material, but the claims made for its freedom from maintenance are sometimes extravagant. When I built the *Dawn Treader,* one of the disadvantages of fiberglassing was the cost of materials. Since then, the petroleum crisis has affected the supply of polyester resin, and I can't predict how costly it may become in the future.

Fortunately, there are degrees of fiberglassing. Some builders use fiberglass only to tape the seams. Some do the hull but not the topsides.

The theory of the process is that polyester resin can bond woven glass to wood. Repeated coats of resin, sanded between applications, cover the fabric and provide a strong, smooth, rigid surface. The tensile strength of the glass reinforces the plastic and keeps it from cracking. Epoxy can be used instead of polyester for hulls with special bonding problems, such as oak planking or metal, but the additional cost of epoxy makes its use with fiberglass rare.

When you discover that pigments are available to color the polyester before you apply it, visions of springtime without painting the hull year after year will dance in your head. But you're wrong. Adding the colors prevents you from being able to tell whether the cloth is sufficiently saturated with wet resin. If you make a mistake, the coating will delaminate. In any case, you'll wind up painting fiberglass eventually.

With the *Dawn Treader,* I stirred the standard yellow pigment into the polyester. The finished job looked bilious compared to the lovely light lemon yellow available in paint, and certain screw heads were left uncovered.

After I had fiberglassed the whole hull while it was conveniently upside down, I realized that the cockpit construction, which I was delaying until the hull was righted, would require a few screws through the transom from the outside. So I painted the hull the less aggressive yellow, taking advantage of its convenient position. Later, I merely puttied the transom screw heads, which came above the waterline, and touched them up with matching paint.

Taping the Seams

In any case, the first step is to tape the seams. You start with a roll of fiberglass tape four inches wide. (See Figure 7-1.) For each seam, cut the tape long enough to run the entire length of the hull. (See Figure 7-2.) Mark guidelines beside the seams showing where to spread the polyester. At the stern, it's a good idea to run an extra length of tape around the perimeter of the transom to cover the ends of the seam tapes. (Do this also at the stem if you're not covering the whole hull.)

Now prepare to stir up the chemicals. A batch of polyester comes with the resin itself in a screw-top can with a small bottle of catalyst. Unlike epoxy glue, which is usually mixed half and half, polyester cures with as little as 1 percent catalyst added. Go to the drugstore and buy a small graduate with markings to measure cubic centimeters as closely as five at a time.

I learned what happens if you don't have a measuring device that's accurate enough. I was experimenting by mixing just a little

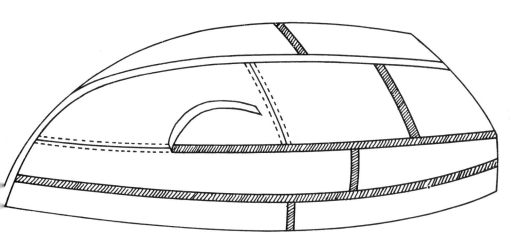

Fig. 7-2. All the seams and planking joints of a plywood hull should be taped with fiberglass and resin. The hull can then be painted or completely fiberglassed.

to become familiar with the material before slopping it on my hull on a large scale. According to the label, I needed to add 2½ cc. of catalyst to a partly filled juice can of resin. The measuring devices I had on hand could cope with adding vermouth to gin or vanilla to cake batter but were vague on such tiny amounts as a couple of cubic centimeters.

I could tell my estimate was faulty when the liquid began coagulating. It was like cooking scrambled eggs. I fished out the lumps, put them in another container, and hurriedly used up the rest on the work in progress. By the time I had finished, the lumpy resin in the second can was as hard as a coral reef.

Before I mixed any more, I bought the most precise graduate I could find. (See Figure 7-3.) It was marked in 5 cc. increments, which proved sufficient, since I could estimate the halfway points well enough.

Fig. 7-3. This is the type of graduate you need to measure the proper amounts of catalyst to use with polyester resin. You can buy one at most drugstores.

Other facts to remember:

• Polyester has a brief shelf life, ranging from a few months to a year. It varies according to formulation. Don't buy it until you're almost ready to use it. If you stock up and something unexpectedly delays your work in the shipyard, keep it in the refrigerator.

• Ordinary polyester has to be used at temperatures around seventy degrees. Manufacturers provide instructions on varying the ratio of resin to catalyst to compensate for temperature and maintain a pot life of about thirty minutes. In hot weather or direct sun, it tends to set too fast. It won't set at all below about sixty degrees.

• Special formula polyester is available. There's a low-temperature resin for use between forty-five and fifty-five degrees. High viscosity resin is designed for vertical and overhead surfaces. These special resins cost more.

• All polyester should be used cautiously, with rubber gloves and plenty of ventilation. It irritates the skin, and the fumes are toxic and explosive. When the resin and catalyst are mixed, they generate heat. So only small batches should be made, to prevent spontaneous combustion as well as avoid wasting material that sets faster than you can spread it.

• Brushes can be cleaned in acetone if you do it before the resin sets. There is a styrene thinner for reducing the viscosity of the resin, but you can't use the brush cleaner for thinner. And once the resin sets, there's no solvent that can clean up any spills.

Needless to say, you won't want to use your finest mink tail paintbrushes to spread polyester. I found that cheap rollers of sponge rubber-like plastic worked well and could be thrown out instead of cleaned.

When you spread the polyester between your pencil marks beside the seams, you'll find that the fiberglass tape sticks to it nicely. Your main concern will be to smooth out all the wrinkles before the resin sets. Any wrinkles in the fiberglass eventually will delaminate.

The second coat of polyester can be put on over the tape at once. The object is to have both the cloth and the underlying plywood drenched with resin before it sets. Properly wetted cloth has a translucent appearance. If it looks milky anywhere, slop on more resin. This coat should be allowed to dry, then sanded to feather the edge of the tape. If you don't feather the tape now, the finished hull will have its underwear showing.

The third coat of resin, over the sanded tape, probably will leave it smooth and unobtrusive. Sand it a little more with a fine-grit paper. If you're fiberglassing only the seams, a fourth coat of polyester may be desirable to make the tape perfectly smooth.

In working with fiberglass, you have to be careful never to sand it so much that the fabric is exposed or weakened. Put on more resin instead.

I fiberglassed all the seams for the *Dawn Treader* in fifteen hours of work sessions that also included painting the centerboard, shaping a bow cap, and completing other small tasks while waiting for coats of resin to cure.

Covering the Hull

For the next step, you have a choice of methods and materials.

The conventional way to cover the hull is to coat one whole side of it with resin, then unroll a sheet of fiberglass over it. Fiberglass comes in rolls up to five feet wide. The fiberglass has to be smoothed down so that there are no wrinkles or bubbles anywhere before the resin sets. At the stem and the keel, the fiberglass overlaps from both sides, so you don't have to try to do the whole hull at once.

I found it easier to start with a substitute for fiberglass called Dynel, which is more elastic and absorbent. Dynel is stapled to the hull before any resin is applied. Because of its moderate elasticity, it's easy to fit to the hull without wrinkles.

You staple it on the far side of the stem and the keel. At the stern, you pull it tight around the corner and staple it onto the transom. Use short staples; later, you'll pry out as many as you can reach.

Turning the corner at the transom is like wrapping a Christmas package. You find yourself with extra material. The solution is to snip out wedges of fabric so that it will lie flat, with cut edges butting against each other.

Only when you're satisfied with the lay of the fabric do you start with the resin, which soaks right through the Dynel into the wood. This way, you can avoid being haunted by the thought of polyester molecules grabbing each other by the millions and turning rigid too soon.

If in doubt whether any spot is wet enough, never hesitate to put on more resin.

The fabric-first method also is sometimes used with fiberglass by expert practitioners, but with Dynel it's easier for the resin to soak in, and an amateur shipwright can feel more confident that it won't delaminate.

The Dynel method assumes three coats of resin. The first and second coats are sanded before the next coat is applied. You try to get the hull as smooth as you can without sanding into the fabric. Usually, the third coat sets up smooth and glossy.

Do the transom last, using a separate piece of fabric to cover the ends of the pieces you brought around from the sides.

It took me 30½ hours to apply the Dynel and the three coats of polyester. Most of the time went into sanding. This was a big job that used up package after package of medium- and fine-grit sanding disks. As I mentioned earlier, I changed my disk sanding attachment back and forth between two electric drills because the steady load made them heat up.

Part of the time was spent mulling over what to do about the staples. I couldn't find any instructions anywhere covering this point. I finally concluded that the thing to do was pry out the ones that were exposed at the end and ignore those that could be paved over by Dynel and resin.

The hardest part was coaxing the Dynel to cover the hull projections, especially the skeg. I faltered for once in my resolve to think each step through until I felt sure I knew what I was doing. The problem was to round the ninety-degree angle between the hull and the keel. With my caulking gun lying nearby, it seemed like a good idea to run a thick bead of caulking compound along the whole length of the keel on both sides, filling the bottom of the corner.

After a couple of seasons of sailing, I have learned why this was a mistake. Maneuvering a boat on and off a trailer in all kinds of weather inevitably leads to some hard knocks on the hull. It's particularly difficult to manage the boat when the wind is pushing it from astern. The keel is likely to hit the trailer frame instead of a roller at some point. A strong crosswind also makes things difficult if you're working without a crew. Consequently, the *Dawn Treader* got two or three bumps that punched through the coating into the relatively soft caulking compound along the keel. This required prompt repair. If water gets under the coating, it can cause delamination of the plastic and rot in the wood. I had to cut away the affected areas, let them dry out, fill them with something hard, like epoxy putty, and repaint.

It would have been wiser in the first place to have finished the coating before the keel was applied, or to have filled the corner with a compound that set harder or with long strips of wood planed down to triangular cross section. (See Figure 7-4.)

As for the skeg, that was the place where having put pigment in the polyester prevented me from observing that the fabric wasn't bonded sufficiently to the wood. This problem solved itself rather simply. In the wear and tear of cruising, the plastic coating wore away where it was loose. So I sanded down the broken edges and painted the skeg over the bare wood.

Righting the Hull

On July 21, a year and a half—and 404½ working hours—from the beginning of the project, the hull was completely finished and ready to turn over.

I had prepared for this day by buying a boat trailer. I was going to need the trailer anyway, and having it early eliminated the need to construct a cradle for the hull in its upright position.

To turn the hull over, I intercepted my eldest son's softball

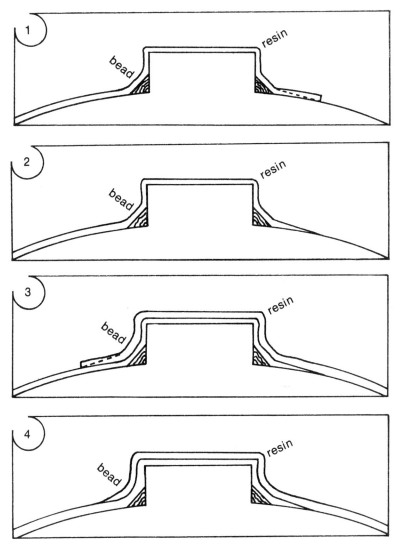

Fig. 7-4. When you fiberglass a hull, the material usually has to be lapped over the keel. Fill inside corners first with a bead of wood or other hard material like epoxy putty or plastic wood. Feather the edge of the first layer with your sander. Then apply material from the opposite side of the hull. Feather the second edge, too. Resist the temptation to fill the inside corner along the keel with caulking compound. It's too soft and will make trouble for you later.

team before a game. We all just grabbed it, turned it over, and set it down on the trailer while I shouted orders to which no one paid the least attention. Although the hull must have weighed four or five hundred pounds without decks and cabin, and offered few handholds as it began to turn right side up, there was no difficulty at all with seven or eight helping.

Lacking the softball team, I would have prepared a soft bed of old mattresses, tires, sand bags, or whatever else could be most easily scrounged. Jacks could have lifted the inverted hull off the stocks and lowered it until the stem and stern rested on the floor. Then a block and tackle pulling from the side would have rolled her onto the bed, with some provision—ropes or stacked tires—to prevent damage as she flopped over. (See Figure 7-5.) She could

Fig. 7-5. If you have to turn the hull over by yourself, you can do it with a block and tackle over a bed of old tires or mattresses. But it's much easier to stand a round of milkshakes for a softball team and let them just grab it and put it back down the way you want it.

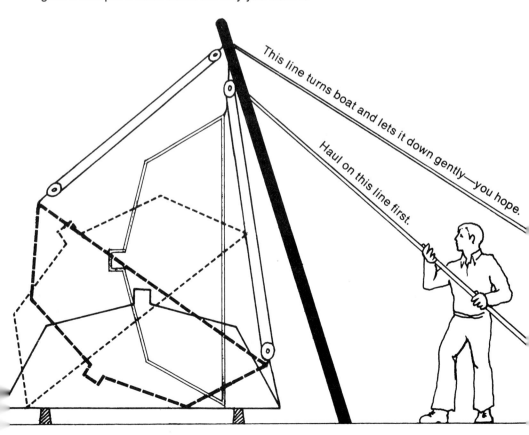

have been raised with jacks again and the trailer backed under.

That sounds like a lot of work. You're better off to buy a round of milkshakes for a softball team.

Appearance

I decided not to fiberglass (I guess that's the verb to use even when the material is Dynel) anything but the hull. One reason was the expense. Another was the complicated shape of the cabin and cockpit coamings. And I liked having an infinite choice of colors.

Having painted the hull a delicate yellow, I thought I would paint the decks and cabin exterior white—easy to touch up—and the inside of the cockpit gray. For the warmth of the wood grain, I would maintain varnish on the tiller and on the mahogany rubrail all around the gunwales.

A boat that's all painted or all fiberglass or all metal can't be truly salty, but varnish takes extra maintenance, so don't overdo it.

Naval architects say the sheer line is one of a ship's most beautiful features. It should be accentuated by different colors above and below. High deckhouses appear less prominent if painted light gray or light blue. A band of black or dark blue makes staring port holes less prominent. Dark colors on decks and cabins make them too hot in the sun.

I can live with the *Dawn Treader*'s present white and yellow, but I can see how her appearance could be improved. The cabin is a bit high and boxy because I raised the roof line four inches. The ports, for reasons I'll explain later on, are squinty. The next time she needs to be entirely repainted rather than touched up I may try a light blue deckhouse with a dark blue band along the port holes as advised.

Michael Verney, in *Boat Maintenance by the Amateur*, divides yachts into three groups. Class A ships always look new. The owner is either a fanatic or, like J. P. Morgan, who never asked what it cost, can afford a professional crew. Class B ships are well cared for and start the season dressed for the ball. In Class C are boats belonging to skippers who prefer to sail at every opportunity, doing their maintenance workboat fashion—just enough to

"Class A ships always look new. The owner is either a fanatic or, like J. P. Morgan, who never asked what it cost, can afford a professional crew."

keep her functional, prevent physical deterioration, and avoid extreme shabbiness.

The only time such a skipper's "blissful existence may be shattered," says Verney, "is when he attempts to come alongside a Class A yacht for a well-earned night in a strange harbor and is received by black looks and a lack of cooperation."

My own inclinations waver between B and C. I do think it's saltier to sail than to sand and paint. But I also think a sailing craft possesses an inherent beauty that should not be defiled by neglect.

A Blizzard of Butterflies

The esthetics of sailing were impressed upon me on a bright clear day in early fall. Playing hooky in midweek after the children had started back to school, my wife and I glided out of Waukegan harbor with just enough breeze to fill the sails from north-northwest.

It was a little before noon. I was hopeful that the wind would pick up during the afternoon, as it often does in warm weather. A monarch butterfly attracted my attention. I was surprised to see it flying straight up the channel from the open lake. Then we were surrounded by monarchs, flying from three to ten feet above the water with that strange combination of purposefulness and erratic fluttering that carries them up to thirty miles a day on their migrations.

We rounded the light at the end of the breakwater and turned toward the unbroken horizon. Out on the lake the rise and fall of a long, low swell proved that a hard wind had been blowing somewhere within recent hours. It made my crew queasy, but she couldn't stop watching the butterflies.

They kept coming by the thousands, across the wind, from the northeast. It was like the beginning of a blizzard, when the flakes drift down large and flat. But these flakes were black and orange, not white, and the temperature was in the seventies.

The butterflies flew through the rigging and dodged around our heads, a foot or two away. A few dropped to the deck or caught hold of a rope for a moment's rest, then flew on. After a summer of munching on milkweed they were on their way to the Gulf Coast.

It seemed a pity that some had fallen into the water. I saw one struggling nearby, fished it out, and put it on the cockpit coaming. It sat there gratefully, slowly opening and closing its wings to dry in the sun.

The wind increased. The *Dawn Treader* heeled slightly and picked up speed. Since the butterflies were coming in the opposite direction, toward the harbor mouth we had just left, they seemed to be flying faster.

For the butterfly on the coaming, this may have enhanced the feeling that it was being left behind. With a desperate flap it tried to catch up, fluttering out over the water astern. I could now see its problem, the reason it had been in the water in the first place. There was a crack in the main rib of its port wing. In a few seconds it crash landed in the water for the last time.

I wondered how it could have damaged its wing in the middle of the lake, or how it could have crossed so much water with a wing that was already broken. No clues to this mystery were furnished.

The flock kept coming for over an hour, more butterflies at one time than the cumulative total of all I had seen in my whole life up to that moment. I've never seen the elephants dance or found the place where the whales go to die or glimpsed the golden sea serpent, but encountering the monarch migration at sea was a splendid enough sight.

Somehow I was glad, with a sky filled with butterflies and sunlight glittering on the water, that while the *Dawn Treader* was scarcely in Class A condition at the end of summer she at least was not unworthy to have spread her white wings among the butterflies. (However, I probably ought to warn you that milkweed is very bitter, and you'll never get used to the taste.)

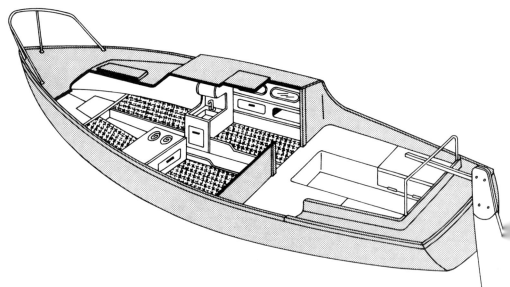

Fig. 8-1. Typical sailboat cabin squeezes in four bunks. Finding space for provisions and baggage for that large a crew can be a real challenge.

8 Cabins: Nobody's Above Going Below

A CABIN is what makes a boat a ship. With a cabin, a ship invites you to toss some provisions into a locker along with the treasure map and sail away for a year and a day, or at least overnight.

Recognizing the sales appeal of cabins, some designers crowd four berths into small craft where there's actually just room for two. Although ingenuity can provide additional bunks in very little space, you can't actually cruise with those extra people aboard. There isn't enough room for provisions and baggage. Also, you have to think of long afternoons at anchor with all hands in the cabin waiting for the weather to improve. If a ship is large enough to cruise with a big crew (I almost said "in comfort," but that is perhaps a landlubber's phrase), the berths arrange themselves naturally without straining the designer's cleverness. Still, I can't find fault with the impulse; four bunks are saltier than two even if you never go cruising. (See Figure 8-1.)

The progress of a ship building project seems to slow when you start on the cabin and the decks. When I turned the hull of the *Dawn Treader* right side up there was no reason I couldn't have launched her that afternoon. The exterior of the hull had been

Fig. 8-2. Spreaders (made of common lumber with knots in it) continue to brace hull until deck beams can be installed.

fiberglassed and painted. Some of the temporary spreaders were still in place to strengthen the hull until the deck beams could be installed. (See Figure 8-2.) Although there was no rigging, I could have clamped my outboard motor to the transom for a sea trial.

Yet, it would be 300 more hours—from July to the following spring—before she would be finished. Much of that time would go into constructing the cabin and dealing with the complexities of joinery that cabin and decks involve.

It would make a good story at this point to confess that after all that work we never used the boat for cruising, but kept chickens in it instead. That, however, was not the case. We went cruising at the first possible moment, and I knew that the work was worthwhile the first night. As the sun dropped behind the trees at the water's edge, the last boats in sight chugged past, bearing determined fishermen home to dinner at last. They tied up at piers already hard to see in the shadow of the trees. The fishermen disappeared into their cottages.

At anchor just inside the sheltering arms of the cove, we had already eaten and washed up. I sat out on deck leaning against the cabin, grateful to be partly in the lee as a cool evening breeze sprang up. I watched the display in the sky, first of scarlet sunset, then of stars, satisfied that the show could not be seen quite so well by anyone else. I zipped up my jacket and hunched around a hot cup of tea, feeling both snug and smug. In a moment I would go below out of the wind and crawl into a warm sleeping bag.

If you can't understand why this was a delicious moment, you probably never wanted a tree house as a child, and there's no hope for you.

People who haven't tried it sometimes wonder whether sleeping aboard a small boat is comfortable. I'll tell you. During the night, the wind shifted, maliciously, to the precise angle that allowed it to bowl waves directly at us through the mouth of the cove. As it blew harder, the waves built up to two feet or more— high enough to make the *Dawn Treader* quite lively at the end of the anchor line.

The wind slapped the halyards against the hollow aluminum mast. Clank. Clank. Clank. Although my sleeping bag was soft and cozy, I began to worry about the anchorage. Maybe the anchor was dragging. Maybe the anchor line was chafing through.

Down below in the cabin, the noise and the motion suggested a minor hurricane—precisely the circumstances in which a sea captain shows his mettle.

Before roaring, "all hands on deck," I decided to investigate. I wriggled reluctantly out of my sleeping bag and went out into the night, feeling much more like a clipper captain intent on making San Francisco in eighty-nine days than like a cold middle-aged man in his underwear.

Fortunately for the crew, who remained asleep throughout, there was no need for emergency action. The night was clear. The anchor was holding. The anchor line, brand new for the voyage, showed no signs of chafe where it fed through the bow chock. I hushed the clanking halyard by taping it to a side stay to keep it clear of the mast. (I later learned that a short length of elastic shock cord is ideal for this purpose.) What seemed like an incipient typhoon below was actually only a breezy summer night. Seeing no reason to take to the lifeboats, I went back to my bunk and slept soundly till morning.

As Theodore Roosevelt once said, going to sleep in wet

blankets after trailing a rustler on horseback all day in the rain, it was "bully."

Cabin Construction

Boat plans show the basic construction features of the cabin, the decks, and the cockpit. (See Figure 8-3.) They don't usually go into much detail about the handling of storage space, cabinetry, the galley, and other nonstructural refinements. Owners have different requirements for a ship and different opinions about how the accommodations should be arranged. Suppose some bachelor with hopes of success among the Sirens had to operate from a ship on which the bunks had been made especially cramped in order to provide more room for fish bait. One of the significant advantages of building a ship is being able to fit the cabin interior to your own interests.

A ship that is to be used for cruising has to provide for the following basics:

- Sail and gear stowage
- Oilskin stowage
- Food stowage
- Water and fuel tanks
- Seats
- Cooking and dining space
- Berths
- Chart and navigation space
- Toilet
- Ventilation below decks

On a small ship, where the entire cabin may not be much bigger than a piano crate, this requires ingenuity.

As much as possible should be done inside the cabin before you put the roof on. Now is one of your rare opportunities to use a level. If you have been paying attention, you have left some of the original spreaders that supported the frame on the stocks in place. They are parallel to the waterline, so you can use them as a reference point to level the hull. If the hull is on a trailer, block the frame so the springs can't allow the hull to dip out of plumb as you

Fig. 8-3. You build the cabin from the floor up. (The large round holes in the photo are to ventilate the interior of a laminated box that forms the base of the *Dawn Treader's* mast support.)

move around inside. Because the hull will remain vulnerable until the deck beams are installed, it should be well supported at this stage.

One of the first things to do is to install the bow eye fitting that takes the line from the trailer winch. This doesn't appear on the plans because the designer couldn't know what kind of trailer you have or how the winch is positioned. You'll have to figure out for yourself where to drill the hole so that the bow eye will line up with the winch. The bow eye is bolted through the stem and backed up on the inside by a large washer or metal plate.

My journal records that I somehow drilled this hole in the wrong place, unlikely as such an obvious error seems. Fortunately, the cure was simple. I glued in a dowel of the proper size.

The plans show the framing for the floors of the cabin and cockpit. This part of the work is just basic carpentry, cutting lengths of mahogany to fit and fastening them with screws and glue. Once that's finished comes another time to sit and think a while. You want to figure out the best sequence for installing the various parts. Work that isn't done at the right time may be hard to reach later on.

You'll probably want to paint the bilge before starting to put down the floor boards. Otherwise, you'll have to take them up again later. You'll need a vacuum cleaner. Working inside the hull produces mountains of sawdust and small shavings, which accumulate in the bilge and can't be removed any other way.

Floors

Under the cabin floor is the best place to store heavy items, such as water, because that keeps the weight low and central. Cabin floors should be made in small sections and fastened with the fewest possible screws so they're easy to take up. You need access to the bilge both for storage and for boat maintenance.

In the *Dawn Treader*, there are two small sections of flooring lying right over the deepest part of the bilge on either side of the centerboard case that aren't fastened down at all. This simplifies drying out the bilge whenever water accumulates from rain, spray, or leakage.

"Under the cabin floor is the best place to store heavy items."

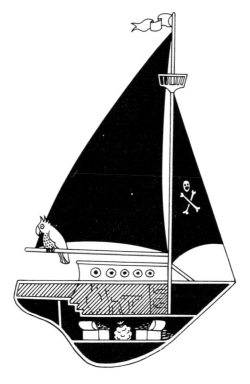

Fig. 8-4. Framing for the port bunk. Note the storage space available under it.

I have also hinged part of the port bunk. (See Figure 8-4 and Figure 8-5.) Underneath is where I store the anchor and other ground tackle. It rests on the keel and surrounding framing, not the thin planking.

Some cockpit floors are self-bailing. This means that the floor is higher than the waterline. Any water that gets in such a cockpit

Fig. 8-5. Floor boards and bunks should be left loose or hinged to provide convenient access to storage space and to ventilate bilges.

will run out through holes drilled in the transom (or short lengths of hose if that's how the design works). A self-bailing cockpit should be made watertight with glued joints. Otherwise, the bilge under the cockpit should also remain accessible by removing a few screws.

If you put a water tank under the floor, it should run fore and aft. Water sloshing from side to side in a tank doesn't help a sailboat's stability. Some authorities question whether a small ship used only occasionally for cruising should have a built-in water tank at all. Individual jerrycans of water offer several advantages: they can be hosed out between voyages and kept free of the stale taste built-in tanks often develop; they can be moved around on board to help trim and stabilize the ship; they're not likely to leak all at once; and they're easy to remove to lighten ship for trailing or to float you off a sandbar. For cruising, you need a gallon per person per day.

Fuel tanks have to be installed so that fumes can't collect anywhere and blow you up. This subject is discussed in detail in the chapter on engines.

Decks

After you finish the flooring, you can start on the decks. (See Figure 8-6.) Complete amateur plans provide a full-size pattern for

Fig. 8-6. Flooring should be finished before starting with the deck beams.

Fig. 8-7. Ends of deck beams are notched into the gunwales with a chisel the same width as the beams.

cutting out the curved deck beams and show how to fasten them, usually with the ends set into notches cut with a chisel the same width as the beams. (See Figure 8-7.) There is a danger at this point of spoiling the appearance of the ship. The highest points on the crowns of all the deck beams should form a continuous, flowing line. If you make a mistake in the length of any of the beams, you may not notice at once because the beam can be sprung a little flatter to bridge the space. But this will spoil the flowing line of the deck crown. So check that line with a long piece of scrap while the beams are merely set in place before you glue them in and it's too late. Mistakes can be remedied by planing or shimming out any beams that don't fall into line.

Once the deck beams are installed, you can remove the remaining spreaders. But don't rest your weight on the deck beams while installing the planking unless the ship is a large one with heavy beams. The usual small boat design requires the plywood in place over the beams to achieve full strength.

Because the deck beams run athwartship instead of fore and aft like the hull framing, you'll be reminded of the studs used in house construction. You'll be tempted to think of the decking as similar to wallboard and cut it to end on the center of a beam. You think you'll save the trouble of backing up the joints with butt blocks as you had to do with the hull planking.

That's a mistake. Deck joints backed only by the width of a beam are weak and tend to leak. It's better to treat the decking as if it were bottom planking and back up the joints with wide plywood butt blocks, securely glued.

A deck made of boards is undeniably the saltiest, the fittest for a captain to pace. It is also the leakiest. That's why so many older boats have decks covered with canvas. Plywood decking won't leak if properly installed. (See Figure 8-8.) It can be covered with

Fig. 8-8. The center joint of plywood planking is backed along its entire length by a wide strip set into the deck beams. Properly glued and fastened, this joint will never leak. (One hazard of boat building is that your family tends to use the decks as temporary shelving. In this case, the apple barrel was removed before any snoopy cabin boys could conceal themselves in it.)

fiberglass, left textured to avoid slipperiness, or simply painted with a nonskid paint, which has fine sand or other gritty material stirred into it or sprinkled on while wet.

I have been satisfied so far with painted plywood decks, although the Douglas fir plywood has checked to some extent, a trait for which fir is notorious. I didn't want to spend the additional money for mahogany plywood or more fiberglassing, once the hull was done.

Accommodations

By the time a shipwright has reached the cabin-building stage, he has had plenty of practice with his tools. Constructing the cabin interior to suit himself is easily within his powers. Some recommended dimensions:

Standing headroom (impossible except in large boats): 6 feet, 3 inches

Minimum headroom: 40 inches

Headroom over a seat: 3 feet

Height of a seat: 12 to 19 inches

Width of a seat: 16 inches preferred; 12 inches minimum

Counter height, full headroom: 36 inches

Counter height, sitting headroom: 28 inches

Berths, ideal size: 6 feet, 6 inches by 30 inches

Berths, minimum size: 6 feet by 21 inches

Hatches: 18 by 18 inches preferred; 14 by 18 minimum

Width of doorways and passageways: 20 to 24 inches

Width of hanging locker: 7 inches minimum

Ship ladders: 16 to 30 inches wide; 5- to 8-inch treads; 10- to 14-inch step rise

You can't always get what you want in a small ship. (See Figure 8-9.) Even though I raised the ceiling of the *Dawn Treader* to the maximum advised by the plan source, the beams are still only forty-two inches above the cabin floor at the highest point. Over the only permanent seat in the cabin, the headroom (apt phrase in more than one sense) is twenty-five inches. This is cramped, but it suffices.

Fig. 8-9. Accommodations on a small ship require the crew to be on rather intimate terms.

The entrance to the cabin is forty-seven inches wide, a convenience for tall persons ducking into the low cabin with the centerboard case sticking up in the middle. (See Figure 8-10.) During construction I considered making it narrower, which would have resulted in a snugger cabin, but I decided there would be many more occasions for scrambling in and out of the cabin with armloads of gear and provisions than for battening down the hatches and avoiding bad weather.

Since then, the designer has begun recommending a thirty-inch hatch to insure that the cabin won't swamp in case of a capsize. The designer also has belatedly recognized the need for a strip down the center of the cockpit floor to brace your toe against when the ship unexpectedly heels. Otherwise, as has happened to me, you slide off the cockpit rim and flop butterside down on the deck.

"Hitting the deck" is a phrase I prefer to associate with turning out the crew for breakfast and raising sail on an inviting summer morning afloat.

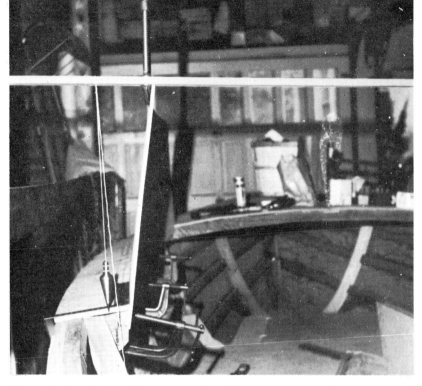

Fig. 8-10. Detail of cabin construction: You can measure from the plumb line to give the cabin side the correct slant. A scrap brace and clamps hold it until roof beams are fitted.

Making Fits

While building the cabin and the cockpit, you're likely to meet measuring and fitting problems that defy familiar methods, although they're easy enough to cope with once you see how the appropriate techniques work.

One example is fitting a large panel against a vertical surface that isn't square. The cabin floor butts against the curving side of the hull and has to fit around the vertical ribs.

Figure 8-11 shows the easiest way to mark the plywood for cutting. Use a stick about two feet long with a notch in the side near one end. You temporarily clamp or tack a piece of scrap about where the piece to be fitted will go. With a pencil held in the notch, the stick is run along the hull curve and around the obstructions—always at ninety degrees to the centerline of the ship. The pencil in the notch reproduces the shape of the hull side.

You put the marked scrap next to your plywood and repeat

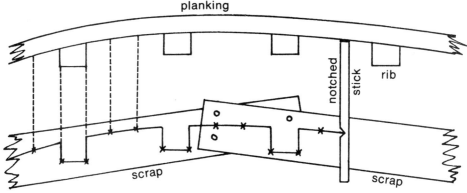

planking

notched

stick

rib

scrap

scrap

Fig. 8-11. To fit a panel against a curved vertical surface, possibly with projecting framing, make a template of scraps fastened together in an approximation of the curve. Use a notched stick with a pencil to copy the changing contours onto the template. Cut out the template and see if it fits. It may need a little adjusting. When it does fit, use it as a tracing pattern to cut out the finished piece.

the notched stick trick, copying the outline onto the plywood, which can then be cut.

Sometimes the piece to be fitted is very large and complex, such as the bulkhead next to the cabin door. It's usually shaped like a fat lower-case b (starboard) or d (port). To determine the precise outline, you construct a template of scraps in approximately the right shape. (See Figure 8-12.) Then you use the notched stick trick to mark the outline on the template. Cut the template as marked and see if it fits.

Fig. 8-12. The scraps of plywood in the photo are a template that has been cut to the outline of part of the cabin bulkhead.

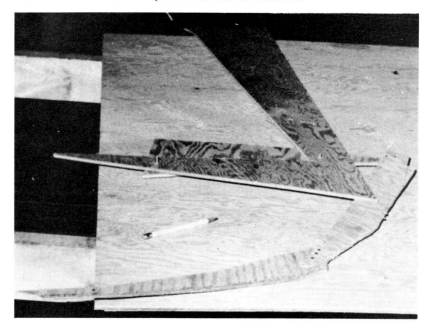

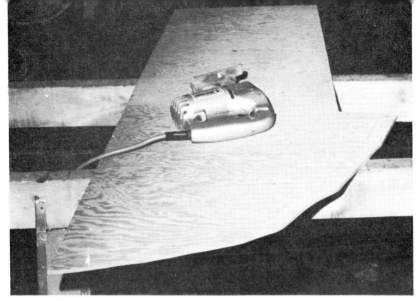

Fig. 8-13. This is the cabin bulkhead cut from a panel of marine plywood. Because a saber saw sometimes gets away from you a little, always cut outside the guideline. Then you can take down the excess with a plane or rasp.

It probably won't fit the first time, so make the necessary refinements and try it again. Now it should fit. When it does, use it as a tracing pattern to cut out the finished piece. (See Figure 8-13 and Figure 8-14.)

Fig. 8-14. Bulkhead in place on port side.

Sanitation

A bucket once was considered to be all the sanitation facilities a small vessel needed. Now, with concern about water pollution almost everywhere, it is considered bad form to dump the contents of the bucket overboard.

Marine suppliers offer a large variety of marine toilets. The simplest, an up-to-date version of the bucket, is a folding seat that uses specially made plastic bags. The bags are tied shut and disposed of ashore. Meanwhile, there is a small stowage problem. You don't want to put the bags where they can be accidentally punctured.

Many builders prefer the type that contains a fresh water reservoir, a flushing pump, and a sealed holding tank. A special chemical is kept in the holding tank to prevent formation of gas and odors. The small holding tank can be detached and taken ashore to be dumped into any convenient sewer. The chemical and the sealing valve really work. You don't have to dump the holding tank until it gets full, even if that takes several weeks.

Installation couldn't be simpler: two screws into the floor of the cabin. Various brands advertise forty or fifty to eighty flushes.

For larger ships, there are more complex models. The aircraft type recirculates chemically treated water for greater capacity. Some offer electric flush, chlorinator-macerator units for discharge overboard, and other refinements. Large holding tanks can be pumped out at dockside in an increasing number of marinas.

Any plumbing required can usually be handled with rubber hose instead of rigid pipe. Exceptions are pointed out in your boat plans or in the instructions that come with various equipment.

Lighting

Depending on your requirements, lighting also can be simple or elaborate. For limited night sailing, you can buy riding lights that operate with self-contained batteries. The next step up is a system of running lights and cabin lights wired to a big central dry cell. You can switch the lights on and off from a central switch panel, which is more convenient and safer.

If you use dry cells, always keep fresh spares on board. Mark the date on new batteries when you buy them. This will help you avoid thinking of them as "fresh" batteries long after their shelf lifespan has passed.

Even without a generator on board, some builders install a wet cell battery, which can be recharged between cruises by an inexpensive battery charger. Special marine batteries are made with spillproof caps to keep the acid inside. A full-size marine battery weighs about forty pounds; a smaller size weighs twenty pounds or so.

To save weight and expense on a small ship, you might consider a motorcycle battery. Some weigh as little as five pounds.

Any kind of wet cell battery should be installed so that it can't be jiggled by the motion of the boat or trailer. It should be surrounded by noncorrosive material in case any acid does spill. Plastic boxes are available that are made especially to hold marine batteries. Batteries also need ventilation because explosive gas is generated during charging.

As I write this page, I have just read of a new wind-driven trickle charger made in England and designed to keep a marine battery charged while the boat sits at its mooring or cruises under sail. Such a specialized item naturally costs much more than an ordinary charger, but in some circumstances it could be well worth the price. By the time you read this, wind-driven chargers may be in general distribution.

Inboard engines long have had electrical systems like those of cars, with electric starters and batteries charged by the engine. Now even some outboards provide the same facilities. I see in the catalogs that an outboard as small as 9.9 horsepower—a good auxiliary size for medium-sized cruising sailboats—comes with an optional 5-amp alternator that can charge the battery for lights as well as electric starting.

Tinkerers with a knack for engines have been known to run automotive alternators attached to smaller outboards with a drive belt around the starting rope pulley or flywheel. A man in Blooming Grove, New York, claims that his system, based on a 6-

horsepower outboard, produces power for an electric refrigerator that keeps his beer cold.

For ships up to about forty feet long, a 12-volt system is sufficient. Plan circuits to use the least wire possible; this reduces voltage drop. You can compensate for voltage drop on longer circuits by using a larger size wire. Solder all connections, and twist any wires that pass near the compass around each other to avoid creating an electromagnetic field that will distort the compass readings.

Galley

You don't have to cook inside the cramped cabin. Some builders plan on cooking in the cockpit, where there's more room. They assume that any cooking will be done at anchor or while tied up at a marina. In the rain a tarp can be rigged over the boom to cover the whole cockpit. If you adopt this idea, you can build storage for utensils under the side decks and use the side deck itself as a cooking surface with a stove that's put away when not in use. I've seen one boat with a sink set into the side deck, with a plywood cover to sit on when sailing.

I don't like this approach, only because it's not as salty as having the galley inside the cabin, where Noah put it on the Ark to set the pattern most builders have followed ever since. (See Figure 8-15 and 8-16.)

Counter tops and cabinets inside the cabin need be only water-resistant. You can get away with ¼-inch exterior grade plywood cabinet sides and brass screws and hardware instead of marine plywood and bronze.

Stoves should stand in a shallow pan that can catch grease, drippings, and the spilled sauce cordon bleu. Surrounding woodwork should have scorch protection such as a sheet of asbestos or stainless steel with air space behind it. Above a stove a minimum of eighteen inches clearance is recommended. Gimballed stoves simplify the cook's life, but there may not be room for them to swing in a small galley.

Any surface used for cooking or eating should be surrounded

Fig. 8-15. Galley idea on factory-built boat. Foot of bunk extends under cockpit. Stove is stored there when not in use.

Fig. 8-16. Another factory boat galley. Stove can be put away under counter top. Counter space on a boat is so valuable that you have to be able to use it for more than one purpose.

Fig. 8-17. Shelves and racks on a sailboat have to be made so that nothing can fall off when the boat heels.

by fiddles about ¾ inch high to prevent utensils from sliding off when the boat moves. The fiddles should provide for drainage at intervals or be removable so you can use the same table for navigation charts at other times. Some builders, instead of using fiddles, snap on shock cord at a height of about two inches when needed. In addition, racks and cabinets can be designed to hold dishes and utensils securely. (See Figure 8-17 and Figure 8-18.)

Galley stoves are fueled by kerosene, alcohol, or propane. The familiar gasoline camp stove that's so convenient on a canoe trip is not welcome in a seagoing kitchen. Gasoline fumes are heavier than air. If anything goes wrong, they can collect in the bilge and blow you up. Propane is easy to use, but you have to be able to replace the containers. It, too, can be dangerous if the piping leaks.

Traditionally, kerosene has been widely available and cheap. Although kerosene doesn't fill the bilge with explosive fumes, a ker-

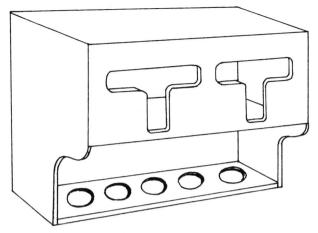

Fig. 8-18. Idea for galley cabinet. Upper compartments hold plates. Lower cutouts hold glasses. (Cups can be hung by their handles on hooks.)

osene flare-up can be a menace. You can't throw water on it, because water spreads any oil fire.

That's why I chose a single-burner alcohol stove for the *Dawn Treader*. Flaming alcohol can be extinguished with water. It didn't take me long to put this advantage to the test. One night, lying at anchor and chatting in the cockpit, we decided to heat up some water for tea. The moonlight was so bright that I could almost see what I was doing. I set the stove on deck, pumped it up, let a little fuel run into the priming cup, and lighted it with a match. In the dark I had not noticed that a little of the fuel had slopped over the side of the priming cup and run across the deck. The instant I struck the match, tongues of flame raced down the sides of the stove and across the wooden deck — not far from the can of gasoline for the engine.

With kerosene I would have had to shoot off the fire extinguisher at once. Since the fuel was alcohol, I could put out the flames simply by dipping my tea cup over the side and splashing a little water around. The alarum didn't even slow up heating the tea kettle.

There's a kit available for converting leading brands of gasoline camp stoves for use with alcohol. I didn't get one because I still use my camp stove on canoe trips, and gasoline is better on shore because it's hotter and faster.

Sterno stoves are safe and in some ways convenient for marine use, but the builder should be warned that Sterno is very slow to boil water compared to any of the liquid fuels.

Windows

It's salty to use marine terms—*bulkhead* for wall and *porthole* for window, not to mention *carline, breasthook, keelson,* and worse. I am avoiding marine terminology as much as possible in this book because boat building is arcane enough without unfamiliar jargon. Of course, everyone knows that ships have portholes instead of windows. The trouble is that the ports I installed in the *Dawn Treader* look like windows.

Usually the boat plans detail the window outlines. For appearance's sake, the sides of the windows should parallel the outlines of the cabin instead of being round or square. (See Figure 8-19.) On

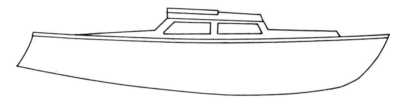

Fig. 8-19. For better appearance, edges of windows should parallel the cabin outline.

small ships the windows are fixed. The main hatch alone provides enough ventilation below. Larger ships carry ports that can be opened or fastened to be leakproof even when submerged by a wave. This type of port is heavily constructed, usually of bronze, and very expensive.

In building the *Dawn Treader,* I postponed a decision about the windows. (Figure 8-20.) Instead of cutting out plywood and plexiglass according to plans, I went ahead and completed the cabin exterior with the ship looking blind, like a pupfish. I thought there would be occasions when I'd want to use the *Dawn Treader* like a houseboat on the Upper Mississippi River, a favorite cruising ground we have visited many times with canoe and tent.

There it would be desirable to have windows with screens. In one catalog I found a small, lightweight aluminum window that wasn't unduly expensive. It came with its own screen and a panel of plexiglass that could be opened or closed with a knurled cam. So I bought two for the front of the cabin and one for each side.

Finishing the cutouts for the windows was one of the dramatic moments of the two-year project. The *Dawn Treader* suddenly acquired a personality. Like the fish-hunting caiques of the Mediterranean, she had eyes and could see.

I could make a screen for the hatch by sewing Velcro tape around a piece of screening and gluing more Velcro to the wood around the entrance. Velcro is the material that sticks to itself and can be fastened and unfastened countless times. To keep the flying fauna of the Mississippi sloughs out of the cabin at night I would merely smooth the edge of the screening with my thumb. The open windows, also screened, would provide cross ventilation.

This fancy proved to be a mistake. The windows were designed for houseboats with vertical sides, not sailboats. My cabin front is tilted back at such an angle that rain and spray collect on the window sills and seep in around the loosely fitting plexiglass. The side windows don't leak ordinarily, but the same thing happens on the windward side when the ship heels far enough.

Fig. 8-20. Until window holes are cut, a ship looks blind. (It's easier to cut the window holes before installing the cabin sides if you're making your own.)

If the *Dawn Treader* ever capsized with the side windows open, water would gush in, which could be serious. A shipwright should keep this possibility in mind. Some designs place the window plexiglass in a rubber channel from which it could pop out under pressure at an inconvenient time.

When I get around to it, I am going to replace those handy little windows with fixed panels of plexiglass—just as the plans specified in the first place.

A ship is never really complete. There continue to be ways to improve the accommodations and the rigging as long as you own her. If I weren't replacing the windows, I'd be installing davits for a motor launch or perhaps an aircraft catapult.

A builder who lives in an area where the industry puts on a boat show can learn by browsing through stock boats to see what the professionals are up to. Bring a camera or a sketch book to take visual notes. I don't think you'll be especially impressed by the galley and stowage arrangements. Building for the market requires holding down labor costs as much as possible. Seeing a variety of finished boats, however, will stimulate your own ideas. Boating magazines also publish countless ideas for improvement of storage space. (See Figure 8-21 through Figure 8-26.)

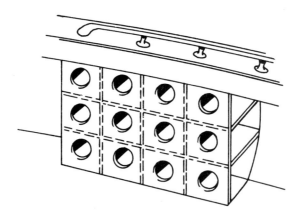

Fig. 8-21. Idea for stowing small items under gunwales. Access ports can be about six inches in diameter.

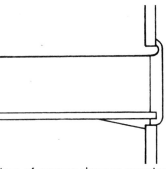

Fig. 8-22. Side view of proper drawer construction for sailboat cabins. Notch prevents drawer from opening until you lift up.

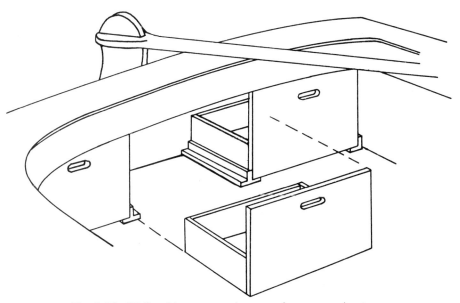

Fig. 8-23. Sliding bins can make use of space under transom.

Fig. 8-24. A chart board can be hinged to swing down from the cabin ceiling. Space above holds extra charts.

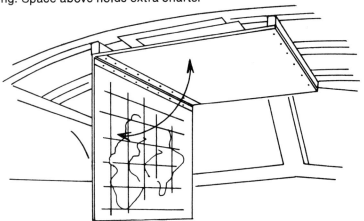

Fig. 8-25. Hinged hatch cover folds down to become cockpit table.

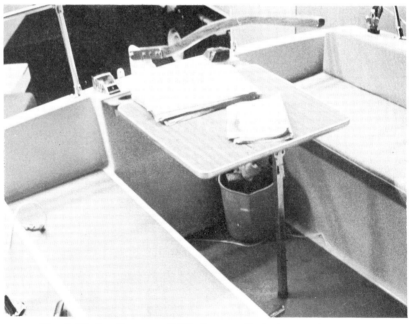

Fig. 8-26. Another possibility for a self-storing cockpit table.

In exercising your ingenuity, there are some rules to keep in mind:

- No part of the boat should be cut off from free circulation of air. Bins and racks are preferable to drawers and lockers with doors. If drawers and doors are used, they should include ventilation holes.

- If the boat regularly rides the highway on a trailer, take into consideration the effect of rough pavement and sudden stops on heavy items stowed in a lightly constructed cabinet. I imagine a loose iron skillet could come right through the side. For cruising the highway, such objects can either be transferred to the car or securely fastened down.

- Remember that a boat, particularly a sailing ship, routinely heels to angles you don't encounter on shore when sober. I heard about one man sailing alone who went below to use the head, located in a tiny compartment with a door. The wind suddenly increased and the ship heeled. A drawer slid part way out of a cabinet in such a way that it blocked the door. He was trapped below until the ship, with no one at the helm, finally worked her way around onto the opposite tack. The ship heeled to the other side and the drawer slid back in, releasing the only captain ever locked in the brig by his own ship.

The story has more than one moral. At a minimum, you should infer that drawers and doors ought to be designed to act less mutinously. You may also conclude something about the modern tendency toward finicky elaboration and too much complexity. When I related this episode to Martin Frobisher, who happens by from time to time looking for the Northwest Passage, he swore that in all his voyages nobody had ever been trapped below decks by a bucket.

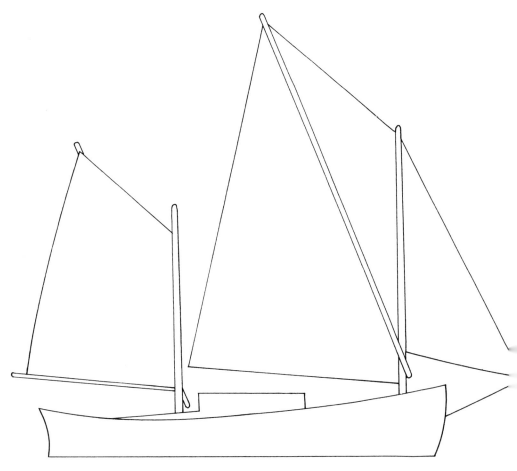

Fig. 9-1. The spritsail rig could be made to work without the expensive complex of stays, shrouds, and turnbuckles found on modern yachts.

9 Rigging: What Goes Up Better Not Come Down

THE Pharaohs were just starting out in local politics, taking a little graft on the irrigation bond issues, when some lazy Egyptian realized that the prevailing spring and summer winds in the Nile Valley would blow him back upstream without paddling if he hoisted something to catch the breeze. By 2000 B.C. Egyptian ships already had sophisticated sails and salty-looking bowsprits.

The reason galleys and oars became so prominent in ancient history wasn't that the Argonauts and their friends didn't know how to sail; the trouble was that on the Mediterranean the wind tends to blow either too hard or not enough to be dependable.

People often think that sailing against the wind was a recent discovery. Not so. On the Indian Ocean, where the wind is more cooperative, the lateen sail appeared at an early date. The Vikings knew all about tacking against the wind. They hauled their big square sails around fore and aft and used them like lug sails. This capability of the Viking rig was one reason a modern replica of the Gokstad ship was able to sail across the Atlantic in twenty-eight days.

Another refinement of sail control—reef points sewed to the sail for partly furling it in strong winds—can be observed on thirteenth century coins depicting English ships.

Some builders say that the modern sailing yacht has become unnecessarily complicated and expensive. For instance, a common rig on nineteenth century workboats was the spritsail (illustrated in at least one Winslow Homer painting I can think of). The spritsail was hung on a rather short mast, with a long gaff that braced the high peak of the canvas. The shape of the sail was an irregular trapezoid (or trapezium, as the geometricians say). Among its virtues was the elimination of several expensive hardware items. The mast required no stays, which meant no turnbuckles, no chainplates, and few mast fittings. The sail itself contained no battens and was easy to handle. (See Figure 9-1.)

This suggests that there is no one rigging plan that is ideal for all boats. In fact, many blueprints show alternate rigs for the same hull—Bermuda or gaff rigs for a small sloop. A larger sloop may also be rigged as a yawl. Such is the glorious diversity of the human spirit that workers in a boat yard may sometimes be simultaneously employed in changing a sloop to a yawl for one owner and a yawl to a sloop for another.

The beginning builder should not attempt any variation not shown on his plans. The total sail area must remain in proportion to the stability of the hull, and the balance of the rig, which must tend to turn the ship into the wind, has to be maintained.

Spars

As explained earlier, I chose an aluminum mast for the *Dawn Treader*, although it would have been easy enough to build a hollow spar of Sitka spruce. Michael Verney says, "Making spars is one of the simplest but most enjoyable tasks in boat building. One should never feel chary about this work, for providing the correct materials are used, a failure is exceedingly remote." Howard Chapelle agrees. "Solid spars, or those pieced up of two halves, can be built by a beginner; the box-shaped hollow spars are but little more difficult."

Your plans show the mast construction details. The trick is to build a jig long enough to hold the mast straight while the glue sets. (See Figure 9-2.) You can probably do it on the basement floor up

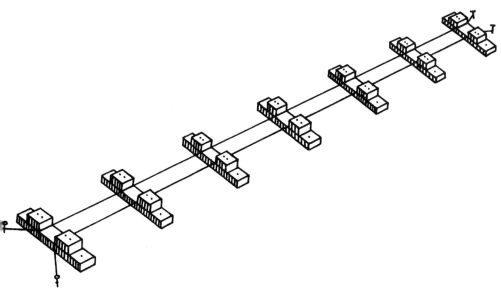

Fig. 9-2. To laminate a spruce spar, you can make a long jig fastened to the floor of your work space. Stretch a long string to make sure it's straight.

against a wall. Wedges can be used to avoid having to buy a bushel of clamps (Figure 9-3). (Be sure you can get the spar out through a window afterwards. Low basements with window wells may be unusable.)

Don't jump to the conclusion that the boom is the same as the mast. Construction is no different, but the cross section is always smaller.

I would never have felt comfortable with a wooden mast. I twice broke one at sea, and I remembered the scene in *Captains Courageous* where the mast of the fishing boat has come down, tangling Spencer Tracy in the loose rigging so that Freddy Bartholomew can't rescue him when it has to be cut away to save

Fig. 9-3. To hold spar parts while the glue sets, wedge them into the jig.

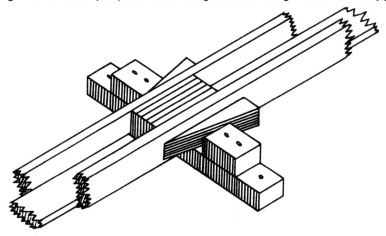

the ship. I didn't want any goings on like that aboard the *Dawn Treader*.

There is a choice of ways to find out which of the standard aluminum extrusions is correct to substitute for a wood spar of a given size. You can consult *Skene's Elements of Yacht Design* and work out a formula that takes most of a chapter to explain. Or you can ask a supplier, who probably can't work out the formula either, but knows from day-to-day experience how to match up spars and hulls. One catalog on my desk rates aluminum masts and booms according to the area of sail they have to carry.

Lengths of the extrusions are in proportion to thickness, the lighter ones for smaller boats being shorter so you don't have to pay for a lot of waste material. The supplier will cut your mast to size at extra cost, or you can do it yourself with a hack saw. Use a fresh, sharp blade and work carefully so that the blade doesn't twist and creep off course. It's a good idea in cutting any kind of pipe to make a wood jig with a pair of slots in it to guide the saw and help you cut square.

Since aluminum doesn't naturally float like wood, you should put flotation inside your mast to make it bouyant. (See Chapter 12.)

Although aluminum masts are available in plain pipe form, most are extruded with a groove that makes a sail track unnecessary. A rope sewed into the sail slides in the groove. You have to remember to tell your sailmaker about this because if he sews the sail with slides for a sail track it won't fit into the groove.

A sail tucked into a mast groove is more efficient because no air can spill around it. And you don't have to worry about the stitching on the slides. However, a sail sliding in a groove is harder for one man to handle than a sail sliding on a track. With track, you just haul on the main halyard and up the sail goes. With a groove, the sail edge tends to stick at the point of entry unless someone is standing right there feeding it in. Also, getting the sail down in a blow requires more effort with a groove than with track.

Sail track is made up in a variety of materials, ranging in cost from brass—the cheapest—to bronze, nickel silver, aluminum, and stainless steel, costing almost twice as much as brass. The standard widths are ⅝ and ⅞ inch, depending on the size of the boat. Wider track is used for special purposes, such as genoa and spinnaker fittings and travelers. Brass or bronze track should not be used on an aluminum mast because the metals are too dissimilar and may corrode.

Stiff at first, a sail slides in the extruded groove more easily after it wears a bit. I can handle the mainsail alone, kneeling on the cabin roof and feeding the sail into the groove with one hand while hauling on the halyard with the other. Of course, the *Dawn Treader* has to steer herself during this maneuver, which adds a certain drama to the occasion, particularly in a good wind with other ships about in a harbor mouth. What makes it possible is that as soon as the main begins to rise it tends to turn the ship into the wind. After the main is up, I can go forward and hoist the jib while the natural balance of the rig keeps the ship from running away. Only when I return to the cockpit, haul in the main and jib sheets, grab the tiller, and set a course does she take off.

It was easier to raise and lower sail in the old days when sails were laced to hoops around the mast. You don't see that anymore because lacing the hoops is too much trouble for skippers who take their sails home between weekends instead of hoisting them every day to go after oysters, whales, or the cargo to be smuggled.

An aluminum extrusion, of course, runs continuously from one end of the mast to the other. You have to cut a gate to permit entry for the edge of the sail and for the gooseneck fitting that holds the end of the boom. This gate should be at least a foot above the end of the boom. Otherwise, the gooseneck may rise enough under the pressure of sail to reach the gate and slide out of the groove. The gate should be six or eight inches long to simplify feeding in the edge of the sail.

You make the gate by cutting away the lips of the groove with a hack saw, then filing it smooth.

Spar Fittings

The plans usually show how to cut your own spar fittings out of a sheet of stainless steel. I could have made everything I needed out of a piece about the size of my desk blotter—if I could have conveniently obtained a piece that size. The sources I tried would have been happy to place a special order for a much larger piece at a high price. So I gave up and ordered standard hardware out of the marine supply catalog.

That's the trouble with having another occupation as well as your career as a shipwright. Things cost more when you don't have time to persevere in finding the best sources and the lowest prices. Fortunately, a ship equipped out of the catalogs is likely to be stronger than a factory boat, because the marine catalog item available for a boat of a given size seems to be heavier and stronger than the comparable hardware you see at a boat show. In order to hold costs down, boat factories have fittings made to their specifications as light as possible, and some factory boat fittings look skimpy. Companies vary in their willingness to give the skipper a performance margin.

The plans will tell you where to attach the fittings to the spars. For smaller ships, you can fasten them to the aluminum with self-tapping stainless steel sheet metal screws. You can also use small bolts as follows. Drill a hole and poke a long wire through until it comes out the bottom of the hollow mast. Then solder the end of the wire to the tip of the bolt, pull it into position, secure it with washer and nut, and snip off the wire. Parts under heavy strain, such as the fittings that hold the upper ends of the mast stays, are bolted through the mast with heavy bolts.

Stays and Shrouds

The ubiquitous Bermuda or Marconi mast requires two kinds of stays. One set prevents the mast from falling overboard; the other, which passes over the crosstrees or spreaders, keeps the mast from curling up like a pretzel from the compression forces that act upon it.

This description fits the basic plan, which includes diamond stays that are fastened at both ends to the mast, passing over the spreaders like guitar strings over their bridge. There's also a way to accomplish the same result with two sets of sidestays or shrouds that both attach to the hull, with only the upper stays passing over the spreaders. The latter plan may be better because you have to snap two shrouds instead of one before the mast falls over. (See Figure 9-4.)

I have never liked the word *shroud;* it suggests what becomes of rash skippers who don't arrange matters to keep masts from falling on their heads.

Most designs today position the chainplates that attach the

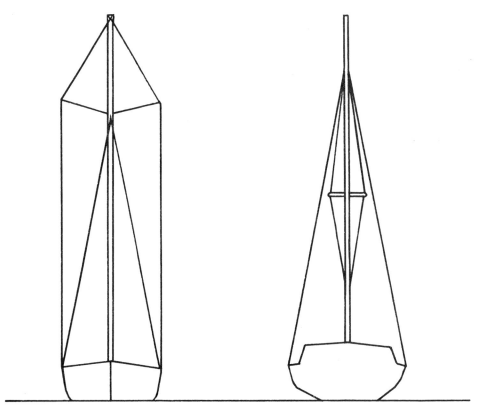

Fig. 9-4. Two ways to rig a Bermuda sloop: with two sets of shrouds fastened to the deck or with one set of shrouds running to the deck and diamond stays fastened at both ends to the mast.

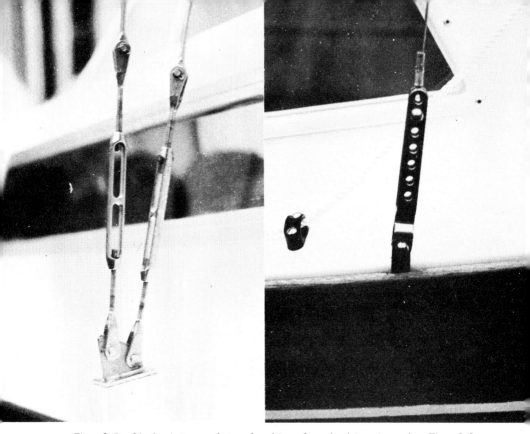

Fig. 9-5. Chainplate and turnbuckles for double shrouds. Fig. 9-6. Another kind of chainplate fastens the end of a single shroud. There is considerable design variation in marine hardware.

shrouds to the hull somewhat abaft the mast. The shrouds and the forestay then brace the mast from three directions, eliminating the need for backstays. (See Figure 9-5 and Figure 9-6.)

To make this standing rigging, you seldom see anything used but 1 x 19 stainless steel wire rope. The "1 x 19" describes a rope composed of one main strand made up of nineteen wires. It is rather stiff and quite strong. The diameter of the wire rope varies with the size of the ship and the stresses expected. The ⅛-inch stays used on the *Dawn Treader* have a breaking strength of 2,100 pounds.

You can't just tie a knot in the end of stainless steel wire rope. In order for the ends to be fastened to anything, the wire has to be bonded to permanent end fittings with special tools too expensive to buy for one boat. (See Figure 9-7.) The procedure is to give the

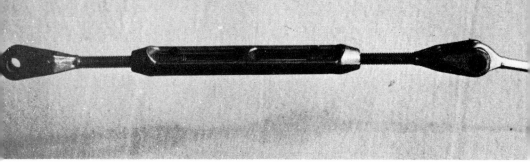

Fig. 9-7. Instead of trying to tie a knot in the end of stainless steel wire rope, you have a special eye fitting like this put on. It fastens to standard turnbuckles with a "clevis" pin passing through the eye fitting and the turnbuckle end. The clevis pin allows the joint to swivel. A small cotter pin through the end of the clevis keeps it from falling out.

measurements to a professional rigging shop. They'll cut the wire to length and attach the fittings securely.

The marine catalogs show various devices and hardware for forming end loops in stainless steel wire rope with 7 x 7 or 7 x 19 stranding. This is a more flexible product sometimes used for running rigging on larger sailboats and should not be confused with 1 x 19 standing rigging.

The turnbuckles that come with the standing rigging are bronze or stainless steel, and you need at least five, so all this is quite expensive. You'll probably wonder whether there isn't a cheaper way to rig a ship. Well, one way would be to select a design that uses an unstayed mast. It probably looks extra salty, with a gaff of some kind. Or you could go back to the old days when standing rigging was made of thick rope and the crew tightened it by hauling on a system of "deadeyes," blocks that were permanently attached to the hull and gave great mechanical advantage. (See Figure 9-8.) The trouble is that wooden blocks and good rope aren't cheap, either, and it's a considerable disadvantage to have thick rigging aloft increasing the windage. Also, ordinary cordage has to be watched for chafing and weak spots.

Getting the right measurements to send to the riggers can be troublesome. A sailboat mast doesn't stick straight up but is raked a little for efficient sailing. On the *Dawn Treader,* a plumb line from the top of the mast touches the cabin roof nine inches abaft the mast step. (See Figure 9-9.) This complicates the geometry of the forestay and the two shrouds. In each case, the length of the stay is

Fig. 9-8. In the old days, standing rigging was made of thick rope fastened to the hull with "deadeyes." The rope had to be replaced frequently. (Photo of *Nonsuch* replica courtesy of Hudson's Bay Company.)

the diagonal of a right triangle. The complication is that it isn't the actual triangle formed by the deck and the mast; it's a mythical triangle that allows for the rake. (You know, of course, that the square of the hypotenuse equals the sum of the squares of the two sides.)

Making the cabin roof four inches higher than the plans called for further complicated my problem with the *Dawn Treader*. The result was that, although I computed the length of the forestay exactly right, I made some stupid error with the shrouds, and they came back from the riggers four inches too short.

You'll be glad to know that the remedies for such errors are simple. An error of an inch or two can be compensated for by adjusting the turnbuckles. If the stays are still too long, you may be able to reposition the mast fittings to take up the slack. At worst,

Fig. 9-9. How to adjust your mast to the proper angle: Suspend a plumb bob from the top of the mast and tighten the stays until the bob is the distance abaft the center of the mast step specified in the plans. Tip: Either use fifty or sixty feet of thin string or do this job on a calm day. There's enough windage on an ordinary halyard to throw a plumb bob off its mark. (Note how mast pivots on long bolt through step.)

you can send the stays back to the rigging shop for recutting, which doesn't cost much since you've already paid for all the materials.

If the stays come out too short, you can add a few links of galvanized chain to the system at the deck end, where it can be regularly inspected and put to use as a handy place to tie down tarps or hang dock fenders. That's what I did, and I'm not sure it isn't an improvement.

Raising the Mast Alone

The mast step, which is on the deck or the cabin roof, should be hinged or pivoted some way so you can raise and lower the mast

Fig. 9-10. Another type of pivoting mast step. (The deck plug and wire are for a masthead light.)

by yourself, particularly if you trail your boat. (See Figure 9-10.) On larger boats the hinge or pivot is arranged so that the mast in the down position lies forward over the bow. The boom is attached to the mast and used as a giant lever to pry the mast up.

Here's how I do it on the *Dawn Treader*. (See Figure 9-11.) First I make sure none of the rigging is fouled and that the shrouds are secure. Then I tie a long line—twenty feet or more—to the end of the forestay, which is loose, of course, when the mast is lying back over the stern and flat on the cabin roof in position for raising. I lead the line through a shackle fastened to the stemhead and back along the deck to the cockpit.

I stand in the cockpit facing forward, grab the hoisting line in my right hand, and start raising the mast out of the support crutch with my left shoulder. I lift it as high as I can above my head with my left hand. I hold the hoisting line tightly with my right hand to keep the mast from slipping back down—this is the only tricky part —while I scramble onto the cabin roof. The shrouds keep the mast from lurching over sideways. Once on the cabin roof, I steady the mast while hauling it the rest of the way up with the line.

Keeping the line taut, I walk along the foredeck to the

Fig. 9-11. Photo sequence shows how a tall mast can be raised without help. The shrouds remain fastened throughout. A rope is tied to the end of the forestay and run through a shackle fastened to the stemhead, then back to the cockpit. You haul on the rope with one hand and lift the mast with the other until you are able to pin the forestay itself to the stemhead.

stemhead fitting and insert the bronze pin that locks the forestay turnbuckle to the stemhead. I remove the hauling line and stow it in a convenient location for reversing the procedure at the end of the cruise.

If you build a boat with the mast stepped on the keel, you won't be able to handle the mast alone unless the boat is very small. Masts aren't heavy, but they have leverage.

The rigging has to be tuned more frequently when you're stepping and unstepping the mast all the time than when it stays up for the season. Racers buy tension meters for twenty dollars and up to adjust the stays precisely. For cruising, you can adjust by feel. The stays should be tight enough to prevent any bends in the mast, but not so tight that you can pluck them like harp strings.

Running Rigging

The rope used to control sails, raise and lower the centerboard, and hang pirates from the yardarm doesn't have to withstand the stress that standing rigging does. However, it sustains much wear passing through pulleys and leads and being fastened over and over to cleats. Manila and hemp have been superseded by nylon, Dacron, and polypropylene, which won't rot and weaken when coiled wet.

Halyards are the lines that hoist sails up the mast, and sheets are the lines that control the angle of the sails to the wind.

Some builders reduce windage by leading halyards down inside the hollow mast to a hole near the bottom. It's worth it to dedicated racers, but I don't like the idea. I can envision halyards fouled somehow inside the mast where you can't get at the tangle.

Dacron, which stretches only a little, is the rope for sheets and halyards. Nylon, being rather elastic as well as strong, is ideal for anchor and mooring lines. Polypropylene, the yellow rope that floats, is substantially cheaper than nylon or Dacron and can be recommended for all the miscellaneous uses around a boat. As a dinghy painter, it floats free of the propeller. As a heaving line, it's easy for the man on the pier to fish out with a boathook when you miss your toss.

The breaking strength of line used for sheets and halyards isn't especially important. You buy thick rope—not for its strength, but to save your palms. The breaking strength of ¼-inch Dacron is 1,750 pounds—far more than any conceivable tension on the main sheet of a small ship. But with the ship heeled to her gunwale a ¼-inch main sheet cuts into your hand like piano wire. A ⅜-inch line in the same circumstances can be handled without discomfort; its 3,600 pound breaking strength is irrelevant.

Larger boats use still heavier lines. I think everybody would like ½-inch line for the main sheet, but that escalates the cost of the tackle. Most standard blocks and cleats for small ships take ¼- to ⅜-inch line. Anything larger means that you must go to the next size for all the hardware, which is something like being in a higher income tax bracket without having a higher income.

Foredeck Fittings

Boat plans show where the fittings go without specifying what kind. So let's start at the bow and examine some of the alternatives. At the very tip of the bow is the stemhead fitting. (See Figure 9-12.) To it are fastened the forestay and the tack of the jib. The stemhead has to be strong and well fastened. There should be a

Fig. 9-12. Typical stemhead fitting provides a place to fasten the forestay that holds up the mast and the tack of the jib.

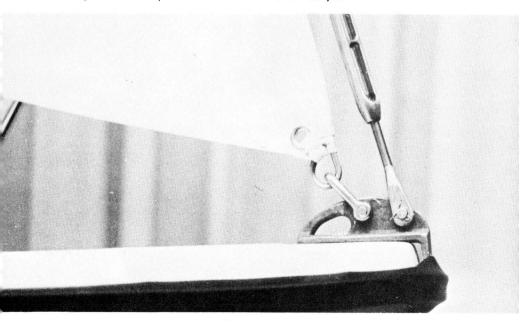

Fig. 9-13. Sailing with a spinnaker requires a small extra boom, or pole, that attaches to the mast as shown here. Fig. 9-14. Outer end of a spinnaker pole.

cleat or bollard in the center of the foredeck for making fast mooring and anchor lines, with chocks port and starboard to prevent the line from chafing on the rail.

You can buy a special fitting to secure the anchor on the foredeck when it's not in use, but your need for one depends on how much you cruise away from marinas. Such a contraption doesn't make sense aboard a boat that is left at a permanent mooring or on a trailer. The marine supply catalogs show how to select the right size anchor for your boat.

The foredeck is the only place to fasten the spinnaker pole, which can also be used to wing out a jib for greater efficiency when sailing downwind. (See Figure 9-13 and Figure 9-14.) Clips are available to hold the pole when not in use. Unless you race, you don't need a spinnaker, but it is salty.

Blocks and fairleads for the sheets come in a variety of materials. The galvanized ones work just as well as the others and cost a lot less. But they have a laundry line look that detracts from the appearance of your yacht. Also, there aren't as many designs to choose from. For example, there's a stainless steel block with a nylon wheel on a mounting plate made in such a way that the block can swivel in any direction with a jib sheet but the block can never slam against the deck. They don't make these refinements in galvanized.

Cleats

Around the cockpit you'll need a variety of cleats. For all-purpose cleats—used to fasten stern mooring lines, tie down the cockpit tent, lash the tiller—the traditional anvil cleat is best. For fastening the main and jib halyards and the jib sheets, jam cleats (Figure 9-15) are convenient. To use a jam cleat, you haul the line taut, place it in the cleat, and let the teeth grab it. To slacken the line you jerk it back until it clears the teeth.

You can make cleats and many other fittings yourself out of hardwood. Although I made my own grab rails for the cabin roof out of mahogany and aluminum tubing, I preferred to buy other fittings. Galvanized cleats are cheapest and least attractive. Black molded nylon is next lowest in price and looks handsome. Other metals—aluminum, brass, bronze—are much more expensive. Although nylon is strong, it lacks the abrasion resistance of metal. When taut lines are hauled across it often enough, with grains of sand adhering to the wet rope, it begins to be sawed through. I used

Fig. 9-15. One type of jam cleat. The teeth hold the line securely until you back it out and lift up. Then it runs freely.

mostly nylon cleats. After two full seasons, only one of them shows sign of wear, so I'm not complaining.

Other Rigging

Every boat has to have halyards and sheets for each sail, but not every boat has a boom vang or a topping lift. The boom vang counteracts the tendency of the boom to lift when the mainsail fills sailing off the wind. Racing sailboats almost always have boom vangs because they improve the shape of the sail and hence its efficiency. I don't have one and don't miss it, although on an extended cruise it would reduce the chafe of the mainsail against the spreader and shrouds when running before the wind.

A topping lift (Figure 9-16) was not specified for the *Dawn Treader*. This is a line that runs from the end of the boom to the top of the mast and down to the deck or to a cleat on the mast. It doesn't do anything but hold the boom up, although in an emergency it could substitute for a halyard. It has no function when you're sailing because the mainsail itself holds the boom up. You don't always need it when the main is down because then the main halyard is available to fasten to the boom end.

But consider your situation coming into a harbor and beginning to lower sail. The instant you release the main halyard the boom drops into the cockpit, trailing yards of line overboard to tangle around the propeller, blocking the action of the tiller, and filling the cockpit with billowing mainsail. You can't start the engine, you can't steer, you can't see where you're going until the sail is stuffed into its bag, out of the way, and the boom lifted again on the main halyard.

Once I installed a topping lift I could start the engine and steer with one foot while I dropped the main, furled it, and put it away—without becoming a menace to navigation.

Reefing

To respond to variations in wind pressure, you can alter the sail area of a boat. In light airs, even day sailers may carry a big spinnaker. If the wind increases, the spinnaker is taken in and

Fig. 9-16. Fastened to the end of the boom to support it when necessary, the topping lift is allowed to lie slack along the mainsail when the ship is underway.

replaced first with a jib, then a smaller jib with a reef in the main, then no jib and another reef in the main, and so on.

You have to decide whether to have reef points sewed into the mainsail so that it can be reefed in the traditional way (Figure 9-17) or to install a special gooseneck that permits the boom to be ro-

Fig. 9-17. The traditional way to shorten sail is to furl part of it around itself and tie up the roll with reef points permanently sewed to the sail at convenient spots.

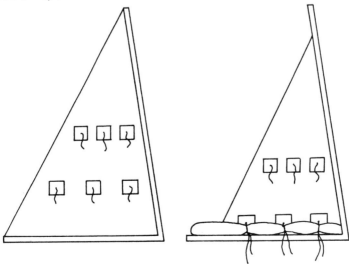

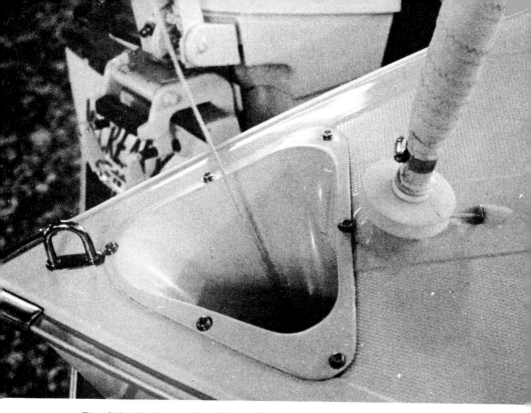

Fig. 9-18. Roller reefing jib. A line running back to the cockpit controls the roller so that the jib can be unrolled like a window shade to any degree or rolled back up again, depending on wind conditions. (The triangular hatch on this factory-built boat is a chute for storing the spinnaker.)

tated, rolling up the main like a window shade. Although faster and easier, roller reefing is not without disadvantages. Because a sail is purposely cut baggy, rolling it up gives it a floppy, inefficient shape unless you tuck in a filler as you roll. Unless the sail was designed for roller reefing, you may have to take out a batten or two. This is hard to do single-handed; you have to hold the main halyard in your teeth while furling. Hand reefing gives a good sail shape, but it's even more difficult to do single-handed.

You can also get a roller system for jibs. (See Figure 9-18.) It works with a revolving drum that furls the jib around the forestay by remote control—a line operated from the cockpit. Jib-furling equipment, even in small sizes, is a more costly option than roller reefing for the main.

With roller reefing you get offsetting savings on the sails. A

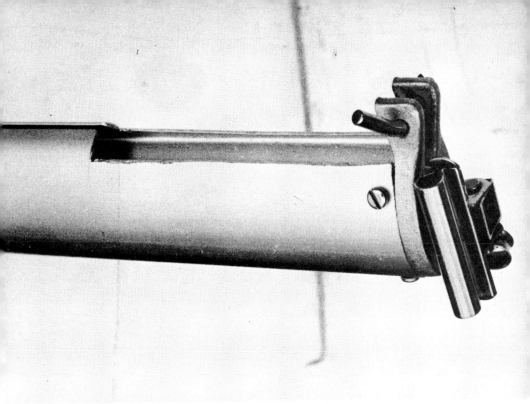

Fig. 9-19. The end of the *Dawn Treader's* boom has a roller reefing gooseneck. The tube slides in the mast groove. A spring in the gooseneck allows the boom to be rotated when desired, rolling the mainsail around it. (Note the gate cut into the boom to allow the rope edge of the mainsail to be inserted into the spar groove.)

main without any reef points is a few dollars cheaper than one with the additional sewing. A roller reefing jib is infinitely variable, so you need only one size.

For the *Dawn Treader* I bought the roller reefing boom gooseneck (Figure 9-19) but decided to forego a roller furling jib. Besides being expensive it looked complicated to handle on a boat that would be rigged over and over instead of left for the season at a mooring.

Winches

You can raise the anchor and control the sails of a sizable boat without a winch (Figure 9-20), yet expensive precision winches are found on rather small ships. The explanation is that for racing it can be difficult to haul certain lines taut enough by hand,

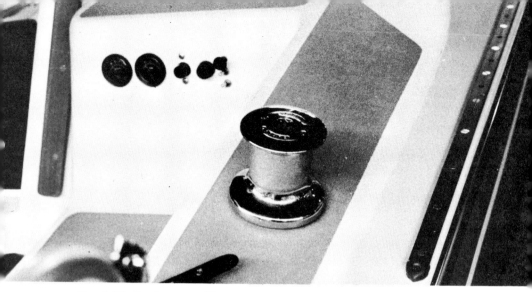

Fig. 9-20. On larger sailboats, winches are used to tighten lines. Make sure you need one before you invest.

particularly the jib halyard. Before you buy a winch make certain you need it.

Sails

You'll find a sail plan in your working drawings. Send photocopies to several sailmakers for estimates. At the time I built the *Dawn Treader*, I found it advantageous to order terylene sails from England—except for one batten that was longer than three feet and apparently would have required a ship all to itself, judging from the shipping cost. I placed the order in December and received it by mid-March, in plenty of time for the sailing season. The duty was only $8.58.

No doubt it is possible for a determined amateur to make his own sails, but few builders do. The reason becomes apparent on a visit to a sail loft when you see the huge triangular tables and industrial sewing machines that simplify the work for professionals.

As the following episode illustrates, even some sail repairs aren't worth struggling over yourself. Four of us were sailing the *Dawn Treader* on an inland lake rather than Lake Michigan's open sea because the weather forecast at breakfast had sounded unsettled. We were glad that we had come because the day turned out reasonably pleasant—light overcast, no rain yet, and a moderate breeze. The fleet of inland scows that raced every Saturday were tilted up on edge as usual, and the *Dawn Treader* drove at a steady pace.

I was looking at my watch, considering whether to steer for the launch ramp and start home for dinner. The wind seemed to be dying away. Someone said, "Look how dark the sky is getting over there."

I glanced over my shoulder. A low black cloud had suddenly appeared over the northwest corner of the lake, with a churning motion that should have warned me this was no ordinary squall. But it never occurred to me to shorten sail. On an inland lake? In fact, we were congratulating each other that the breeze was picking up again, and we wouldn't have to use the motor to scurry in ahead of the probable rain.

Looking at the advancing cloud, I said, "I think the rain will catch us on the water. There are some ponchos in the—EVERYBODY TO STARBOARD!"

A cold blast of wind suddenly laid the ship almost on her beam ends. I yanked the jib sheet out of its cleat and let it fly along with the main sheet. Leaning on the tiller, I brought the ship around on a reach, the most controllable point of sailing.

All of us were instantly drenched by rain and blown spray. The ponchos remained dry in their storage bin. While I held the ship on course, the first mate climbed onto the steeply tilted cabin roof and clawed down the mainsail. The wind continued blowing just as hard as before—forty miles an hour or more, the weather news said later. It was lifting roofs off barns and knocking down big trees in the neighborhood.

The mate now turned his attention to the big jib, which was flapping dragonously, trying to writhe free from the lines fettering its wicked tail. The foredeck pitched and bucked over the biggest waves I have ever seen on a small lake, and the jib kept eluding his grasp.

Our course was taking us toward a line of piers along the shore. In another moment we would be up on the front porch of a lakeside cottage. "Never mind the jib," I shouted over the roar of the wind. "Let's get the anchor down."

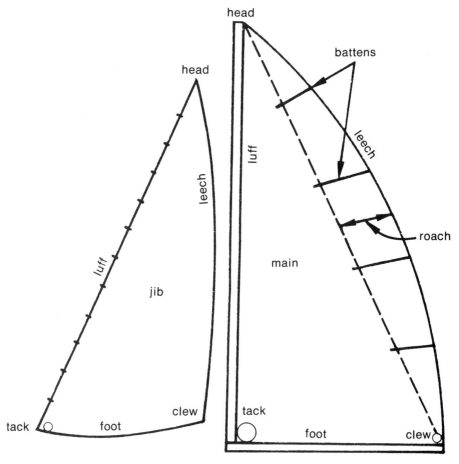

Fig. 9-21. You can't cuss the sails properly without knowing what to call the parts.

The anchor was extracted from under the port bunk, passed forward, and dropped overside while the line was laid through a chock and secured to the bollard. After a moment the anchor bit in and swung the bow into the wind.

We were all shivering from wet and cold. Leaving the jib to flap, we crawled under a dry tarp in the cabin and were immediately restored to warmth and coziness. I peered out one of the little windows to see what had become of the racing scows, with their vast spread of canvas. The entire fleet had capsized and was drifting ashore with their crews hanging on wherever there was a handhold.

The storm had struck with no more than seven minutes' warning. In half an hour it was over. We stowed the sails and the anchor, started the motor, and proceeded a few hundred yards to the trailer ramp, then home without further incident.

A couple of easily replaced battens in the mainsail were cracked. The only other damage, apart from a wetting and a fright —one member of the crew was seen trying to put on two life jackets at the same time—was to the jib, which had spit out the grommet to which the sheets are fastened.

I could have sewed up the small tear in the fabric myself. (Cruising ships should always carry a sail repair kit.) But I couldn't find a large enough grommet in any of the local stores or the marine supply catalogs I had on hand. Finally, I located a sail loft within half an hour's drive. They had a grommet, which they sewed in as good as new while I waited. They charged me two or three dollars and sent me away happy.

The experience wasn't much of a tribute to my seamanship. I had failed to shorten sail at the approach of a storm. I had let the jib damage itself. I had allowed the whole crew to get wet unnecessarily ("not enough sense to get in out of the rain," is the way it's sometimes put). At the same time, the ship I built had performed beautifully, refusing to capsize and standing up to the buffeting without complaint.

I decided I could allow myself a hornpipe or two.

Lightning Protection

Although the deck of a sailing vessel is not a cozy place to be in a storm, the cabin can seem wonderfully warm and snug—especially if you have just changed into dry clothes after having been on deck. Then you start thinking about the lightning crackling overhead and the cabin becomes much less inviting. You know that a boat on the water with its metal mast sticking up is like the lone tree in a pasture, a notorious lightning target. Fortunately, a boat can be protected from lightning damage by grounding the rigging to a conductor below the waterline. The mast then acts like a lightning rod, offering a cone-shaped zone of protection. (See Figure 9-22.)

The ideal underwater ground plate is a copper sheet about one foot square. Connections can be made with number 8 stranded copper wire. Some principles:

• The path from the highest part of the system to the water should be as short and straight as possible. Use a shroud rather than the forestay.

• If you have an aluminum mast, the ground wire can be bolted to the base of the mast (or the step if it's metal).

• A metal keel or centerboard can be used as the grounding plate.

• Any heavy masses of metal such as inboard engines should be individually connected to the ground wire unless they can be kept more than six feet away.

• Arrange the ground system so that it avoids passing through such items as turnbuckles and centerboard pivot pins, which might be damaged by a jolt of lightning.

The Rudder and Tiller

The rudder and tiller can be fabricated in your workshop during the winter; your plans show the details. Every hull has its own rudder design, but here are a few suggestions you won't find on the plans.

You should provide some arrangement, such as a couple of cleats and a short length of rope, for quickly lashing the tiller so the

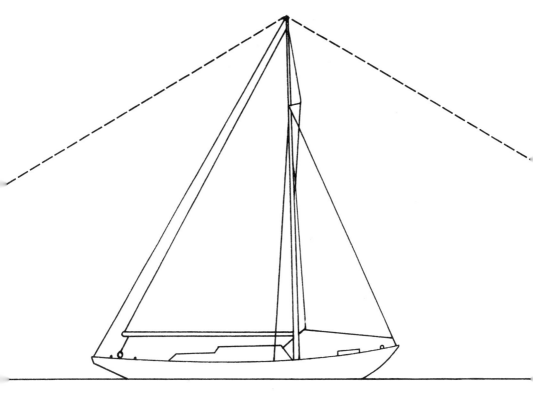

Fig. 9-22. The metal mast or stays of a sailboat offer a conical zone of protection against lightning if they are grounded to the water by efficient conductors taking a direct path.

boat will continue her course while you do something requiring both hands, like starting the engine or furling sail.

The tiller has a pivoting extension handle that lets you steer while leaning far out to windward. This handle becomes tiresome to hold unless you give your fingers something to grip. One solution is to run a short piece of dowel through the extension handle an inch or two from the end so that the dowel projects two or three fingers worth on both sides.

If you follow the dowel suggestion, you can make the exten-

Fig. 9-23. When a tiller has an extension handle, a short piece of dowel through the end makes it easier to hold. Then a hole of slightly larger diameter in the head of the rudder provides a way to fold the extension securely out of the way when you don't want it poking at you.

sion handle self-storing by drilling a shallow hole in the tiller itself where the end of the dowel can rest when the extension isn't being used. (See Figure 9-23.) An extension handle that isn't secured makes a nuisance of itself grabbing sheets and prodding the skipper in the vitals at inconvenient moments.

The superior saltiness of a steering wheel with spokes on the outside is beyond controversy. The difficulty is that a tiller steers better than a wheel except on quite large boats. The solution is to append the Roman numeral *II* to the name you have chosen for your ship. Then you can label a steering wheel "Polaris I" or "Spindrift I" or "Mermaid I" and hang it on the wall of your office to brighten your day until you next set sail in *Polaris II, Spindrift II,* or *Mermaid II.*

The rudder is attached to the transom with pieces of hardware called a gudgeon and a pintle, two of my favorite nautical words. As I said, I'm avoiding salty talk in this book, but *gudgeon* and *pintle* are like *scrimshaw*—decorative.

Unless you're a good sign painter, use standard stick-on numerals and letters. Painting your ship's name is harder than it looks.

10 Goodbye, Old Paint; I'm Leaving Cheyenne

WHEN you start planning to build a boat, the picture your imagination paints for you depicts days and weeks aboard your ship with no cloud in view. The sun shines, a fair breeze blows, and the ship dances across a sparkling sea—a handsome sight. On the question of maintenance, your vision is hazy; perhaps it is done by pretty girls wearing hibiscus blossoms in their hair.

Then you meet a few boat owners. Soon you see yourself spending your weekends scraping, sanding, and painting as if you'd been shanghaied by some particularly sadistic Captain Bligh.

The truth is somewhere in between. Once the *Dawn Treader* was built, I never spent a day painting when I could be sailing. On the other hand, there's no way to escape standing some watches on the end of a paintbrush. A neglected wooden boat rots, and even a fiberglass hull sooner or later loses its luster.

A shipwright should plan the finishes for various parts of the boat at an early stage. Hard-to-reach places should be fiberglassed or painted before later structures get in the way. If you're going to varnish a coaming or a piece of trim, it should be made of wood with attractive grain. Varnish is more trouble to maintain than paint, so you shouldn't varnish anything without a reason.

179

Varnish is used on spars of Sitka spruce because a transparent finish permits inspection of the wood for cracks, glue fractures, and wet spots that can develop into rot. Tillers are usually varnished for the same reason. The warmth of wood grain adds so much to a boat's appearance that no vessel should lack a touch of it. Just don't overdo it.

Antifouling bottom paint is expensive. You don't need it at all if you keep your boat on a trailer, but you can't do without it if the boat is kept in the water all season. Some kinds of bottom paint don't work unless they're put on at the last minute before launching.

Regarding the inside of a hull that is enclosed by decks and a cabin, there is a controversy among the experts. Some say the inside of the planking should not be painted because the paint film traps moisture and encourages rot. Others say paint is necessary in the bilge to prevent spilled gasoline and oil from soaking in and becoming a fire hazard. Also, an unprotected bilge soaks up other kinds of spills and acquires a permanent odor. One alternative is to treat the wood with a sealer or a preservative instead of painting it. Some who are against painting the inside of most wood planking favor painting the inside of plywood planking, which is less likely to rot.

In ancient times, owners poured ordinary rock salt (sodium chloride) into bilges to ward off rot. The fact seems to be that salt water on the outside of a hull is hard on it, but salt inside is good. There are many wood preservatives more up-to-date than rock salt, but read the label carefully. Some can't be painted over. Creosote works, but it smells unpleasant.

Before any painting begins, the whole hull should be examined for nail or screw heads that need puttying. If you used carvel planking, this is also the time to do the caulking. Plywood and glued-strip planking never need caulking. Lapstrake planking is caulked only in large hulls.

The theory of caulking (Figure 10-1) is that cotton forced into a seam will be squeezed watertight when the wood swells upon immersion. You deliberately stuff the cotton into the seam slack and

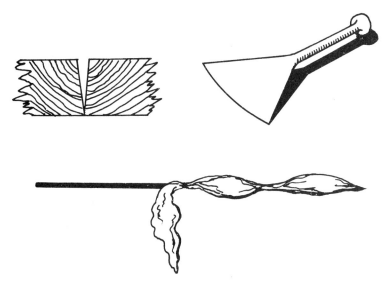

Fig. 10-1. Caulking: The gaps between adjoining carvel planks are filled with tufts of cotton, tapped in with a caulking iron. Then the seam is puttied with caulking compound and painted.

doubled back on itself so that it loops out in tufts every couple of inches. Then you tap it in with a caulking iron. The seams are primed with paint before filling with caulking compound.

Caulking is done from the outside of the hull. The planks on the inside should fit snugly even when the boat is out of water. Don't use the caulking iron too exuberantly or you may split the planking.

The usual schedule for painting, once the preliminaries are out of the way, is:

1. Outside prime coat
2. Inside prime coat
3. Bottom paint
4. Inside flat coat and finish
5. Outside flat coat and finish
6. Final coat of bottom paint

Types of Paint

The place to get the best information on the details of painting is on the label of the paint can. No one is better qualified than the manufacturer to tell you how to obtain the best results with his paint. It is human nature to undergo any amount of torment rather than read instructions, especially if they come free with the product. Nevertheless, paint formulas vary widely, and it really is important to follow the label instructions.

Paint chemists are continually improving their products. At this writing, the newest type of marine paint has an epoxy base. Like epoxy glue, it is mixed with a catalyst, and has to be used up in the time specified. Epoxy paint is much more resistant to weathering than other marine paints, and is especially suitable for fiberglass and metal hulls. However, it costs about half again as much as other marine paints. The solvent is toxic. You should use it with rubber gloves and long sleeves outdoors where the fumes can't get you.

This blend of advantages and disadvantages brings up the philosophy of paint selection. You can argue that because of the labor involved it pays to use only the most durable paint regardless of expense. Or you can argue that a boat needs to be touched up all the time anyway because of the inevitable knocking about during the sailing season, so why not use cheaper paint?

In fact, is there any reason not to use ordinary porch enamel at half the cost of marine deck paint? That's exactly what owners of many workboats do, slopping it on with a roller.

You'll have to make up your own mind. I'll tell you what I did. After trying epoxy paint for the inside of the centerboard well and the blade of the rudder, I decided the fumes were too oppressive and switched to ordinary marine paint for the rest. I might have experimented with porch enamel if the *Dawn Treader* weren't such a small ship that she doesn't take much paint.

Adventures of Barnacle Bill

I learned quite a bit from an experiment I had no wish to make. From the beginning, I had planned to cruise the *Dawn*

Treader out of my garage via trailer. So I never gave a thought to bottom paint. When the hull fiberglass turned out an ugly color, as I mentioned earlier, I just painted it what I considered a more attractive shade of yellow.

Then, a few weeks before she would be ready for launching, I received a notice that the village intended to tear up my street, install new sewers, and widen the pavement. I had to hurry to finish before I was trapped in the garage until the pavement could be relaid. (That proved to be the following fall.) I found a slip at a marina on a lake forty-five minutes away where the sailing would be good, but any further work on the boat would be inconvenient.

The deadline threatened like a deadly reef. I had painted the hull, decks, and cabin long ago for their protection, although some construction details were incomplete. On D-Day minus two, a Saturday, I was still cutting and fitting the rub rails and fastening deck hardware. On Sunday I finished the deck hardware, put a second coat of varnish on the rub rails, and drove her up to the lake, not collecting as much dust on the varnish as I had feared. Monday morning at eight o'clock they mined the harbor—I mean they began tearing up the pavement at the end of my driveway.

In salt water, I knew, an unprotected wooden bottom would have provided a tasty curry for shipworms. My fiberglass coating wasn't complete. They could munch on the inside of the centerboard well and bore in through the skeg. Fresh-water marine life is less destructive, which is mentioned as a partial excuse for my lack of foresight.

Some bright child of five or six will point out that I could have left the boat on the trailer at the marina until I had a chance to apply antifouling bottom paint. So I might as well confess a strong aversion to any unnecessary painting. I slid her into the water (we'll discuss Launching Day later), went for a sail, and tied her up in her slip.

Since it took the paving crew all summer, working with tweezers, to restore the street, the *Dawn Treader* spent the whole season in the water. She grew a green beard of algae on the bottom and all the paint below the waterline flaked loose. I spent many a cold day in the garage that fall and winter on my back under the boat, chipping at dried algae and paint flakes. Safety goggles kept the chippings out of my eyes, but after every session I had to take a shower and rinse my hair, ears, and moustache. I also brushed my teeth and cleaned under my toenails.

In the spring I sanded the bottom and repainted with the same yellow paint, which lasted the second season on and off the trailer in good condition.

Types of Bottom Paint

I hope you appreciate the trouble I experienced in order to give you first-hand information on the consequences of keeping a hull in a slip or at moorings without bottom paint, even in fresh water. There are several kinds of bottom paint:

Soft copper.   With this kind, the boat must be launched within hours after painting to prevent formation of a skin that would block the release of toxic chemicals. If you haul the boat out of the water, the bottom must be repainted before launching again.

Copper bronze.   Copper bronze paint also must be tacky when the boat is launched. It gives a hard, glossy surface that probably makes the boat a little faster, and it costs more than soft copper.

Vinyl copper.   This is the bottom paint to use if your boat can't be kept in the water all the time. You can even apply it in the fall for the following season. In a given supplier's paint line, it usually costs more than copper bronze.

Epoxy.   Like vinyl copper, epoxy antifouling paints have no limit on launching time. They're supposed to be extra durable. Naturally, they cost more than the others.

Working with antifouling paint demands caution. If it can poison a barnacle, it can poison you. Avoid splattering it on your skin or breathing the fumes. Wear a breathing mask when sanding it. Breathing masks are inexpensive and some marine supply catalogs offer them on the same page with the bottom paints.

The metallic content of bottom paints makes them a factor in electrolysis. Read the label carefully before buying any bottom paint for a metal hull. Some paints are formulated for metal; others can be used over metal if properly primed; some can't be used over metal at all.

Not all of the paints are compatible with one another. In general, hard bottom paints can't be applied over soft paints, and vinyl copper can't be applied over anything else. So if you switch types of bottom paint in the future, you may have to sand down the whole hull to bare wood or fiberglass and start over.

You can see why I didn't plan to use antifouling bottom paint on the *Dawn Treader* just in case I might need it someday.

The Waterline

Bottom paint is used only on the bottom, partly because of its high cost and partly because of its restricted range of colors. The upper part of the hull is often painted a different color. So the shipwright has the problem of marking the waterline accurately while the ship is not in the water.

Despite all the curved lines in a ship, certain parts of the cockpit and cabin are built parallel or perpendicular to the waterline. If you put your level on one of these parts, you can jack up the hull and brace it so that it is level athwartship and fore and aft.

The waterline can be measured off at bow and stern from dimensions given on the plans. Then a string is stretched taut at the same height above the floor as the bow and stern marks and tacked to a pair of saw horses. At intervals of about eighteen inches you use your level to mark the hull parallel to the string. Connecting these marks with a long flexible batten gives you your waterline. (See Figure 10-2.)

Fig. 10-2. To mark the waterline, measure off at bow and stern using the dimensions given on the plans. Stretch a string at the correct height above the work space floor. Use a level at intervals to mark the hull. Draw a guideline from point to point.

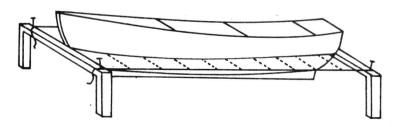

Before sticking on the masking tape and starting to paint, squint along both sides from the bow to see if the waterlines you marked look symmetrical.

How to Paint a Boat

Most of the procedures in boat painting are the same as the ones you have used innumerable times to paint bedrooms and bookshelves. You grasp the brush by the dry end, dip the bristly end in the paint, and so on. There are a few tips that apply specifically to marine work:

• Decks should have nonskid surfaces, especially the foredeck, where you go to wrestle with the anchor and the jib amid flying spray. To produce the needed traction, you sprinkle fine sand or nonskid compound over the paint while it's wet.

• Modern builders usually apply fiberglass on decks and cabin roofs where canvas once would have been used. If, for some reason, you do use canvas, bed it in wet paint; *don't glue it down.* One authority says that when the time comes to replace canvas that was glued down it's easier to sell the boat.

• If you're attaching deck hardware before you paint, use steel screws temporarily to save wear on the slots of your bronze screws when you back them out to paint.

• For boat painting, a brush 2½ to 3 inches wide is as big as you need—except on the bottom, where you could use a bigger brush or even a roller.

• Professional boat painters (if right-handed) always begin at either the starboard bow or the port stern and work clockwise around the boat, backing up for best brush control.

• Plan your work so that you'll be finished with a whole section by mid-afternoon. That avoids lap marks and gives the paint a chance to set up before the evening dew.

• If you're going to varnish something detachable, like a tiller handle, take it indoors to keep dust away. Wiping excess var-

Fig. 10-3. Typical boat number kit. On a light-colored hull you stick on the black numbers. On a dark hull you use the white rectangle surrounding each number like a stencil, letting the hull show through. The material has an adhesive back.

nish from the brush into a spare container keeps bubbles out of the work pot.

● Paint the topsides from the top down, to avoid spatters on the work. Paint the bottom from the keel up and out, to avoid spatters down your neck.

The law requires your boat number to appear on the bows. You may want your ship's name and possibly her home port on the transom. Unless you're already a good sign painter, don't try to do this with paint. It's harder than it looks. Instead, use the standard stick-on numerals and letters that come in white for dark hulls and black for light hulls. (See Figure 10-3.) Make chalk guidelines before you start. Crooked, poorly spaced lettering ruins the whole appearance of a boat.

In scheduling your boat painting, the most important factor to consider is what you were supposed to paint in the house that you haven't got around to yet. If, for example, you start painting the boat on the same day when your wife, tired of waiting for you to do it, begins painting the kitchen ceiling herself, you will be making a very serious mistake. Although the argument of this book is that, with patience, almost anyone can learn to build ships, I have to confess that anyone who would make this particular error is probably beyond help.

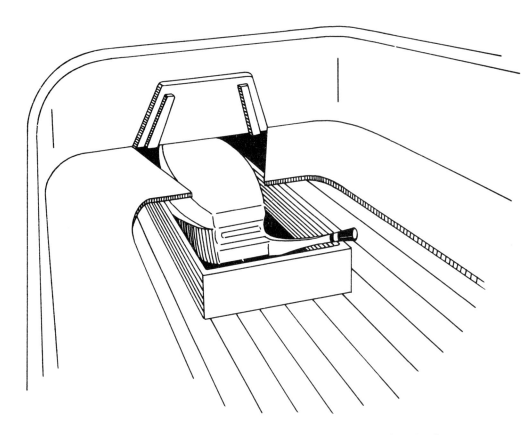

Fig. 11-1. Typical outboard well permits engine to be removed easily for servicing.

11 Good Engines for Ill Winds

A SAILOR noted for long voyages to far places tells in one of his books that his first move after purchasing a new ship was to have the auxiliary engine taken out. Representing the purist point of view, he argued that an engine always fails you in a crisis anyway. It is safer to know you have to depend on your sails and practice better seamanship accordingly. There is some merit in this argument, as I have learned by drifting into places I didn't want to be while fiddling with the engine, when I could have kept clear if I'd left the sails up.

On the other hand, engines do start most of the time. They bring you home in time for dinner when the wind fails, which it often does in late afternoon in summer when the temperatures of land and water reach equilibrium. They also bring you in when the way to shelter lies straight upwind.

Much advice available from blue-water sailors has to be discounted because the source is influenced by what I consider to be his own death wish. An element of possible danger is what adds spice to any sport, but some people can't tell when to stop. There's a difference between a taste for adventure and a compulsion to tempt fate.

In a book published in 1954, *Lonely Voyagers,* Jean Merrien compiled a list of 120 major ocean voyages by one or two persons in small boats between 1849 and 1953. Since then there have been numerous additional ocean crossings, including the well-publicized voyage across the Atlantic by Robert Manry in the tiny *Tinkerbelle,* only thirteen and one-half feet long.

Manry does not seem to have had a death wish. He began by rebuilding *Tinkerbelle* to make her virtually unsinkable. He planned carefully to avoid unpleasant eventualities. He not only shipped a radar reflector to prevent being run down by large ships but even packed an extra one in case the first one somehow fell overboard. While at sea Manry himself was washed overboard by big waves six times. But he always had fastened himself to the boat with a safety harness. Long after his famous voyage he died of a heart attack while riding in a car.

In contrast, Sir Francis Chichester, who sailed much larger ships, displayed an obvious death wish. In his autobiography, he tells of catching a viper by the tail as a boy. It didn't bite him at first, so he pestered it till it did. In 1929, after amassing a bit of wealth in New Zealand real estate, he took up flying, which some death wish authorities consider prima facie evidence of an advanced case. Alone in a 900-pound airplane of paper and string, he flew from London to Australia, from New Zealand to Australia, from New Zealand to Japan. His solo flight across the Tasman Sea was the first. Chichester crash-landed on water, on land, and on various muddy mixtures of both until in Japan he totaled the plane and sustained injuries he didn't get over for ten years.

After World War II he took up sailing because he couldn't afford a private jet, and he was delighted to find out about single-handed racing. In his autobiography, he wrote, "A solo race across the Atlantic from east to west was the greatest yacht race that I had ever heard of, and it fired my imagination. Three thousand miles, plugging into the prevailing westerlies, probably strong, bucking the Gulf Stream current, crossing the Grand Banks off Newfoundland which were not only one of the densest fog areas of the world, but also stuffed with fishing trawlers."

What deep-water sailor with a death wish could pass up the glorious risk of colliding with a trawler in a dense fog on the Grand Banks? It was significant, I thought, that Sir Francis named his series of racing vessels after the Gypsy Moth seaplane that had almost killed him in Japan in 1931.

That he survived his daring voyages to die in bed was a tribute to his skill and irrepressible determination, which saved him from the perils he created for himself. Also, there is the fact that a good ship, like a faithful horse, will try to bring you home if you let it.

So, resisting the influence of the death wish fleet, we will agree that a ship should have an auxiliary engine.

Outboard Wells

Ships less than twenty or twenty-two feet long almost always are powered by outboard engines. The weight and cost of an inboard engine would be disproportionate in ships of that size.

Some hull designs provide for an outboard well. (See Figure 11-1 and Figure 11-2.) This offers advantages: the transom doesn't have to be cut low so the drive shaft can reach the water; the propeller can be located farther forward so it won't come out of the water between high waves; and the weight of the engine can be more centrally located.

There are disadvantages, too: the well may clutter up an already cramped cockpit; sometimes wells collect engine fumes and smell worse than necessary; and in construction, wells are a bit of extra work and, like centerboard wells, may leak eventually.

A well may limit your choice of engines. On the *Dawn Treader*, to reverse the engine I simply swivel it around 180 degrees in its transom clamp. Many wells would not provide room for the engine to swing around. You'd have to have an engine with forward and reverse gear shift.

Horsepower

Matching hulls and horsepower is scarcely an exact science. For sailing auxiliaries, the rule of thumb is a minimum of one horsepower for every 500 pounds of displacement. Every hull is

Fig. 11-2. Outboard well in rear of cockpit permits the propeller to fit between skeg and rudder, almost like having an inboard engine.

different, and some may need more power. Also, it makes a difference whether your engine is needed only as insurance against calms or has to chew its way upstream against tidal or river currents to reach your anchorage.

With crew and equipment aboard, the *Dawn Treader* probably weighs about 1,500 pounds. My 3.5-horsepower outboard drives her at about 4 miles per hour, which is ample under most circumstances. However, her waterline length permits a hull speed of about 6 miles per hour. Under some circumstances a larger engine would be desirable.

For example, I have made canoe voyages on the Upper Mississippi when the current was running about 3 miles an hour. With the same motor on a heavily loaded canoe it takes an hour to move one mile upstream. At 6 miles per hour, the expedition could travel three miles upstream in the same time. Of course, the canoe will not accommodate a larger engine. Maybe I should get a bathtub for upstream work: in 1969 a man named Jackson crossed Lake Michigan in a bathtub driven by an outboard motor.

An engine that's too big just wastes fuel and adds weight and expense unnecessarily.

Skene's Elements of Yacht Design contains data for computing the horsepower needed to drive a given displacement hull at its top speed. You can calculate it theoretically (very complicated) or refer to a chart based on the engines actually installed in fifty-three ships with waterlines of twenty-two to ninety feet. The variations show that the professional designers and builders are far from agreement on what is the proper amount of horsepower for ships of the same size. Table 2 shows some typical installations representing an average.

Table 2

Typical Engine Installations

WATERLINE (FEET)	AUXILIARY HP	MOTORSAILER HP
32	37	37
35	48	62
40	62	100
45	80	150

There isn't as much design data available for smaller ships because the range of power choices is narrow anyway. When I put the question to the experts at Mercury Marine, they conceded "we do not possess specific design data relative to powering displacement hulls with outboards." However, they did calculate for me that if my 3.5-horsepower motor would shove the sixteen-foot *Dawn Treader* along at 4 miles per hour a 7.5-horsepower engine would drive it at hull speed of 6 miles per hour.

Mercury also furnished the results of a test-with a twenty-two-foot sailboat weighing 2,100 pounds, which cruised a test course at its hull speed of approximately 7 miles per hour powered by a 9.8-horsepower Mercury outboard.

So, with this great mass of data plus what can be observed hanging around the waterfront, we can extend the range of typical engine installations to cover smaller ships, as shown in Table 3.

Table 3
Typical Engine Installations, Smaller Ships

WATERLINE (FEET)	OUTBOARD HP
Under 20	3 ½ to 10
20 to 25	10 to 20
25 to 30	15 to 40

Planing Hulls

Fishing boats and other small commercial vessels are designed with displacement hulls and modest-sized engines. Their owners, being businessmen, aren't willing to pay for speed.

An example from *Motor Boating & Sailing* magazine makes the point. Consider two powerboats, both twenty-five feet long. One has a displacement hull and can go at a speed of 7 knots on 10 ½ horsepower, covering 7.5 miles on a gallon of fuel. The other has a planing hull and will hit 25 knots. But its 175-horsepower engine burns a gallon of fuel every 1.65 miles.

To be efficient, a planing hull has to have a broad fanny and lightweight construction. Powerboat plans specify a range of engine possibilities. I'm looking at plans for a twenty-three-foot cruiser. The designer says the minimum power plant is a 55-horsepower outboard. She needs 80 horsepower to pull water skiers. With a 125-horsepower outboard, fully loaded in a test, she raced at 31 miles per hour.

Outboard Features

The major outboard manufacturers change their lines every year and will gladly send you their current catalogs. *Consumer Reports* is able to detect differences in quality, but all of the engines are reasonably reliable if maintained properly. Sailors look for features that may not be important to fishermen or water skiers. Perusing this year's catalogs, I concluded that there is no single model that combines all the most desirable features. I suppose such an engine could be built but would cost too much.

Throttle. You want either a lever-type throttle or a twist-grip throttle that can be locked at the desired speed. On a sailboat you steer with the rudder and don't want to bother touching the motor controls once it's running.

Course-holder. One way or another, the motor has to be held firmly on course. Left to itself, it will vibrate and slew sideways. You can lash down the handle, or you can buy one of the motors that has a lock to hold the motor on center.

Reverse capability. The simplest way to reverse an outboard is to rotate it 180 degrees. As I pointed out in the discussion of outboard wells, there has to be room on your boat for the housing to come around. Also, if there's no course lock, you may have to fumble to release a lashing.

An engine with forward/neutral/reverse transmission is desirable. Neutral is good because you can start the engine and have it warmed up and running steadily before casting off from the dock or lowering your sails.

There's one line of outboards popular with sailors that can't be reversed, either by rotating or by shifting gears. I consider that an important disadvantage.

Shaft length. The standard outboard motor is designed for the fifteen-inch transom of a powerboat hull. You may be able to use a standard engine in some outboard wells or with a bracket attached to the stern. If your motor fastens over the transom, chances are a standard model will be too short. That's why the manufacturers produce sailboat-sized engines with shafts five inches longer.

One low-powered model now available has an adjustable shaft, which seems like an excellent idea. You can lower it for full power in waves or raise it for weeds and tricky shallows.

Gas tank.   The smallest engines come with the gas tank built in like a lawn mower tank. The rest have remote tanks that feed the engine through a flexible fuel line. A few of the integral tank models can be converted with an accessory kit for operation with a remote tank.

For a cruising sailboat, remote tanks are better even for a small engine. It can be a perilous maneuver at sea trying to pour more gas into a little hole atop the engine back over the transom while it bucks and dodges. You or the gas can or both may go overboard. There have been cases where the gas has spilled down over a hot engine and ignited.

My 3.5-horsepower engine cruises for less than two hours on its five-pint tank of gas. With a three-gallon remote tank it would go all day, which would be more convenient on a cruise when the wind failed or turned contrary.

The reason the smallest motors are made with integral tanks is that a remote tank is a nuisance in a small boat such as a skiff or a canoe.

Gas cap.   The cap of the gas tank should be permanently fastened to the tank with a chain or a spring clip. Otherwise, it certainly will roll overboard or into the bilge at the first opportunity. Incredibly, many tanks are still made without cap retainers. Another nuisance: some remote gas tanks lack gauges.

Weight.   The smallest outboards, from 1.5 to 3 or 3.5 horsepower, weigh under 30 pounds and are easy to handle. They're relatively inexpensive, too, and will propel surprisingly large sailboats fast enough to beat paddling. As power goes up, so does weight. The 4- to 6-horsepower motors weigh 40 or 50 pounds or more. You need two hands to put them away.

The sailboat skipper wants the lightest and least expensive motor that will drive his boat. An auxiliary engine isn't used much, and it's foolish to be burdened by it. (However, you should heed the advice of Robin Knox-Johnston, the first man to sail around the world alone and nonstop. Said he in *A World of My Own*, "Out of my experience there is a lesson for people who take an engine cruising; remember to turn it frequently." He didn't run his during his ten-and-one-half-month voyage, so it froze up and had to be replaced when he reached home.)

Inboard Engines

Cruising sailboats between twenty and twenty-eight feet in length are powered either by outboards or by small inboards. Over twenty-eight feet or so, you see few outboards. Inboards are quieter and more reliable and can be installed in a more convenient location. It takes a sizable boat to accommodate the weight. A 6-horse-power Westerbeke-Vire gasoline inboard weighs 117 pounds. An 8-horsepower Palmer weighs 195 pounds. Diesels are still heavier. Volvo's smallest marine diesel, a 10-horsepower engine designed for sailboats, weighs 397 pounds.

When builders check out the weights and prices of inboard engines, having decided against outboards for some reason, they usually are moved to reconsider. Another alternative that suggests itself is converting an auto engine. Maybe they have an old car that still runs fairly well but the body is falling apart and the transmission isn't worth keeping up. The answer is that auto conversions do work, and many boats are powered by them, but it costs almost as much to convert an auto engine as to buy a second-hand marine engine.

Gasoline vs. Diesel

Gasoline is nasty stuff to have around. The fumes are explosive, and they can collect in the bilge, in engine compartments, and in other enclosed spaces. Refueling is always a moment of truth because the fresh liquid pouring into the tank forces out the heavier-than-air fumes, which waft around the boat looking for a cigarette or a spark to ignite them. If the choice were more practical, all inboard engines probably would be diesel. The fuel for diesel engines is a nonvolatile oil that doesn't spread explosive fumes.

Unfortunately, besides being much heavier than comparable gasoline engines, diesel units cost about two and a half times as much. Although diesel oil costs about half as much as gasoline, it takes a long time for the difference in fuel cost to make itself felt. One naval architect, using prices prevailing in the early 1970s, calculated that a diesel engine would begin to pay for itself in fuel cost savings after about 10,300 miles of cruising.

An engine—either gasoline or diesel—uses .6 pound of fuel per hour per unit of horsepower. Gasoline weighs 6.19 pounds per gallon; diesel oil, 7.13 pounds per gallon. Besides costing less, diesel fuel gives better mileage. A ship with a 6-horsepower auxiliary cruising 10 hours (these examples are beginning to sound like algebra problems) would use about 5.8 gallons of gasoline compared to 5.0 gallons of diesel fuel.

Inboard /Outboards

As outboard motors increased in size, designers realized that the larger ones were getting too heavy to sling over the transom. So they developed the stern drive unit, which is installed through the lower part of the transom and offers some of the advantages of inboard engines. One important safety factor is that the stern drive eliminates the need to cut the transom low, which was the cause of many powerboat swampings.

Now there's a similar sailboat drive unit, designed for use with either gasoline or diesel inboard engines. Instead of passing through the transom, it passes through the bottom of the hull. (See Figure 11-3.) Volvo says its version offers lower water resistance than a conventional propeller shaft with comparable propellers. It appears to be easier to install, too, than inboard engines with conventional shafts.

Installing Engines

To install an outboard, you just clamp it onto the place provided—the transom itself, a transom bracket, or an outboard

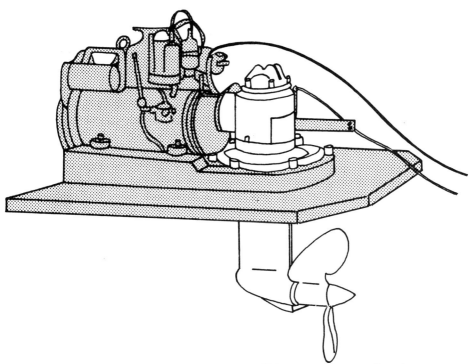

Fig. 11-3. New idea for larger sailboats. Either gasoline or diesel engines can be bought with special drive unit that fits through the bottom of the hull. It's much easier to install than traditional inboards and eliminates some potential sources of trouble.

well. (See Figure 11-4.) Attach a safety chain so that if it ever jiggles loose it won't fall to the bottom of the sea. Adjust the angle of the drive shaft to a vertical position. That's it, unless it has electric starting and a battery to be secured.

Installing an inboard engine requires one operation that is likely to challenge the amateur shipwright: boring the hole through the hull for the drive shaft. I'm glad I didn't have to bother with this for the *Dawn Treader*, but when I read up on it the procedure didn't seem too difficult for an amateur with patience. The most important thing to remember is to drill the shaft hole before building the engine bed. Then, if you don't get the shaft hole exactly right, you can compensate by shimming up the engine.

To find the right location for the hole, you construct a giant template of scrap planks reaching from the position of the engine over the transom and under the hull to the location of the propeller. (See Figure 11-5.) With engine and propeller positions marked on

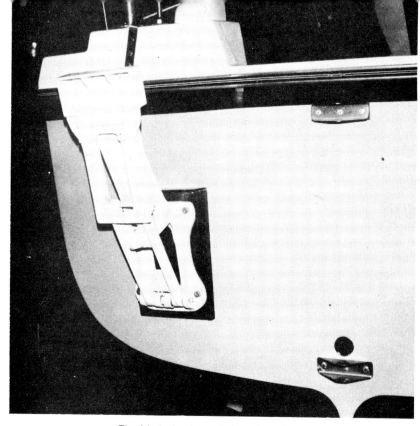

Fig.11-4. Outboard stern brackets.

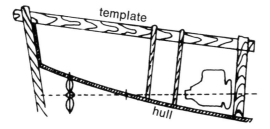

Fig. 11-5. To bore the drive shaft hole for an inboard engine, you construct a giant template of scrap planks, big enough to locate the engine and the propeller positions. Take it out of the hull and mark off the drive shaft centerline with a taut string. Intervening parts of the template then show you where you have to drill, and at what angle.

the template, you take it out of the hull, lay it on its side, and stretch a string across from the engine mark to the propeller mark. Pencil this line on all the intervening parts of the template; then when you put it back in the hull you can see the angle the centerline of the propeller shaft hole has to take.

The hole to be drilled should be ⅛ inch larger than the propeller shaft. You can't just put a bit in your electric drill and go to it, because you can't drill accurately at such an acute angle, and your bit probably isn't long enough anyway.

You have to build a drilling jig (Figure 11-6). It consists of a

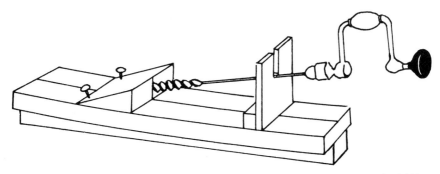

Fig. 11-6. Drilling at an angle is hard. Here's how: Make a jig to hold the shaft of the bit at the proper angle. Fasten a temporary block to provide a flat surface for the tip of the bit to bite into.

wood block, temporarily fastened to the hull at the point where the hole is to be made, and a brace for the drill shaft. The block gives you a flat face into which to drill. The brace supports the drill at the precise angle required.

For a power drill, you may be able to use one of the bit extensions that are standard items in good hardware stores. The longer the drill extension, the easier it is to control the drill angle. The traditional shipwright's solution was to use a special extra long ship auger. A ship auger lacks the usual screw point, which tends to follow grain and wander off course. I don't know of a source where a ship auger can be bought, but you could make one yourself from an ordinary auger bit by nipping off the screw point and welding an extension to the shaft.

If, despite your efforts at precision, the hole is still a whisker off, the traditional cure is to heat an iron bar red hot and improve the hole by scorching.

The installation instructions that come with an inboard engine and the boat plans give the details of the engine mounting. Water is prevented from leaking through the hull around the shaft by a hardware item called a stuffing box.

You can probably lift the engine for a modest-sized sailboat with one helper. If the engine is too heavy for two men to lift, you'll have to figure out ahead of time how you will manage to hoist it in. Rig up block and tackle (but don't pull the garage rafters down on your head) or rent a tow truck with a small crane.

The engine's installation instructions will also tell what to do about water and exhaust piping and wiring.

Fuel Tanks

Shipwrights can save money by salvaging used materials and equipment, but when you're installing a cruising fuel tank you should resist the urge to exhibit a sudden flash of creativity. Make sure you use a tank designed for the purpose. One necessary feature is a set of interior baffles to keep the fuel from sloshing back and forth inside, shifting its weight and making noise.

If your boat was designed for an inboard engine, the plans

should specify the size and location of the fuel tank. Its weight is a factor in the ship's ballast and trim. A 50-gallon tank, for example, might weigh 55 pounds empty and hold more than 300 pounds of gasoline or 350 pounds of diesel oil. Typical dimensions would be sixteen inches in diameter and five feet in length. It goes fore and aft, not athwartship.

The law is insistent about the way fuel tanks and engine compartments must be ventilated. The filler must be located so that spilled fuel will run overboard instead of into the bilge. The vent must be located high in the open air so fumes can disperse, with a flameproof screen covering the opening. Wherever a fuel tank or an engine is enclosed in a compartment, Coast Guard regulations call for "at least one exhaust duct installed so as to extend from the open atmosphere to the lower portion of the bilge, and at least one intake duct installed so as to extend to a point at least midway to the bilge or at least below the level of the carburetor intake."

On powerboats, it's considered good practice to install a drip pan under the engine. Drip pans don't help much on sailing vessels because they'd only spill when the ship heeled under sail.

Never locate a tank where you can't remove it for repairs or cleaning without tearing half the boat apart. Most engine failures at sea are caused, I've been told, not by any malfunction of the engine itself, but by water or crud in the fuel.

Propellers

Chances are you'll use the propeller that comes with your outboard and never give it another thought. But every hull is different, and it sometimes happens that a boat responds sluggishly with an engine that should have sufficient power for the size of the hull. When this happens, it's worth the trouble to investigate using a different propeller.

This is much more important for powerboats than for sailing craft, obviously. There are methods of calculating propeller size and pitch, but I won't go into them because they're complicated and you can't begin unless you have a tachometer to count your engine revolutions. But it may be useful to know that from 25 horsepower up even the outboard manufacturers offer propeller options. As a general rule, with a given engine, propellers of larger diameter and smaller pitch are used on heavier boats.

Propellers are located amidships in line with the keel if that doesn't interfere with the rudder, or on the port side, never to starboard. A port side location offsets the tendency of the propeller to crawl sideways with the stern.

Boats with outboard motors offered the first power steering. When you want to turn, the motor churns its way around. But when the motor stalls or you switch it off approaching a dock you're as helpless as a trailer rolling downhill. Boats with inboard power enjoy a considerable advantage, having independent rudders. Sailboats also steer with separate rudders, so you never lose control completely.

It is romantic to think of being a purist, perhaps sailing a gaff-rigged ketch with spruce spars, tarred rope rigging, and no engine, but I'm not that salty. On too many summer afternoons, at least where I sail, even a brisk wind subsides about the cocktail hour to desultory puffs, mostly from undesirable directions.

Under sail, the last mile could take an hour or more. Then when you arrive at the ramp there are several other boats milling around like waterbugs, waiting their turn. The majority are power-boats operated by skippers who have no conception of a sailboat's limited maneuverability.

That's when I am glad to give the battered outboard a yank— well, two or three yanks—and hear it start. I think of it not as a stinkpot but as a companion that has breasted many a swift river to push my canoe upstream and has brought me home punctually from many a day's sail.

I lash the tiller on course and stow all the sails while the engine throbs. I make sure the centerboard is up. (Trying to get a boat on a trailer when you have forgotten to raise the centerboard makes a lubberly spectacle.) I hang out the dock fenders and organize the rest of the gear as best as I can while underway.

About that time I reach the congested part of the harbor. An outboard runabout cuts me off. To avoid collision, I spin the motor around to reverse and put on the brakes. I may have to turn in tight circles for a few minutes until I'm next in line for the dock.

I cut the engine, steer alongside the dock, and jump ashore with bow and stern lines. A little while later the *Dawn Treader* is secured on her trailer and we're rolling home in time for a drink before dinner after all.

Having read recently that engines thrive when 10 or 15 percent alcohol is added to gasoline—better mileage and less pollution —I reflect that the faithful engine deserves to share a drink.

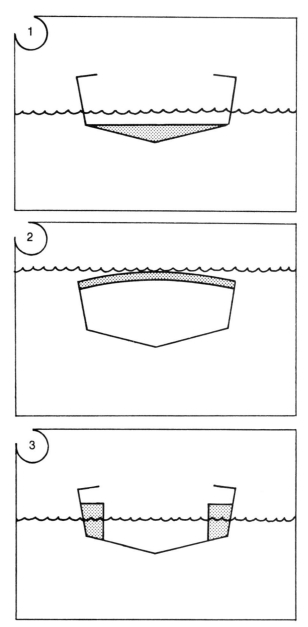

Fig 12-1. Flotation in the bottom (1) makes a boat unstable; if swamped, it may turn turtle. Flotation under the deck (2) may keep the boat from sinking, but the cockpit may be awash and impossible to pump out. A sufficient amount of flotation at midpoint (3) keeps the boat stable even when swamped.

12 How Not to Keep Up with the Davy Joneses

This chapter is about components of your ship that will help prevent it from capsizing, sinking, drifting away, or colliding with other ships.

A sailing vessel always needs something to counterbalance the pressure of the wind on the sails. Designers use various expedients. A wide-beamed hull is hard to tip. Ballast can be secured in the bilge or attached to the keel. Some high-performance boats rely on automatic movable ballast, with a harness provided for a crewman to hang out over the windward side as a routine part of racing. Although the main purpose of a centerboard is to prevent the ship from blowing sideways, the centerboard's weight is also a ballast factor.

The *Dawn Treader* needed a centerboard of steel plate $5/16$ inch thick. I couldn't buy this at the lumber yard and cut it to the pattern with a saw. So I consulted a friend who likes to visit scrap and salvage dealers and places where buildings are being wrecked. He volunteered to look for a sheet of steel plate of the proper size. I was glad I started the search early, while working on the hull. My friend reported that there was plenty of $1/4$-inch steel plate around, but it was a year before he located a suitable piece of $5/16$.

The metal was turned over to a high school teacher, who had one of his students cut it to my pattern with a welding torch. So the teacher got a bottle of scotch, the student got an A on his class project, and I got my centerboard.

What do builders do who need outside ballast for a fixed keel? I made inquiries in case I decide to build a larger ship someday. Four materials are used: lead, cast iron, fabricated steel, or reinforced concrete. Boat plans specify which, since the weights of the materials vary.

Lead is considered most desirable. It resists corrosion and is soft enough to be drilled for bolts after it's cast. Lead scrap is widely available in the form of old water pipe and auto batteries. Amateurs have been known to cast their own lead keels, although that can be dangerous if you don't read up on it first. Lead weighs 700 pounds per cubic foot. When used for internal ballast, it is cast in little pigs that you can lift one at a time. Large centerboarders sometimes need ballast concentrated between the forward end of the centerboard well and the mast step.

With lead and the other ballast materials it would be easy in a moment of rash enthusiasm to cast a piece you couldn't move, and it would block your driveway forever (or until you rented a crane).

Iron casting is beyond the capabilities of a home workshop, but the country is full of small gray iron foundries that customarily handle small orders for their regular customers. You can make the wood pattern yourself, which would be cheaper than having their pattern shop make it from your boat plans. Cast iron weighs 450 pounds per cubic foot.

Ballast keels are also fabricated from steel plates welded together. If you collect the scrap steel, any welding shop can assemble it for you. Steel weighs about 490 pounds per cubic foot.

Concrete reinforced with steel rods forms a keel you can pour yourself. Less durable than other materials, it can chip when you run aground. Plans calling for concrete ballast often specify a hardwood shoe set into the bottom to protect it. Because concrete weighs only 144 pounds per cubic foot, it is sometimes filled with lead or iron scrap to add weight.

Sometimes the plans give you a choice of ballast materials. I have plans in front of me for a thirty-footer that specify a ton of lead ballast attached to a keel of steel plate. The plans include a cast iron alternative. Plans for a forty-footer specify two and a half tons of lead ballast poured into a hollow keel fabricated of steel plate. Don't drop it on your foot.

Flotation

After the turn of the century, when myriad lumber schooners plied the Atlantic coastal waters, some of them proved unsinkable. Although wrecked in storms and abandoned by their crews, these wooden boats with cargoes of wood continued to float until they ran aground somewhere or disintegrated, after months of menacing navigation.

In small yachts that conceivably can be capsized or swamped, you should plan for a flotation reserve. A wooden boat can be sunk by the combined weight of ballast, engine, and equipment. Or a boat that doesn't actually sink may ride so low in the water when swamped that bailing is impossible. Also a swamped boat has little stability and can be capsized by the stomping of roaches abandoning the galley.

The solution to these problems is judicious installation of Styrofoam planks. Don't put them under the floorboards. Placed too low in the hull, flotation material tends to make the hull *more* unstable when swamped. A good location for flotation planks is on either side of the cockpit about halfway up. Here, the planks help stabilize a swamped boat and prevent her from rolling over. It's important for some of the flotation material to remain above the water even when the boat is swamped. (See Figure 12-1.)

Styrofoam's buoyancy factor is 64 pounds per cubic foot. One marine supplier whose catalog I have handy offers Styrofoam planks 20 by 7 inches and 9 feet long. Each plank supports 480 pounds. Half a plank under each of the *Dawn Treader*'s side decks would infringe only a little on cockpit storage space while more than countering the weight of engine, gasoline tank, head and holding tank, water jerrycans, and other equipment and supplies.

Foam flotation is essential, of course, with ferrocement, all-fiberglass, or metal hulls.

Besides Styrofoam planks, there are sheets of polystyrene flotation material (softer than Styrofoam and less expensive) and a polyurethane liquid you mix yourself. It foams and sets in place to add flotation to out-of-the-way places. One quart expands to fill 1.2 cubic feet, providing a buoyancy factor of 70 to 80 pounds.

The foam is a useful product for making hollow aluminum spars float. Just block one end and pour it in—quick. It takes thirty seconds to stir, and it hardens in one minute. I don't think it's necessary to fill a spar completely with foam. If you block the upper end of the mast with it, the rest of the hollow space will remain filled with air in a capsize as long as the foot of the mast is attached to the mast step. (If the mast step is underwater, there's no point in worrying about the floatability of the mast anymore.)

Although polyurethane foam weighs little—only two and a half pounds per quart—any unnecessary weight aloft is undesirable. If the *Dawn Treader*'s mast were completely filled with foam, it would be ten pounds heavier.

There's a standard formula used by the Boating Institute of America for computing minimum flotation: add the full weight of the deck and superstructure to the weight of the hull submerged and .69 of the weight of engines and equipment. Table 4 is used to compute the submerged weights of boat materials.

Table 4

Specific Gravities and Flotation Factors of Boat Materials

MATERIAL	SPECIFIC GRAVITY	FLOTATION FACTOR
Steel	7.85	0.88
Aluminum	2.73	0.63
Fiberglass	1.50	0.33
ABS plastic	1.12	0.11
Oak	0.63	−0.56

Mahogany	0.56	−0.78
Ash	0.56	−0.78
Yellow pine	0.55	−0.81
Fir plywood	0.55	−0.83
Mahogany plywood	0.54	−0.83
Cedar	0.33	−1.95

Take as an example a boat with 200 pounds of deck and superstructure, a 600-pound hull of fiberglass, and 150 pounds of engine and equipment.

$$200 + 0.33\,(600) + .69(150)$$
$$200 + 198 + 103.5 = 501.5$$

Translating math into English, you need something over 500 pounds' worth of flotation. A fir plywood hull of the same weight gives quite different results:

$$200 - 0.83(600) + .69(150)$$
$$200 - 498 + 103.5 = -194.5$$

This is another way of saying that wooden boats float even when swamped. In this example, you would have to have more than 194.5 pounds of gold doubloons stashed in the hold to sink the boat even without added flotation.

The formula is difficult for the amateur to work out accurately because although you may know the total weight of the boat you can only estimate how much of the weight is concentrated in the hull. But that doesn't matter. You want to allow a considerable reserve buoyancy to provide for the weight of the crew, which hasn't been figured in above.

Keep track of the weight of all equipment you put aboard. Even the natural buoyancy of a wooden hull can become overburdened.

Calculate your flotation requirement and make sure you wind up with a substantial margin. That will more than compensate for any error in your calculations.

Anchors

Many skippers sail for weeks and months without touching the anchor. Even cruising, you may go from marina to marina and always tie up at a pier. But, as novice outboarders keep discovering to their dismay, boats don't have brakes. When you need an anchor you really need it.

The builder has to provide a place to keep the anchor. If you are likely to use the anchor frequently, it's worth the trouble to install a device that snugs down the anchor on the foredeck where it's

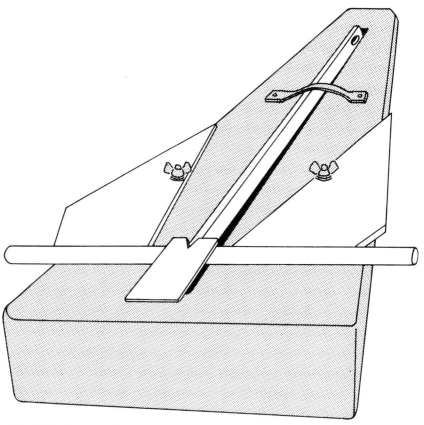

Fig. 12-2. If you cruise a lot, it's convenient to install anchor stowage on the foredeck. Otherwise, it's just something to trip over when you have to take down the jib in a hurry. (Drill holes for bolts in the flukes.)

always handy. (See Figure 12-2.) There's also hardware to keep the anchor poised over the water and to retrieve it by remote control. If you seldom use an anchor, these gadgets are just something to clutter up the foredeck and trip over.

No one type of anchor is perfect under all circumstances. Look around your local harbor and see what's popular. Chances are that it will be a Danforth type anchor, which depends for its holding power on its design rather than its weight. To give an extreme example, a 22-pound Danforth has the same holding power as a mushroom anchor weighing 650 pounds. There is also a high-tensile-strength version of the Danforth with stronger, thinner flukes that gives even more holding power per pound.

Except on a rocky bottom, an anchor digs itself in, often completely out of sight. The sand and mud abrade the anchor line, so it's considered good practice to attach a few feet of chain to the anchor, even for a small boat. The chain also helps weigh down the shank of the anchor to the angle at which the flukes bite best. Marine suppliers make up six-foot lengths of anchor chain with neoprene or vinyl coating to protect the rail of your boat as the anchor goes and comes over the side.

Almost as important as the anchor itself is the length of the anchor line. That's where the expression "plenty of scope" comes from, scope being the ratio between the length of an anchor line and the depth of the water. A ratio of five to one is regarded as minimum, with seven or eight preferred and perhaps fifteen to one as the maximum practical scope under severe conditions. So you have to provide a place to store one or two hundred feet of line along with the anchor.

Nylon rope is favored for anchor line because its elasticity cushions shocks, and it won't rot if you have to coil it up and put it away wet. There's no advantage in using thicker line than necessary for a given boat, because that merely reduces the elasticity factor. It's desirable to mark anchor line every twenty feet or so. With such markings you can judge how deep the water is when you drop the anchor and know when enough line has been payed out to provide enough scope.

Table 5

Recommended Ground Tackle Sizes

LENGTH OF BOAT (FEET)	DANFORTH-TYPE ANCHOR WEIGHT (POUNDS)	HIGH-TENSILE ANCHOR WEIGHT (POUNDS)	NYLON ROPE DIAMETER (INCHES)	ANCHOR LINE LENGTH (FEET)
10	$2\frac{1}{2}$	—	$\frac{1}{4}$	100
15	4	—	$\frac{1}{4}$	100
20	8	5	$\frac{1}{4}$	120
25	8	12	$\frac{3}{8}$	150
30	13	12	$\frac{3}{8}$	180
35	22	18	$\frac{3}{8}$	200
40	22	18	$\frac{7}{16}$	250
50	40	28	$\frac{1}{2}$	300

These recommendations assume moderate shelter from heavy seas, average holding ground, and seven-to-one scope. Many boats carry more than one anchor. You can use a size smaller as a "lunch hook" to hold the boat while you eat or go swimming. One size larger—a storm anchor—might be needed if winds exceeded thirty knots. The working anchor sizes given are adequate for overnight anchorages and most emergencies that occur in cruising.

A spare anchor of any size is useful in several ways. Sometimes you want to anchor bow and stern or put out two anchors ahead at the same time. Then there's the obvious use of a spare: as a spare. One deep sea voyager with a death wish made his first stop on a voyage from Panama to Australia memorable by throwing his only anchor overboard without fastening the end of the line to the boat.

Running Lights

Any boat that might conceivably be caught out after dark—and that's almost every sailboat larger than a sailboard—needs lights. (See Chapter 8 for a discussion of sources of electrical power.) The regulations on lighting are confusing because they're not standard for all waters and because your sailboat legally becomes a motorboat, with slightly different lights, the minute you start running the engine.

You no doubt have seen the light chart. It has been published everywhere, even on boat cushions and cocktail napkins, so I won't go into all of the details here. I'll merely try to summarize what a shipwright needs to know.

There are four sets of rules: International, Inland, Great Lakes, and Western Rivers. For the builder, all the continental rules are basically the same. International rules may be followed anywhere, but the continental rules aren't legal on the high seas.

Well, then, why not just simplify matters and install lights according to the International rules? The trouble is that they call for a masthead light when you use your engine. This is fine for a ship with a permanent mooring and a mast that remains undisturbed all season. It's a considerable nuisance for a boat that goes on and off a trailer every weekend or has to dip its mast frequently to pass under bridges. If you don't break your masthead light in the process, you'll strangle yourself in the wiring.

The variation problems are confined to white lights. All ships on all waters must show a green light on the starboard bow and a red light on the port bow. These can be separate 10-point lights on the side of hull or cabin or a 20-point combination light on the bow, depending on size.

The description of lights in points derives from the traditional 32 points of the compass, one point being roughly 11 degrees. A 10-point light is visible through an arc of about 110 degrees. A 12-point light covers 135 degrees. Twenty points equals 225 degrees, somewhat more than half a circle. A 32-point light is visible from all directions. Table 6 shows what you have to install.

Table 6

Light Requirements

INTERNATIONAL RULES, SAIL ONLY

Length of ship	White lights	Red/green lights
Under 40 feet	12-point stern light visible 2 miles	Side lights or combination visible 1 mile
40 to less than 65 feet	12-point stern light visible 2 miles	Side lights visible 2 miles

INLAND RULES, SAIL ONLY

Length of ship	White lights	Red/green lights
Under 26 feet	12-point stern light visible 2 miles	Combination visible 1 mile
26 to less than 65 feet	12-point stern light visible 2 miles	Side lights visible 1 mile

Under International rules, when you turn on your engine you must also switch on a 20-point white masthead light visible for three miles. "Masthead" means higher than the head of the jib.

Under Inland rules, when you turn on your engine the stern light must be raised higher than the bow lights and become visible from all directions. If your boat is twenty-six feet long or longer you must also turn on a 20-point bow light.

Exceptions: Where Western Rivers rules apply, the red and green lights of vessels under sail should be visible for three miles. On the Great Lakes in lieu of a continuously burning stern light a sailing ship may show a white light to an overtaking vessel. Small sailboats without engines and rowboats don't need any lights except a strong flashlight to light if another boat approaches.

How do you tell how far away a given light is visible? It would be awkward to put your wife in the dinghy on a dark night and sail off for two miles to see if she can still see the lights. An easier way is to follow the recommendations of the Coast Guard on bulb numbers, as shown in Table 7.

Table 7

Recommended Bulb Numbers for Boat Lights

Distance in miles	1	1	2	3
Color	Red	Green	White	White
6-volt with fresnel lens	82	88	64	82
12-volt with fresnel lens	90	94	68	90
6-volt without fresnel lens	1130	1130*	82	1130
12-volt without fresnel lens	1142	1142*	90	1142

*The Coast Guard doesn't recommend green lights without fresnel lenses because green is basically dim. Fresnel lenses transmit more light for a given wattage than ordinary lenses.

There has been talk in Congress about making the continental rules more uniform and more like the International rules, but nothing has been done at this writing. The changes proposed probably won't affect pleasure boating much anyway, having more to do with the difference between a tugboat with two barges and two fishing boats with one net.

To summarize: for a sailboat of a given size the law describes appropriate running lights. When the auxiliary engine is used, that ship becomes legally a motorboat and must alter her white lights accordingly. The red and green lights remain the same.

Installing Lights

Because the construction details of boats vary so much it's not always obvious where lights should be installed. (See Figure 12-3.) A red and green combination light on the foredeck may interfere with anchor and mooring lines. With red and green side lights, you have to screen them—usually with the cabin—so that the wrong light can't be seen from the wrong side.

Obviously, lights don't serve their purpose if they're obstructed by bollards, railings, coamings, hatch covers, or other parts

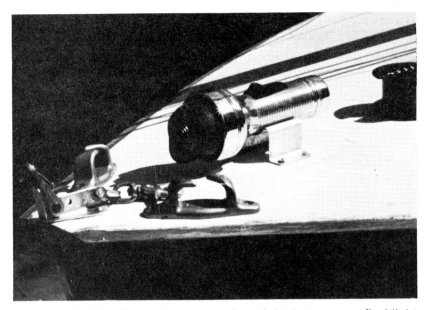

Fig. 12-3. Combination red and green bow light that runs on flashlight batteries is adequate for ships that don't sail much after dark.

of the boat. This problem solves itself if you wait until last to position the lights.

Your chief difficulty with lights will be in providing both a 12-point stern light for sailing and a 32-point stern light for power. One answer is to have the 12-point light permanently attached, low and out of the way—perhaps set into the transom. The 32-point light can clamp on the transom when needed or slide up out of a retractable socket. It has to be high enough to be visible over the top of the cabin.

But you can't have the 32-point light sticking up that way all the time. The boom may knock it off. Or it will foul the traveler or the main sheet. Because every cockpit is different, I can't be more specific. Just make certain the light staff won't goose the helmsman at a moment of crisis. (See Figures 12-4 through 12-6 for illustrations of various lighting arrangements.)

The other light you have to provide for is the anchor light—a 32-point white light visible for at least two miles and positioned forward where it can best be seen. On a sailboat, this can be an electric or kerosene lantern that you slide up the forestay with the jib halyard.

Fig. 12-4. Battery-powered stern light in lowered position is visible only from astern, which is correct when ship proceeds under sail. When ship proceeds under power, stern light is raised to make it visible from any direction as required by rules for motorboats and auxiliaries using their engines.

Fig. 12-5. Expensive factory-built boat has stern light on retractable post for conversion back and forth from sail to motorboat lighting. Wires to electrical system are inside the post.

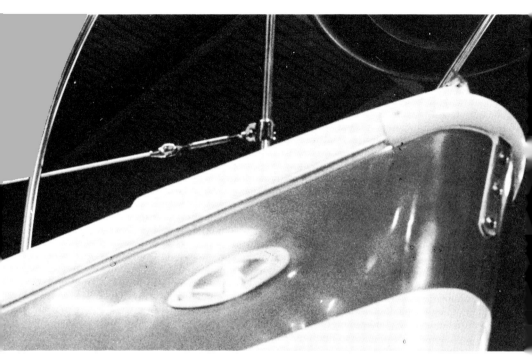

Fig. 12-6. Bow lights set into hull on either side are less likely to be damaged than lights on deck.

If you're planning to do much cruising, all these lights, except the anchor light, should be wired to a central power supply with remote switches. Self-contained lights powered by flashlight batteries are less reliable and more trouble, as you'll discover the first time you have to crawl up on the foredeck to switch on the bow light at dusk when rough water is tossing the bow up and down.

Judging the life expectancy of dry cells is hard because some of it could have been used up on the shelf before you bought them. In my experience, if an anchor light is burning brightly when the crew turns in, it still will be going strong in the morning. (There's one rather expensive battery model that turns itself off at dawn. I suppose in time the savings in batteries would pay for it if you cruise a lot.)

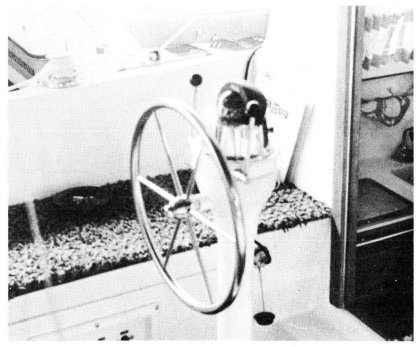

Fig. 12-7. Traditional location for the compass is best when the cockpit is large enough.

Compasses

The price range of compasses is astounding, considering that you can obtain roughly the same information from a steel needle stuck through a cork and floated in a pan of water. The differences are in refinement of construction. The $250 compasses have large, easy-to-read cards that don't wobble. They can be precisely corrected. For $7 or $8, the card probably is too small and moves too much to give a truly accurate reading. But don't rush out and buy an expensive compass. A cheap one may be adequate for the kind of navigation you do, poking around inland and coastal waters, seldom out of sight of land.

Any compass should be installed within easy view of the helmsman. (See Figure 12-7.) A line through the center of the compass and the lubber line on the dial must be parallel to the keel. The compass should be as far as possible from any masses of metal, such as the engine or the centerboard plate. It should also be out of harm's way when lubberly crewmen are scrambling around the cockpit trying to cope with some sailing crisis.

On most small yachts, there isn't any place that meets all these requirements. You just have to make the best arrangement possible.

Any electrical wires that pass near the compass should be twisted around each other to avoid creating a magnetic field. For sailing at night, the compass can be lighted with a tiny red bulb.

On a large seagoing yacht whose skipper is determined to make a precise landfall after 1,200 miles at sea, special craftsmen come aboard and compensate or correct the compass, making minute adjustments of small magnets to counteract the magnetic disturbances created by metal parts of the ship.

Small sailboats are too bouncy for such refinements. The instructions that come with your compass tell you how to adjust it yourself for deviation on your boat, with less accuracy because everything is so close. Just putting the steel centerboard up and down can throw off your compass a little no matter what you do.

Deviation is not to be confused with variation. Deviation is caused by the boat itself. Variation is the difference between true north and magnetic north and changes according to your geographical location. Navigation charts give you the information you need to allow for compass variation.

Since deviation is caused by the boat, it changes from one course to another, regardless of where you are on the seven seas. After a compass has been adjusted as well as possible, you have to make a deviation chart to use in navigating.

To work out your deviation chart, find a place where you can get a positive directional fix, such as the mouth of a harbor with range markers. Sail across that range line on a series of courses, fifteen degrees apart according to your compass. On each crossing, note the difference between the direction your compass says you're sailing and the direction you're really sailing according to the range markers and the chart. You wind up with a list of twenty-four deviations, one for each of the twenty-four courses you sailed. (I am told that this takes two men all afternoon. You can't do it by yourself.)

When I read about the tedium of adjusting compasses and correcting courses, I can't help reflecting that all through the age of sail, navigators found their way around the globe using compasses with the thirty-two traditional divisions—north, north by east, north northeast, northeast by north, northeast, and so on. (I think all thirty-two of them have been book titles at least once.)

Now we have a compass divided into 360 degrees. You can't steer a small boat within a single degree of a desired course, so all course directions such as 270 degrees (instead of west) are to some extent fictional.

I intend to work out a deviation chart and sharpen up my own navigation, which at present is about good enough to guarantee finding the state of Illinois even in the dark unless I slide off a little northward and hit Wisconsin instead.

Anyone who sails on a large body of water has to rely on his compass sooner or later. The waters I like to sail are notorious for fog early in summer. In contrast to a morning fog that burns off by noon, a day sometimes starts out merely hazy and grows thicker. You're sailing along, enjoying the day, when suddenly you realize that the distant shore, which you've been aware of out of the corner of an eye, is no longer visible. Without a compass, that could be scary. If the wind shifted, you wouldn't know which way to steer for home.

A squall can cut visibility without warning. Late one afternoon on a cruise, I was steering a course south by east, more or less. As we raced along with a freshening breeze, a dark cloud appeared in the sky to the northwest and began chasing us. After a time I calculated, correctly, that it would miss us. It passed to the north, catching us only with a spatter of light rain.

Then a second angry cloud came over the horizon. This one had us right in the crosshairs. There was nothing to do but shorten sail, snap tight our foul weather clothes, and see what happened next. The whole sky turned black. Gusts came hissing across the choppy water to tilt the *Dawn Treader*'s deck. We were relieved that the gusts weren't as violent as the darkness of the sky threatened.

Then the rain came down so hard that it hammered the waves flat, despite the wind. I could no longer see the land, or anything else much past the bow. We might have sailed over the edge of the earth before we could even see the drop-off. But I knew where we were when the squall hit, and I knew where we wanted to go, so I kept on steering south by east, still more or less.

The light began to brighten. A towering wall of opaque light slowly advanced on us from the west while the rain fell harder than ever. Then the eerie wall of light passed over us and we were suddenly in sunshine, with visibility not only restored but enhanced by the vigorous scrubbing of the atmosphere.

I was reminded of something William Albert Robinson wrote in *To the Great Southern Sea* after a violent storm off the Pacific coast of South America: "During the hours of trial I had thought of nothing but security, comfort—even of quitting the sea forever and using *Varua* as a houseboat. Now, after a good night's sleep, the dual nature of the seafarer asserted itself, and I realized that probably never, in any other life, would I feel as fit as I did now."

As we continued on our course, running the jib back up now that the squall had passed, a rainbow appeared in the east, a complete semicircle with clear, intense colors. While we admired it, a second rainbow came onstage, dimmer than the first but equally complete. I can't think of any other rainbow display I ever saw to match it.

The crew said he was reminded of a double-dip ice cream cone made with fruitbowl revel sherbet. The mention of food immediately gave all hands keen hunger pangs. Fortunately, before mutiny broke out or we were reduced to whitened bones drifting aimlessly about the Sargasso Sea, our destination appeared off the starboard bow. Our compass course of south by east had brought us to the entrance of Point Comfort Cove, neither more nor less.

We turned into the cove, dropped anchor, and in no time at all sizzling sausage patties heated on the alcohol stove were being used as ballast for a plate of buttered buns.

Fig. 13-1. The *Dawn Treader* on her trailer. The tarp makes a cockpit
cover to protect the boat from weather. It can also be hung over the
boom to form a tent that provides extra living space at anchor.

13 There's Many a Slip twixt Mooring and Trailer

Before you settle on a boat plan, you should have decided where the boat will be kept when it's finished. There are advantages and disadvantages to all the alternatives.

Moorings

Many large yachts tie up to a buoy fastened to a permanent anchor in a harbor. The permanent anchor is heavy—a surplus concrete patio or the equivalent. You row out to the ship in your dinghy. This is very salty and adds immensely to the pleasure of owning a yacht.

There is also the simplicity of getting ready to sail. You just run up the sails while at anchor, cast off from the buoy, and sail away. And keeping a wooden hull in water is good for it. The hull won't twist or hog and the seams stay tight.

On the other hand, sun and water are attacking the paint and the fittings day in and day out. You have to keep the bottom painted with antifouling paint to ward off barnacles, algae, and other marine organisms looking for a home at your expense.

Near population centers, the seasonal rental for moorings is likely to be stiff. Because each boat must be free to swing around

227

the buoy as the wind changes direction, moorings consume the available space in a harbor rapidly. In many areas, no moorings are open. You have to get on a waiting list and hope that some of the boats now in the harbor sink and create vacancies.

On balance, I think I would prefer a mooring, but knowing the problems I decided from the first to build a boat that could be kept in the garage on a trailer. (See Figure 13-1.)

Slips

More and more boats are being kept in slips, which make much more efficient use of the space in a harbor. They also offer some conveniences. Instead of having to lug supplies and equipment out to your mooring in a dinghy or to fetch your ship and wait for a chance to tie up at the pier, you just walk alongside and dump everything into the cockpit.

Electricity is often available at marina slips to recharge batteries or to run power tools if you have repair work to do, and you can listen to the radio while you paint. I personally consider that a disadvantage, because the scurvy swabs in the next slip invariably exhibit deplorable taste in the choice of programs on *their* radio.

In tidal waters, the piers are usually designed to float up and down with the tide, which is a superior arrangement. While I was keeping the *Dawn Treader* in a fixed slip on an inland lake, a week of torrential rains raised the water level a foot or two. My mooring lines, which had to be rather tight to keep the hull clear of the pilings on either side of the narrow slip, couldn't provide enough slack to accommodate that much change in water level. As the hull floated higher, the line under the most strain pulled an eye ring askew, splintering the coaming around it.

A boat kept in a slip needs plenty of protection in the form of fenders between hull and piers. You can make the nest more comfortable with cushioning materials nailed to the pier and the pilings with galvanized roofing nails.

Seldom can you sail away from a slip. The wind is usually from the wrong direction, and the surroundings are too congested anyway. Backing out of a slip with the engine is easy enough, but

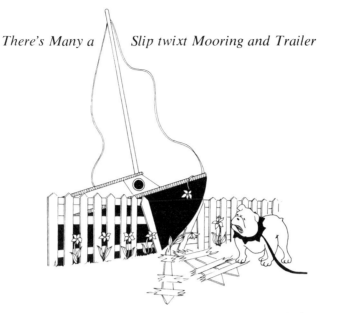

Nosing back into a slip can be challenging in a crosswind . . . nobody can win them all.

nosing back in can be challenging in a crosswind unless you're carrying at least two crewmen to fend off and jump ashore with mooring lines.

With practice, I became fairly good at tying up single-handed without ramming and sinking the parking lot, but nobody can win them all, as several chips in the *Dawn Treader*'s rails attest.

Trailers

With trailers, you don't have to pay rent for a slip or a mooring, although there may be fees to use launching ramps. You don't have to worry about storm damage or buy expensive bottom paint. You can safely leave equipment in the boat between voyages without fear of theft (unless valuables tend to disappear from your garage). You can do maintenance work comfortably and conveniently at home.

Hauling a trailer-sized boat slows you down on the highway only a little, and skill at backing up can be acquired quickly with practice.

The main disadvantage is that you have to put the mast up

Fig. 13-2. One of the disadvantages of sailing your boat off a trailer: waiting in line for a turn at the trailer ramps (Waukegan, Illinois).

and down for every cruise. Getting the boat off and back onto the trailer, securely fastened down, is also time-consuming. A strong crosswind or a pushy tailwind can be even more of a nuisance when you're trying to coax your boat back onto the trailer than it is with a tight slip. If you bungle, the keel may miss the rollers and hang up on the trailer frame, or perhaps one of the fenders, causing expensive wear and tear on both the hull and the trailer.

Choosing a Trailer

When you build your own boat, you have to design, in a sense, your own trailer. The rollers, supports, and other fittings on a stock trailer are bolted on and can be moved around to some extent to permit you to adjust it to fit your hull.

Most trailers are intended for powerboats, with two strong longitudinal supports (called bolsters) under the stern to take the weight of the engine. Some experts argue that a sailboat trailer should have its bolsters positioned forward to support the deepest part of the hull. Sailboats have light engines and strong keels, so they don't need bolsters under the stern. However, the manufacturers don't seem to agree, judging from their catalogs. The trailer models they specifically recommend for sailboats either have the bolsters at the stern or provide long bolsters running the length of the trailer.

Before buying a trailer for the *Dawn Treader*, I took my hull plans and a steel tape measure to the dealer's, where I spent an hour or more measuring trailers, checking the measurements against the plans, noting how much the components could be adjusted and making sure the hull would fit—as it does, more or less. The bolsters are under the stern and can't be repositioned forward without creating a problem with the tie-down hardware. Following are some desirable features for a boat trailer:

•   The frame should contain numerous extra bolt holes to permit flexibility in adjusting fittings. (See Figure 13-3.)

Fig. 13-3. Note the numerous extra bolt holes punched in the trailer frame. They permit adjusting a standard trailer to fit many different hulls.

• Wheel bearings should have grease fittings and spring caps so you can keep them lubricated with a grease gun. It's a bother to have to take off the wheel and repack the bearings every time they need grease, which is often for a boat trailer.

• Capacity of the trailer should be several hundred pounds heavier than the boat itself to allow for the weight of added equipment.

• The tongue should be hinged so that the bed of the trailer can be tilted without unhitching the tongue. Trailers with tilting beds come with locks to prevent tilting at the wrong time.

• It's worth paying extra to get wider rollers, particularly the rollers at the stern. No trailer can have too many rollers. (See Figure 13-4 and Figure 13-5.)

Fig. 13-4. Extra wide roller at rear of trailer simplifies recovering your boat and helps avoid damage.

● If the trailer doesn't come with a wheel and jack on the tongue, buy one as an accessory. Except for the smallest boats, the convenience is worth the cost.

When the boat is on the trailer, it should be balanced so that a slight majority of the weight falls forward. The frame should be bolted to the wheel and axle assembly. Then you can move the fulcrum forward or aft as required.

The tow hitch should be welded to the frame of your car. Bumper hitches are too insecure. The ball part of the hitch comes in different sizes. Before you buy one, find out the size required for your trailer. The ball should be kept lubricated and protected from rust in winter through some clever stratagem such as taking it off and putting it away.

Fig. 13-5. No trailer can have too many rollers.

Fig. 13-6. Extended winch support on this trailer also holds mast when boat rolls along highway.

Any support bolsters or chocks should be positioned to bear on framing or a curved part of the hull, not on flat panels that could flex every time you hit a bump.

The best kind of tie-down is fastened to the trailer frame with springs. This system holds the boat on the trailer, but not too tightly. Protective covers for boats on the highway should have drawstrings. At highway speeds, a tarp with a rope fastened through grommets tends to rip around the grommets and pull loose.

Trailers That Failed

If you already have the equipment and skill for welding, I think building your own trailer would be worthwhile. Plans are available from boat plan sources. As I'll explain, I don't much like the trailer I bought.

Building a trailer of wood doesn't pay. I cite the testimony of a skipper who built a double-axle model weighing 1,200 pounds. He said he did it because he already had the tools and materials on hand. His conclusion was that a steel trailer could have been built more cheaply and with less work. And it would have weighed less, too. That's why you almost never see a wooden boat trailer at the marina.

I have several minor complaints and one major one about my trailer. Recovering the boat, I found that with any crosswind blowing it was very difficult to center the bow on the first roller, which I couldn't see under the turbid waters of most launching ramps. When the forefoot of the boat missed the roller, it ran aground on the frame, chipping paint. I solved that problem by installing a new roller a foot wide.

The transom tie-down clamps were fastened to the trailer frame with chain. Obviously, the chain would saw into the hull at every bump. I had to cut sleeves from an old bicycle inner tube to put over the chain and protect the hull. (See Figure 13-7.)

The spring lock on the tilting bed hinge was difficult to release. Mostly, I do without it because the ramps I use don't require the bed to tilt.

My serious complaint about this trailer is that it almost dumped my boat on the highway. One day I happened to notice that the welded seams at the point where the tongue joins the trailer bed were cracking. A few more bumps and the tongue would have

Fig. 13-7. Tie-down clamp with spring holds hull securely without exerting damaging pressure. A length of old bicycle inner tube protects hull from chafing by chain fastened to trailer frame.

pulled away from the trailer. The front edge of the trailer bed might then have dipped to the highway at fifty miles an hour, which sounds like the beginning of a spectacular accident.

I secured the seams temporarily with C clamps and crept a short distance to a welding shop, where repairing the seams was easy and cheap while I waited. What I didn't notice was that in the process the tongue had twisted so that the trailer winch was no longer on the centerline of the rollers. Consequently, it was no longer possible to center the boat on the trailer. The winch pulled the bow to port.

Now there's an interesting problem for the home craftsman. The first step obviously was to write a heated letter of complaint to the president of the trailer company to see what, if anything, would be done about it. I was told to see the dealer.

So the next step was to call the dealer, who said that they no longer handled this kind of trailer. Whether any warranty would apply would be up to the trailer company, who would have to send someone around to look at the trailer. The service department expressed skepticism about the possibility, since the warranty period had expired and the welds that failed had been already covered up by the emergency repairs.

The suggestion was made that if I could leave the boat and trailer for a couple of weeks the dealer would look into the problem. In any case, they probably would have to order a whole new tongue from the factory, and, with labor, the job might cost fifty or sixty dollars.

As we go to press, it is too soon to report the outcome. I have written only three letters to the president of the trailer company. I have not picketed the corporate headquarters. I have not snitched to Ralph Nader. It may be that in the end, with persistence, I may be able to persuade the manufacturer to pay for the repairs.

You are invited to make your own prediction, based on your experience with automobiles and major appliances.

Traveling with Trailers

One benefit of this experience was that it emphasized the importance of checking and maintaining a trailer carefully to prevent accidents. The winch and rollers should be lubricated regularly. All bolts should be checked and tightened. Lights should be inspected before every trip. I'm told that a loose ground wire is the commonest source of trailer lighting problems.

The small tires of trailers receive more wear than your car tires because they make so many more revolutions to cover the same mileage. The sidewalls of trailer tires usually go long before the treads. It's unusual for trailer tires to last beyond 10,000 miles.

Your auto jack and tire wrench probably don't fit a boat trailer. You need a scissors jack or a hydraulic jack to put under the trailer axle and a scrap piece of plywood, perhaps a foot square, to support the jack where the ground is soft. If you buy a four-way wheel lug wrench, it will fit almost all equipment made in the United States.

Many trailer tires require higher pressures than can be registered by an ordinary tire gauge. You need a truck tire gauge that reads pressures beyond sixty or sixty-five pounds per square inch.

You'll be tempted to load gear and baggage into a boat for a trip because there's so much room. Don't do it. The tires can't stand that much more load. In fact, you should transfer as much heavy gear as possible from the boat to the car. Light objects such as sails and sleeping bags can travel in the boat if you arrange matters so that they won't bounce out or be stolen.

Traveling long distances, many skippers contrive a shield of plywood or hardboard to protect the hull from flying gravel.

It is possible to trail a boat wider than eight feet, but you have to obtain a special permit from each state you pass through. Some states also require separate brakes on trailers above a certain weight. Of course, the larger stock trailers come equipped with brakes anyway.

For a boat the size of the *Dawn Treader*, you don't need brakes on the trailer. I never notice the extra weight in braking, although the boat and trailer do reduce the acceleration and gas mileage of my four-cylinder van from about twenty-four miles per gallon to nineteen.

With good side mirrors, hauling a trailer isn't troublesome if you're not the type of driver who is frantic to make good time. About the only difficulty comes when you want to park somewhere other than at a marina or a gas station. One suggestion is to time your arrival at restaurants along the road before or after the usual mealtimes when the parking lots aren't crowded.

Don't leave a lightweight outboard motor on the transom. If you can lift it, so can a thief. Lock it in the car.

Going cruising with a trailer widens the horizon of your seascape. You can range up and down a coastline, exploring waters you couldn't reach otherwise without weeks of sailing. Or you can follow the good weather, avoiding the foggy side of the peninsula.

But your ship's log does read strangely when the first page of the entry for every voyage records items like the new detour to avoid on Lake Avenue and the name of the cafe where the rude waitress never brought any mustard for the hamburgers.

Fig. 14-1. Boat registration numbers in proper position on bow.

14 Fitting Out and Fitting In

I LIKE the phrases associated with the beginning of voyages —"fitting out," "casting off," "weighing anchor." They lift the spirit, suggesting that you will soon leave the land and its jungles behind for a while. The prospect makes endurable a few more days of editing catalog copy or attending sales meetings or whatever occupies your time between voyages.

The world has become more complicated since a mariner could sail as he pleased and walk ashore anywhere in the world without a passport. Now, besides having the necessary equipment and provisions on board, you have to be registered and insured so that if you spear an olive in the yacht club's Harbor View bar some windy day with your bowsprit it will be only a breach of etiquette rather than a crime or a personal financial disaster.

You can be ordered ashore by the Coast Guard or fined for failure to comply with regulations.

● Your boat must be numbered. The number is issued by your state with a validation sticker, except in New Hampshire, Washington, Alaska, and the District of Columbia, where you go directly to the Coast Guard. The number must be permanently attached on each side of the bow in characters at least three inches high and in a contrasting color. (See Figure 14-1.)

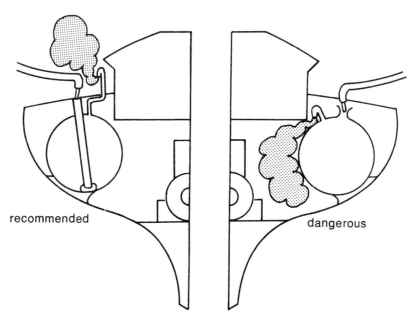

recommended

dangerous

Fig. 14-2. A safe gasoline tank installation spills fumes from vent into the open air. A vent below deck permits fumes to collect in the bilge, where they can blow you up.

• There must be a flotation device for each person aboard all watercraft, even the smallest. On boats under sixteen feet long and all canoes and kayaks the familiar floating seat cushion is acceptable. Over sixteen feet, each passenger must have a wearable flotation device, such as a life jacket or a ski belt, *and* a throwable device (life ring or seat cushion).

• You must carry a fire extinguisher if you have an engine unless on a completely open outboard-powered boat where no gasoline fumes could possibly accumulate. (See Figure 14-2 for safe gasoline tank installation.) The protection of a fire extinguisher is required if you have permanently installed fuel tanks, closed compartments under thwarts and seats for portable tanks, double bottoms not sealed to the hull or filled with flotation material, or closed living spaces or storage lockers.

- If there's a deck, there have to be at least two ducts ventilating every engine and fuel compartment and the bilge.

- On boats from sixteen to less than twenty-six feet long, you're supposed to carry a signal whistle—hand-, mouth-, or power-operated—audible for at least one-half mile. Over twenty-six feet, you need a ship's bell and a whistle audible for at least a mile, operated by hand or power because you can't blow a whistle loud enough to be heard for a mile.

- For rules on lights, see the previous discussion in Chapter 12.

On larger boats, you're expected to carry additional fire extinguishers—two extinguishers when the length is twenty-six to less than forty feet, three from forty feet to less than sixty-five. There's also a rule about backfire flame arrestors on the engine, but it seems unlikely that any engine you'd be installing at this late date would not already be so equipped.

Capacity Information Label

One new requirement you may not have heard about before is the U.S. Coast Guard Capacity Information Label, which is supposed to be attached permanently to the hull of all powerboats *under twenty feet* built after October 31, 1972, assuming that the boat will be sold. Complying with the law is not unduly bothersome. The label must show the following information: name and address of builder, date, hull identification number, maximum weight capacity, maximum horsepower capacity, and maximum persons capacity. This regulation doesn't apply to the backyard boat builder who constructs a boat for his own use—until he wants to sell it—except for having a hull number.

The regulation doesn't apply to sailboats, canoes, or kayaks, either. I think Congress realized that people expect these boats to demand skillful handling. Powerboats give innocent landlubbers a false sense of security because so many of them look like seagoing cars, and certain unscrupulous small companies have produced unsafe hulls. So the law says that without the required label "no

"Powerboats give innocent landlubbers a false sense of security because so many of them look like seagoing cars."

person who manufactures, constructs or assembles a boat or associated equipment may deliver that boat or equipment for the purpose of sale."

Hull identification number.   The hull identification number (not to be confused with your bow registration number) consists of twelve characters. The first three are your own manufacturer's code. The next five are a serial number. The last four record the date of construction. You get your manufacturer's code from your state or from the Coast Guard simply by asking. Who says you're not a shipwright? The government gives you your own label, like a cattle brand.

If your state hasn't set up a hull identification system yet, write the Coast Guard: Commandant, GBBC, 400 Seventh Street, S.W., Washington, D.C. 20590.

Maximum weight capacity.   Maximum weight capacity is

one-fifth of the maximum hull displacement minus one-fifth of the weight of the boat and minus four-fifths of the weight of any inboard or inboard/outdrive engines.

Maximum persons capacity. To calculate the maximum persons capacity, you divide the actual weight the boat will carry without sinking or capsizing by 0.6.

Maximum horsepower capacity. Plans usually show maximum horsepower.

The regulation says:

Gradually add weights along one outboard extremity of each passenger carrying area, at the height of the seat nearest the center of that area and distributed equally forward and aft of that center in a plane parallel to the floorboards until the boat assumes the maximum list or trim, or both, without water coming aboard.

I wrote to the Coast Guard, complaining that the regulations as published seemed a burden to amateur boat builders, who would be tempted to give up and ignore them. (As a practical matter, some are not enforceable at the backyard level.) Vice Admiral T. R. Sargent, vice commandant of the Coast Guard, replied that a backyard builder wishing to determine capacities may use "any method which is easy or most convenient for him. The requirements are really rather simple, once you have studied the sections of interest and become familiar with the legal language."

The maximum hull displacement is information that can be obtained from the designer. Admiral Sargent says a boat under twenty feet can be weighed one end at a time on a household scale or taken on its trailer to a coal yard scale. Weight of engines is always shown in manufacturers' catalogs and specification sheets.

Reading the regulations, I envisioned a builder who, after a year or two of labor and much expense, takes his new boat to the water on a calm day. He adds test weights as directed until the boat "assumes the maximum list or trim, or both, without water coming aboard." Oops, slight miscalculation. The last weight is a bit too heavy, and down goes the boat, brand-new engine and all, to the bottom of the harbor.

Admiral Sargent said the shipwright may "use less precise methods, if they are conservative." He gave the following example:

> The builder might desire to rate the boat for 540 pounds of persons (three at 180 pounds) even though he might be able to rate the boat a bit higher if he went to the absolute limit of the allowed capacity. In that case he would need 324 pounds of test weight (0.6 × 540 pounds). Any practical weights would do, and there have been instances where even people have been used, though we do not recommend it if there is any doubt as to the boat's stability. When these weights are moved outboard and the boat does not ship water the builder knows that he meets the requirements with a margin. The test is easy to do, requires little calculation and the results are immediately apparent.

Or, to simplify further, estimate how many persons the boat

will hold. Get that many friends (who can swim) and carefully experiment with all of them sitting to one side.

There is a rule of thumb for estimating how many persons you can safely carry in normal weather. Multiply overall length by the maximum beam (to the tenth of a foot) and divide by fifteen. That formula gives the *Dawn Treader* a capacity of eight, which actually is too many to be comfortable on a cruise of more than a hour or so. At least two of the eight would have to spend the whole time sitting in the cabin or on the spray-drenched foredeck.

To avoid all these tests and computations entirely, be a nonconformist: build a sailboat.

Recommended Safety Equipment

Besides the safety equipment required by law, there are several other items required by common sense. A change of warm clothes, for example. People don't realize how cold it can get in and on the water, even in summer. During World War II, the British learned that fliers in good physical condition seldom survived longer than half an hour in the forty-degree water of the English channel. At thirty-two degrees, you may have only fifteen minutes. Human beings become incapable of conscious, life-saving decisions when deep body temperature is lowered by only seven degrees Fahrenheit. In many boating accidents, crews perish from cold rather than drowning. Small pleasure craft can be swamped or capsized, but seldom actually sink.

On a cool, cloudy day far out on a large body of water, it wouldn't be unusual for the summer temperature to sink to fifty degrees in many parts of North America. If the wind were blowing twenty-five miles an hour, the wind chill factor would be thirty—the equivalent of thirty degrees with no wind. Yet, because the day seems warm in the harbor, people set sail in bathing suits with perhaps nothing extra but a light jacket.

If a boat is too small for a clothes locker in the cabin, extra clothes can be brought along inside a plastic bag. (Some skippers also pack clothes for dining out ashore when they go cruising.)

You should also keep on board a box of tools that is never

raided for household repairs. This kit should contain hammer, saw, drill, pliers, screwdrivers, adjustable wrench, assorted fasteners, and fresh spark plugs for the engine. A sailboat should carry enough extra rope to replace any of the lines on board and a sewing kit for repairing the sails.

Naturally, you'd pack a first aid kit and personal essentials just as you would on a camping trip or any other outing where you're dependent upon your own resources.

Marine catalogs offer many devices to use in signaling for help. At night you can fire rockets or flares or flash a battery-powered strobe light. For daytime, there are smoke flares and dye packets. You can also use mirrors or signal flags or wave your arms. How elaborately you should equip your ship depends on the waters you cruise and the ambitiousness of your voyages.

Some provision must be made for bailing out the bilges. A small open boat can be bailed with a scoop or a bucket. A hand pump is convenient on any boat with a floor. If you equip your boat with electrical generating capacity, you may as well enjoy the luxury of an electric bilge pump. But have an alternative in case the water rises high enough to short out the battery. Farley Mowat, the Canadian writer, for years sailed a ship that perversely developed strange leaks. As he wrote in *The Boat Who Wouldn't Float*, a whole book devoted to the subject, he often would swing his legs out of his bunk in the morning to discover the water already halfway to his knees in the cabin.

If you cruise in shipping lanes, you should have a radar reflector so the big ships can pick you up on their radar screens instead of running you down. (In an emergency, you can also use a large mass of aluminum foil, a frying pan, or another sizable metal object that can be run up the mast.)

Then there's the electronics section of the catalog. For several hundred dollars, you can have a radiotelephone to call up the office and tell them you won't be in next week, either. Or you can report to the Coast Guard that pirates are swarming over the port rail. While you're spending money, you can also have a radio direction finder, an electronic depth finder, and your own radar.

More practical is a portable radio that picks up the weather information broadcast on the marine band. Some models are inexpensive, and they play music besides.

The *Dawn Treader*'s radio shack contains a four-dollar transistor radio that brings in weather information from local AM disc jockeys. I can be sure that any forecast I hear is local because the radio can't pick up distant stations.

I'm not arguing against better equipment. I plan to buy a weather band receiver in time. My point is that not every cruising boat has to be equipped as if she were bound for the Antarctic for six months.

Insurance

The marine liability coverage you need may be included in your homeowner's policy if you own a house. Apparently, insurance companies think that if the careless maniacs on their policyholder list are out sailing they can't be home at the same time smoking in bed or pushing guests down the stairs, so there isn't much difference in risk.

Read the fine print. Your liability may be covered for sailboats up to twenty-six feet, outboards up to twenty-five horsepower, inboards up to fifty horsepower. If the dollar limit of liability seems low compared to your automobile policy, you can ask your insurance company to increase your coverage for a modest premium.

A typical hull policy insures your boat against theft, collision, grounding, sinking, damage on the highway in transit, and the other usual marine hazards. The premium may run from $2\frac{1}{2}$ to 5 percent of insured value, depending on the deductibles, the waters sailed, and the length of the season. My policy limits the *Dawn Treader* to "inland waters of the U.S." and requires that she be laid up ashore during the winter months.

Having built the boat yourself, you'll have to establish a value for it with your insurance company. This isn't as difficult as you may think. Check the ads in boating magazines or the annual *Boat Owners Buyers Guide* or *Sailboat & Sailboat Equipment Directory* for the prices of factory boats similar to yours in size and equipment. If you take the average price of three or four stock boats, no one can argue that your valuation isn't fair. Whether your boat would command more or less than that on the market is hard to tell unless you put up a For Sale sign and see what happens.

Many home-built boats are worth more than factory boats the same size because the owner worked with loving care, used the best materials and hardware, and made his boat stronger. On the other hand, some well-made factory boats enjoy high resale value because buyers recognize the brand name and respect it. They might be suspicious of your ability as a shipwright.

The insurance company probably will ask for a photograph of your boat before they issue the policy. They like to know that the boat really exists, and that it looks like a boat rather than the bastard offspring of a barge and a front porch.

There's one other kind of "insurance" you ought to carry—on board the ship. That's a copy of *Piloting, Seamanship and Small Boat Handling* by Charles F. Chapman, which is frequently updated like an encyclopedia. It's a big, heavy book you can count on as part of your ballast. The comprehensive contents answer important questions that may come to mind out at sea when there's no old salt around to ask for advice.

A sensible person learns what he needs to know about the everyday rules of the road before leaving the shore, but some of the more specialized details will never stay in your head. You know that red and green lights mark port and starboard bow, respectively. But what if you see red and green lights, two white lights, and a flashing amber light looming out of the dark some night? You might think it was a flying saucer. But quick consultation of your reference library informs you that it's a submarine coming straight toward you on the surface, and you'd better get out of the way.

Some skippers consider a lead line a necessity. They can feel their way around in the dark or in the fog by checking depth of water and the nature of the bottom, then consulting the chart.

"The depth is twenty-seven feet, Cap'n, and the bottom is solid beer cans. Where do you suppose we are?"

"Two miles due east of Revelry Park. North of here the bottom is sand. Farther east, the water is deeper. Closer in, it's shallower. To the south, the bottom is old tires."

One other item of equipment is essential. That's the skipper's hat. You need something to keep your nose from being sunburned and your brain from being baked in the shell. The trick is to find one that is practical, inexpensive, and salty, but not too pretentious.

Although I subscribe to the general rule that favors wearing the wrong kind of hat for every sport (golfing caps are fine for horseback riding and western hats for hiking), I hold a prejudice against a cap emblem made of crossed putters aboard ship. On the other hand, a genuine officer's cap with white cover and gold braid on the stiff peak should be worn only by professionals or—insouciantly—by the skipper of a very small craft.

I am not offended by a hat that looks like a baseball cap and has a crossed-anchor decoration sewed to it. This looks less salty than the Baltic style yachting cap but is less expensive to replace when it blows overboard—a good compromise. During the sailing season, I lose, on the average, one hat every six weeks.

"I can never understand the people who say they get bored in a sailing ship."

15 The Last Day of Creation

I COULDN'T stand the suspense any longer. I launched the *Dawn Treader* before she was completely finished. I hadn't installed the rub rails yet; the decks sloped down to an edge of raw plywood; and the mast hardware still hadn't been fastened, so we couldn't sail. But there was no reason why we couldn't take the outboard motor and go for a cruise on the Fox River.

At the launching ramp in the state park, I unfastened the transom tie-downs, removed the winch line, and ran lines from bow and stern to my crewmen on the pier. Then I backed the trailer into the water and braked. The *Dawn Treader* slid off the trailer and floated free for the first time.

I was relieved to see that she sat gracefully in the water, not lopsided. The Chicago Symphony Orchestra and singers, concealed in the shrubbery along the water's edge, burst forth with Handel's *Hallelujah Chorus*. Several journalists and historians were taking notes.

This was the culmination of almost two and a half years of working, hoping I was doing things right but not really sure until this moment. I was reminded of the indenture of apprenticeship signed by Donald McKay, builder of the best clipper ships, at the age of sixteen when he undertook to learn "the art, trade and mystery of a ship carpenter."

An apt phrase. It is rather a mystery coping with construction when few lines are straight, few corners square, and your usual source of advice at the local lumber yard doesn't know what you're talking about.

Six of us dined aboard the family yacht that evening as we motored up the river through a wildlife refuge. The popping of a champagne cork frightened off a great blue heron, who rose from the bank to a tall tree and glared at us while we ate our chicken sandwiches in the rain. Oh yes, it was raining, but no one paid any attention. The rain just made it cozier for those in the cabin.

By the following weekend, the mast and rigging were complete, so the ship could be taken for her first sail. This is when the builder finds out about the idiosyncracies of the vessel's personality and the various inconveniences that need to be put right.

Bring along a notebook on your first cruises to record anything that doesn't seem to work the way it should. Try all the basic maneuvers under varying wind conditions. If you let go of everything—tiller and sheets—she should round into the wind on her own. Tack a lot. Run before the wind. Jibe. With the jib backed and helm lashed down, she should lie quietly hove to. Drop the anchor and retrieve it to make certain you can do it again when you have to. Practice reefing.

Some characteristics of your ship are inherent in the design. Long, low hulls are fast but sail wet. High, stiff hulls are drier on deck and slower. Short-ended, beamy hulls that are good for cruising are particularly sluggish when the breeze is light. There's nothing you can do about these traits but build another boat from different plans.

On the *Dawn Treader*'s sea trials I discovered that the boom crutch had to be taken down before the tiller could be used. (See Figure 15-1.) The line that was supposed to let the centerboard down was too short to run through the pulley system. The halyards needed end snaps. Two more cleats at the stern would be handy. A topping lift was essential. The mainsail was hard to hoist because the brand-new rope sewed into the sail was stiff and tight in the mast groove.

Fig. 15-1. One of the things I discovered on launching day: With the mast in the support crutch it is impossible to use the tiller.

But with her sails up she came to life and pranced across the water, not at all self-conscious about her continuing lack of rub rails.

I felt more lubberly than usual. It takes a while to get the feel of a new boat—to know how much wind she can stand up to, how far she'll coast on momentum when you round into the wind, how much leeway to anticipate in sailing a course, how closely she can point into the wind, how easily she goes about.

Two full seasons later, I still have a list of changes to make aboard the *Dawn Treader*. I plan to replace the two small windows in the forward part of the cabin with larger fixed windows that won't leak. I'm going to add galley shelves. Also, I intend to rethink the storage space around the cockpit to see if I can make it more functional. I may lead the jib sheets to a different location. The way the leads and cleats are positioned now, someone is always sitting on the jib sheets.

No boat is ever truly finished. The builder can always think of improvements to make, especially in ways to simplify handling the ship when sailing alone.

Strictly speaking, it takes at least two to handle any sailing craft larger than a sailboard. Even on a sailing canoe with only one sail a crewman can make himself useful. However, any number of mariners have roamed the world single-handed aboard ships of all sizes, large and small. In *American Sailing Coasters of the North Atlantic*, Paul C. Morris tells about a short-tempered New England sea captain named Parker Hall who decided about 1907, after a crew mutinied and tried to rob him, to get along without the aggravations of having employees. So he sailed single-handed in the coastal trade for the next thirteen years. He constantly steered in and out of harbors, tying up at docks and keeping sharp watch in crowded waters. His ship during these years was a ninety-foot schooner, with two topmasts carrying extra sail to handle.

Obviously, single-handing is possible. And when the options are staying in port for lack of crew or taking on the extra work of single-handing, you'll be willing enough to be captain, mate, forecastle hand, cook, and all.

This is an argument for not building too big a boat. I think sixteen feet is about the minimum length for a ship. On anything smaller, it's difficult to fit a functional cabin for cruising. Eighteen to twenty feet or so gives you more room and can still be sailed, rigged, and retrieved onto a trailer by one man. Up to perhaps thirty feet, one-handed sailing isn't too hard, but getting a boat over twenty feet onto a trailer by yourself can be a struggle.

I see that one sailboat manufacturer advertises a twenty-five-footer (so heavy it needs a four-wheel trailer), which is supposed to be designed so that one man can do everything, including raise the mast and winch the boat back onto the trailer. And I suppose it is possible under good conditions. But let's say the day turns nasty and by the time you return to the marina, the rain has driven away anyone who might be standing around the pier to help. There's a gusty wind astern. Thanks to your skill with the engine in reverse and your natural sure-footed agility, you manage to lay the ship alongside the pier and put a mooring line ashore without mishap. Then you back the trailer down the ramp and fasten the winch line to the bow eye.

Now all you have to do is persuade that big, heavy hull to ignore the wind for a moment, sidle away from the pier far enough to center herself off the end of the trailer and allow herself to be winched in instead of dashing up the ramp by herself the instant you release the mooring lines. Good luck if you want to try.

Racing vs. Cruising

A sailing vessel is especially well suited for voyages of the spirit. When Robin Knox-Johnston sailed around the world nonstop, he was alone at sea on a thirty-two-foot ketch for ten and a half months. "I can never understand the people who say they get bored in a sailing ship," he wrote. "In a power driven vessel, yes, whether a large liner or a small cabin cruiser, because somehow using an engine instead of the natural forces seems to take the poetry out of the movement. Watching the ever-changing waves alone can keep me happy for hours on end; there is so much variety. And when the sea is flat calm suddenly it comes to life with small marine animals that you never notice as a rule."

A yacht race gives participants the impression of tremendous speed and power, particularly when sailing closehauled with the bow throwing spray over the top of the cabin. You forget that the top speed, depending upon the size of the boats, is about six to eight miles an hour with a strong wind.

Many sailors become devoted to sailboat racing and would rather be first around a buoy than collect a $10,000 fee. (Although in many yacht races more than a few $10,000 fees are spent to come in first. One racing skipper told *Newsweek* that you could get a feeling for the sport by standing in a cold shower while tearing up twenty dollar bills.)

There's no denying the satisfaction of edging ahead of other boats because you have made a superior appraisal of wind and weather and responded more skillfully than the other skippers. If you have also built the fastest hull yourself, the America's Cup runneth over. Many racing sailors leave their moorings only for races, scorning any other outing as a mere "sailboat ride."

Maintaining a boat in racing condition is more expensive than maintaining it for cruising. A cruising skipper doesn't have to replace anything as long as it's safe and serviceable. A racer has to concern himself constantly about all the factors that might affect the decisive tenth of a knot that separates winners and losers.

If you build a boat to race, be sure to pick a design that is raced in your area. Many racing fleets are composed of one-design boats, so that the variables are the skill of the crews rather than differences in boats. You can build a one-design boat from the plans like any other boat. To qualify it for a racing fleet, the usual procedure is to have someone representing the class association examine and certify it. The examiner fills out a measurement form to show that the boat's dimensions and specifications fall between stated minimums and maximums.

Uptight racers get to the point where before a big race they won't eat any vegetable with iron in it. The crew has to remove coins from their pockets and cut the tips off their shoelaces before coming aboard. The captain doesn't even allow heavy breathing.

Advertising in the boating magazines would have you believe that the same boat can be ideal for both racing and cruising. That's something of an exaggeration. When you look at close-up photos of the serious racing machines, like America's Cup contenders, they conjure up no images of fishing or swimming over the side or leisurely conversations in the cockpit. Most designs are compromises.

In my view, sailboat racing is tainted by its appeal for perfectionists and compulsively competitive personalities. Too often, the same hard-driving men who contribute so much to the tenseness of life ashore are the skippers who lead the fleet across the finish line, driving their boats and crews as much by force of will as by wind. I go to sea to get away from all that.

Piloting

Knowing more or less where you are in coastal and inland waters is no less important than on the high seas. Otherwise, you are likely to run aground or otherwise inconvenience yourself and the Coast Guard. Piloting is fun. You start the game with a chart of the waters you're cruising. At first, you may wonder why it provides such a wealth of information. You may not care that the bottom eight feet down is green sticky mud since you have no intention of going there. But someday in fog this fact, ascertained with a hand lead, could become your warning that half a mile ahead the bottom is only one foot down—and it's rock.

All landmarks visible from the water are charted. The church steeples and distinctive buildings help you take bearings and avoid shoals. Channels are marked by buoys, which are identified on the chart according to their size, shape, color, number, and type of light at night. In a typical channel, Buoy Number Seventeen may have a white light fifteen feet above the water emitting a four-second flash. Numbers Sixteen and Fifteen will be unlighted. Buoy Fourteen may flash red.

If you think you are cruising this part of the channel at night and see a buoy flashing *green*, you should heave to until you figure out where you went wrong, or return to GO and save $200, at least.

Thanks to the interest of the government in keeping boats

from unexpectedly obstructing traffic on highways that parallel the sea, many bodies of water are marked well enough to be navigated at night without elaborate equipment.

One night I was a passenger on a small boat cruising up the Potomac to see Mount Vernon by moonlight. Our principal navigation equipment was a flashlight, which proved especially useful because there wasn't any moonlight that night. The cloudy edge of a storm hovered overhead, making the night dark except for distant lightning flashes. To stay in the channel, we steered from one lighted buoy to the next. It often took a minute or two to pick out the next light, perhaps a mile away, against the confusion of lights on the shore. To pinpoint our position between lights we watched for the unlighted buoys. This wasn't wasted effort. We had to watch for them anyway in order not to run into them.

When we saw an unlighted buoy suddenly rise against the lesser blackness of the sky, we steered alongside and shone the flashlight on it till we could read the number. This is how we knew when to leave the main channel, feel our way cautiously inshore, and watch for Mount Vernon on the hill beside the river. Presently, our navigation was verified by a lightning flash that backlighted the silhouette of the cupola and chimneys above the trees.

Flashlight navigation also helped us return to our launching site without blundering around in the dark and running out of gas. The only difficulty on the entire cruise was that we were using the flashlight from my car and my brother-in-law forgot to give it back.

Living Aboard

There are sailors for whom cruises stretch into months and years. Couples with a bit of income have lived on small ships and sailed the world for fifteen and twenty years. Some of them write books about their cruises, which provide money for more cruises, which beget more books. This is better than a chicken ranch.

Surprisingly, many of these experienced sailors cherish ships about thirty feet long, which don't provide much space to live in year after year. One reason is that boat maintenance costs rise in proportion to the cube of the waterline length. Everything costs more—insurance, depreciation, mooring fees, and anything else the shore pirates can stick you with after they see you come ashore from a big yacht. Long-term cruisers say that cruising and living aboard a forty-footer costs two to four times as much as on a thirty-footer. Also, a thirty-footer isn't a little easier to handle by yourself; it's a lot easier.

Living aboard a small ship full time offers more escape than I need. Yet I rejoice that the open sea still calls voyagers to solitude and self-reliance in a world where, as the *Wall Street Journal* reported recently, there is talk about building an oil refinery at Pago Pago.

The day I declared the *Dawn Treader* officially completed, one of my crew, without requesting leave to address the bridge, inquired whether I intended to start building another boat the next morning. I should have had the swab keel-hauled; it wasn't his first offense. Instead, I pondered his facetious question.

I had been a shipwright during most of my spare time for two years and four months. Now was the season to move on to other enterprises, including sailing and enjoying the ship I had built. When Thoreau had lived at Walden Pond for two years and two months, he moved back to town.

But I knew that there never will come a morning when, granted respite from the press of other matters, I won't be happy to spread out the plans and begin building another tall—and salty—ship.

The *Dawn Treader* at sea.

Appendix: Where to Buy What You Need

Few of the materials needed to construct a ship are in everyday use around home, office, and shop. You can't just walk into any hardware store and ask for a couple of gudgeons and a two-foot auger. Oh, you could *ask,* but they'd probably give you the same treatment they reserve for jokesters who come in for polka dot paint and left-handed screwdrivers.

Part of the art of ship building is knowing where to get things. It's beyond the scope of this book to go into competition with the Yellow Pages, but I can give you some useful information about leading sources.

Plans

Clark Craft Boat Company
16 Aqua Lane
Tonawanda, NY 14150

Clark Craft is a major supplier of plans, patterns, and kits for all kinds of boats, power and sail, from sailing dinghies to forty- or forty-five-foot cruisers. For the more popular designs, they offer hardware and rigging kits. They also sell sails.

Glen L. Marine
9152 East Rosecrans
Bellflower, CA 90706

Headed by Glen L. Witt, himself a naval architect, this company also offers a wide variety of plans—more than a hundred—with backup items including kits, hardware, sails, and even spars. Glen L. provides clear, helpful instruction books on a variety of topics from inboard engine installation to sailboat rigging.

Luger Industries, Inc.
1400 East Cliff Road
Burnsville, MN 55378

Luger supplies fiberglass boat kits. Your boat comes in large molded pieces that you stick together with resin according to instructions. These boats are for people who want to save money and don't mind doing some assembly work. I don't consider this really ship building—no salty tradition. The prices are less than for comparable factory-built fiberglass boats and compare favorably with the cost of a plywood boat you build yourself by the time you add in plans, lumber, fasteners, finishes, and the other components. But the Luger kits do require a substantial outlay right in the beginning.

I don't know of any other plan sources that try to offer a complete line of plans for everybody, including houseboaters, water skiers, fishermen, and speed maniacs as well as cruisers and sailors. Despite their extensive plan catalogs, however, the choice may be rather narrow in any one category.

For example, all three companies together offer only half a dozen designs for cruising sailboats under twenty feet. If you don't see anything you like in their catalogs, you may want to turn to the much more numerous sources that specialize in certain types of plans.

I mention the following as examples. There are a great many more listed in marine directories and boating magazines.

International Amateur Boat Building Society
3183 Merrill
Royal Oak, MI 48072

The IABBS has sponsored competitions to develop new plans for boats that are particularly well suited to construction by amateurs. The society has discontinued its publication, *Amateur Boat Building,* and hasn't answered my letters recently, so I'm not sure of their operating status. However, someone still owns the rights to the plans and will no doubt continue making them available to boat builders one way or another.

Tri-Star Trimarans
Box 286
Venice, CA 90291

Tri-Star offers plans for trimarans from eighteen to sixty-five feet long, designed by Edward B. Horstman, who has sailed his own trimarans in many ocean races. Tri-Star offers full-size patterns for ships up to forty-eight feet long and instructions along with the plans. The company also sells all necessary materials and equipment, including engines, to fit their trimarans. The exception is plywood, which is always cheaper locally because of shipping costs.

Lumber

Somewhere in your area there may be an accommodating lumber yard that will be willing to get you marine-quality lumber at a reasonable price as well as marine plywood. Or, if the plans you like can be obtained from the source with frame kits, that's usually a good value. The frames themselves are curved pieces that have to be cut from wide planks, which can be costly and involve waste.

For the *Dawn Treader,* I bought my Philippine mahogany framing lumber from Craft Marine Supplies of Elmwood Park, Illinois, a small dealer specializing in boat lumber and supplies for the Chicago area. Duffy-Evans Plywood of Mount Prospect, Illinois, ordered my marine plywood for me and accommodatingly obtained additional pieces of mahogany one or two at a time when I needed them.

M. L. Condon Company
252 Ferris Avenue
White Plains, NY 10603

This company advertises a complete line of boat lumber, which they are prepared to ship anywhere. In the Chicago area I found I could get lower prices locally, but Chicago is a transportation center where many things can be found that aren't readily available elsewhere.

Epoxy
Chem Tech
4481 Greenwold Road
Cleveland, OH 44121

Chem Tech is a direct source for a special boat building epoxy, T-88, which can be used in cold weather down to almost freezing. It comes in quart kits with a graduated plastic measuring cup and a supply of thickener to make epoxy putty. The epoxy and the catalyst are in separate plastic squeeze bottles, very convenient to use.

Hardware and Supplies
Sears Roebuck and Montgomery Ward show more marine supplies in their mail order catalogs all the time. You can check their prices against those of the dozen or so major marine mail order specialists.

There is no one house that stocks everything. You have to have several catalogs on your workbench to rummage through and find various items you need. There are several complications. For instance, many of them charge a dollar or two for sending their catalogs to persons who have not previously ordered and might not be serious customers. Some quote the price in the catalog. Others give a fictitious list price and enclose a discount sheet giving the real price for orders of a certain size, say fifteen dollars or more. (It doesn't take much in the marine field to add up to fifteen dollars.) This discount sheet has a nasty habit of slipping out and hiding under the filing cabinet.

Some marine mail order suppliers insist on a minimum order. This can lead to troublesome exchanges, like the following:

SUPPLIER: In reply to yours of the 16th inst., "CNF" means "cannot furnish."

We are aware that you have a credit for $2.76 with us and suggest that when you place another order, including the J113 ⅝ × 6″ bronze machine bolt, you make mention of same.

With the marine season not too far ahead it is well to anticipate your requirements to be assured of having the items you require.

CUSTOMER: I still don't understand about the bronze machine bolt (J113 ⅝ × 6″). If you are temporarily out of stock, when should I reorder—thirty days, six months? Also, what about your minimum order rule? Since I just bought supplies from you, I won't need anything else for a while. So where does that leave me? Waiting till I have another ten-dollar shopping list? By that time you may again be out of the bolt I need. How do I get this item without a lot of complications?

SUPPLIER: In reply to yours of the 30th ult., we enclose check in the amount of $2.76, which is the refund for the bronze machine bolt. We cannot specify when we will have it as the promises from the manufacturer are not reliable. We look forward to being of further service.

CUSTOMER: May the gods of the sea cover your house with a great flood reaching to the top of the chimney while relays of piranhas gnaw on your bones for a thousand years. And while the boys are there please give them the address of that bolt manufacturer so they can swim around and see him, too.

There are only two ways to deal with this nuisance of minimum orders. One is to save up a list of nonurgent items to toss in with the things you need. The other is to place all or nothing orders: "If you can't supply at this time the first two items listed, please cancel entire order and return check."

I have spent whole evenings poring over the catalogs, finding the items I needed, comparing prices, and trying to make the minimum orders work out. One place has the right size bolts, another has the right stemhead fitting, and another the best prices on rope. To fatten up orders and reach the minimum, I might plan ahead and order a boat cushion from one company along with the rope and a couple of cleats I wasn't ready for yet along with the stemhead fitting.

The *Dawn Treader* was completed before the era of shortages; even so, I experienced many disappointments. It took six weeks to get the first batch of bronze nails and screws I ordered. Even the U.S. Plywood warehouse in Chicago was out of stock for four weeks at one point with the size of marine plywood I needed.

Explorers Ltd. Source Book, edited by Alwyn T. Perrin. Published by Harper and Row.

This is a 384-page large-format paperback book sold in bookstores. It lists books, periodicals, and equipment sources for all the blood-tingling activities from aerial photography and backpacking to wilderness living and winter bivouacking. There's a section on offshore sailing. Also, the backpacking and camping sections can be helpful to anyone fitting out a boat for cruising. If you can carry something in your pack, you can stow it aboard a boat, and many pieces of equipment are equally useful ashore or afloat.

James Bliss & Company, Inc.
Route 128
Dedham, MA 02026

The catalog ($1) comes with a discount sheet for orders of $15 or more and shows a complete line of marine equipment of all kinds in 284 pages. Minimum order is $10.

Algonquin Distributors, Ltd.
8499 West River Shore Drive
Niagara Falls, NY 14304

The discount schedule is published in the catalog: from 10 percent on $10 to 25 percent over $400. The catalog is 265 pages, shows a wide range of marine equipment (somewhat less complete than Bliss) and adds skiing, diving, and fishing equipment not shown in most marine catalogs.

Defender Industries, Inc.
255 Main Street
New Rochelle, NY 10801
Defender offers no discounts, but the prices published in the catalog are low. The 160-page book costs 75 cents and is cheaply printed on pulp paper—one reason for the low prices. Minimum order is $10. Defender carries a particularly broad line of resins and other marine chemicals, also hardware items not available elsewhere. I have bought quite a bit from Defender, but you have to know what you want in hardware because you can't tell much from the poorly printed illustrations.

E & B Marine Supply
257 Bertrand Street
Perth Amboy, NJ 08861
The 180-page catalog ($1) shows list prices with the E & B price under each item. There is no discount sheet and the minimum mail order is $10. It's not always easy to compare prices because quite a few of the better known brands say either "list price: much higher" or "write for E & B special price." However, there are some genuinely discounted items shown with firm prices ($54.95 instead of $69.95, for instance).

Goldbergs' Marine Distributors, Inc.
202 Market Street
Philadelphia, PA 19106
Minimum mail order is $4, no discounts. A complete marine assortment is shown in 204 pages. Prices appear mostly average, with some items shown below list price. Inquiries are invited on special "low" prices for Evinrude outboard motors.

Fore and Aft
Box 27125
Riverdale, IL 60627
Minimum mail order is $2.50. Catalog (25 cents) is 5½ by 8½

inches, 72 pages. Fore and Aft tries to offer competitive, below-list prices on basic marine items. The lack of an index makes the catalog inconvenient to use.

Land's End Yacht Stores, Inc.
2221 North Elston Avenue
Chicago, IL 60614

Land's End's 336-page catalog costs $3, and it's worth it. Beautifully printed, it shows every item in meticulous detail. Informative captions even tell you what fasteners to buy for hardware items. There is no minimum purchase, and there are no discounts. This catalog is oriented toward the racing sailor who wants strong, first-class equipment and doesn't mind paying for it. Service is prompt. They carry some items not readily available elsewhere, such as aluminum spar extrusions, many sizes of stainless steel fasteners, and an extensive line of mast and rigging hardware.

Leigh Dinghy Stores Limited
215-221 Chapel Street
Leigh, Lancastershire, WN7 2AR, England

Boat building and sailing are popular in England, and many items are cheaper than here—even after you've paid duty and shipping charges. The Leigh catalog of 160 pages (25 pence) includes a comprehensive line of marine hardware and some supplies. Of special interest are off-the-shelf sails made up for a number of racing classes, including G.P. 14s, Snipes, Albacores, and 5-0-5s—all popular in the United States. Prices are given in pounds and pence. Work up a list and write for an estimate.

Manhattan Marine & Electric Company
116 Chamber Street
New York, NY 10007

Minimum order is $10, and a discount sheet can be used with orders of $15 or more. The catalog runs 436 pages. Manhattan Marine and James Bliss & Company (see earlier entry) seem to publish the most comprehensive catalogs. Even with discounts, though, prices are about average.

Freeport Marine Supply Company, Inc.
47 West Merrick Road
Freeport, NY 11520

The 308-page catalog describes standard marine equipment and supplies. Prices also appear to be standard, with discount sheet for orders over $10. Minimum order is $10.

National Marine & Electronics Corporation
Box 870, Main P.O.
Miami, FL 33101

Minimum order is $5. This 240-page catalog ($1) concentrates a bit more on mechanical equipment—marine refrigerators, engine controls, electrical equipment—than most other catalogs. Prices appear to be genuinely discounted from manufacturers' list.

Ripley Marine Supplies
66-45 Grand Avenue
Maspeth, NY 11378

Ripley has a discount sheet and a minimum mail order of $10. The catalog of 152 pages costs $1, is poorly printed so that illustrations don't always show much. Prices are competitive on some items, including inflatable dinghies.

Rodi Chris-Craft, Inc.
2550 South Ashland Avenue
Chicago, IL 60608

As might be expected, this Chris-Craft dealer publishes a 164-page catalog ($2) oriented toward powerboat owners. It offers outboard motor ignition parts, for example, although there are a few pages of sailboat hardware. Prices appear to be manufacturers' list.

West Products
161 Prescott Street
East Boston, MA

The only pocket-sized catalog has 208 pages and offers 20 percent discount on orders of $250 or more. Other prices seem high. The catalog provides an additional retail outlet for the Sea/Line marine products manufactured by West, which include nylon and Dacron line, duffel bags, sea anchors, storm suits, and many other items, mostly nonmechanical.

Publications

Boat Owners Buyers Guide, published annually by *Yachting* magazine.

You'll find this publication on newsstands for $2.50. It runs 300 pages and lists all manufacturers of boats and marine equipment that the editors could locate. For instance, it lists a hundred or more U.S. sailmakers, plus others in Canada, England, Hong Kong, and Australia. It also lists all mail order suppliers. It contains illustrations, but the accompanying advertising provides additional information—and pictures.

Sailboat & Sailboat Equipment Directory, published annually by *Sail* magazine.

This is another newsstand source, costing $2. Less comprehensive than *Boat Owners Buying Guide,* it concentrates on sailboats and their gear. Photographs accompany plan drawings of stock sailboats.

Boats & Harbors
Crossville, TN 38555

For $2 you get this publication three times a month for a year. It has a tabloid newspaper format and consists *entirely* of advertising. Most readers are commercial boatmen, judging from the contents. It's a good place to watch for bargains in heavy duty pumps, used diesel engines, surplus mine sweepers ($35,000), and the like. It's where old lobster boats go to die.

Tools

Brookstone Company
15 Brookstone Building
Peterborough, NH 03458

There's no marine emphasis to this "hard-to-find tools" catalog, but it includes some tools that a shipwright could use and wouldn't ordinarily come across in a hardware store. Some examples: plane and chisel blade sharpener, super versatile clamps, rethreading files to salvage external threads, nut splitter for removing jammed nuts, extractors for broken off screws.

Other Equipment

Nashcraft Marine Products
32906 Avenida Descanso
San Juan Capistrano, CA 92675

This company supplies kits that convert Coleman or Sears two-burner gasoline camp stoves to burn ethyl alcohol, marine stove fuel, or shellac thinner. The kits include an instruction booklet as well as the necessary parts.

David Jolly
Lytchett Minster
Poole, BH16 6JD, England

This is the first source that came to my attention for the Aerocharge wind generator that recharges 12-volt batteries by wind power while your boat lies at anchor. The unit is designed to recharge at an average rate of .25 amps whenever the wind blows 10 to 20 miles per hour or more.

INDEX